The LDC Theory
Highway Code Workbook

This workbook contains **all the official theory test questions and answers** as used in the UK theory test for car drivers. This Crown copyright material is reproduced under licence from the Controller of Her Majesty's Stationery Office (HMSO) and the Secretary of State for Transport.

Published by: Teaching Driving Limited
Telephone No. (01977) 691818

Version: 2006/07

ISBN: 0-9529035-9-8

Compiled and written by: Paul McArdle and Val Wood

Graphic Design by: Michael Bedford

The LDC Theory Test CD-Rom

Price £7.99

The ultimate learning tool for the theory test for car drivers and motorcycle riders

Call Freephone **0800 400 777**
or visit **LDC** on the web at
www.learnerdriving.com

2 CD Set

ISBN:
0-9529035-8-X

Theory Test

Excellent Theory Test simulation. Nothing can compare to the quality of our multiple choice and hazard perception test simulations.

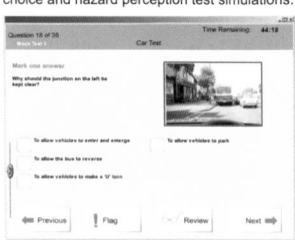

Three unique learning quiz programmes for car drivers and one specially for motorcyclists. Each learning quiz takes you through every question in the official databank in a different order. DSA, Highway Code or in-car lesson learning sequence. The only product that is designed to go hand-in-hand with the Highway Code or your driving lessons.

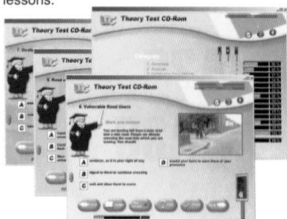

Unique traffic light question monitoring and feedback system so that you know exactly what's been covered and already learnt.

Six carefully balanced pre-set mock tests using what we consider to be the most commonly used questions on the actual theory test based on our extensive experience of successfully getting people through the test.

Random mock test facility giving you virtually an unlimited number of mock tests.

FREE Bonus: Printable version of the Theory Test Highway Code Workbook in PDF format. Valued at £4.99 on its own.

Master progress report records each user's multiple choice and hazard perception progress.

Hazard Perception Test

Official Hazard Perception practice clips. We provide all the official DSA Hazard Perception practice video clips (10 in total) as part of a fully working mock test. Making this first mock test, of six available, particularly realistic. We also provide an additional 90 clips of our own giving you 100 Hazard Perception clips in all to be tested on.

Six realistic pre-set mock tests. Each with 14 different clips, plus 16 separate practice clips.

Random mock test facility giving you several hundred unique hazard test combinations.

Unique review section showing you exactly where you clicked and where each section of the scoring window starts with the option to slow down or speed up the action. A great learning tool.

Weakest clips league table to enable you to identify and be retested on those hazard clips where your score was insufficient to pass the test.

Detailed hazard perception test video tutorial and the DSA hazard test introduction video clip. Two great videos to help you understand what a developing hazard is and how the test really works.

Practical hazard perception lesson plan to help you put the theory into practice on the road.

Highway Code

The digital Highway Code plus. Cross linked to each of the official test questions and pop up hint screen with click on text voiceover. View or print the rules by Highway Code section or subject index via the Key Information Browser.

Learn 2 drive

Follow the highly acclaimed LDC tuition programme. 20 carefully designed lessons to follow with detailed explanations and extensive graphical illustrations of the skills you need to develop and the procedures you need to learn.

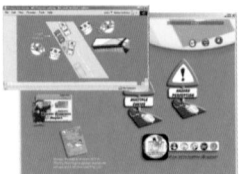

Driving Test

Everything you need to know about the theory and driving tests for car drivers. Detailed descriptions with graphical illustrations.

Includes the DSA Driving Test Exam Report. Find out exactly how the examiner will mark your test. Check list of common driving faults by DSA exam category.

Show me - tell me training notes with extensive video training tutorial.

Full live driving test simulation on video via the Internet (needs broadband connection). Watch the action to see if the learner passes or fails.

Contents

Introduction

This book covers all the information you need to know to book, take and pass the UK theory test for car drivers first time.

Multiple choice

This is the only book where the official UK theory test questions have been restructured to enable you to easily learn the Highway Code as you prepare for the UK theory test. This will not only help you to learn the Highway Code (essential for a lifetime of safe driving) it will also help you to better remember the correct answers to the theory test questions. This is because most people find it easier to remember things they understand or have studied rather than things they have just tried to memorise.

Most of the other books containing the official questions present the questions in the same order as they were provided by the Driving Standards Agency (i.e. in 14 standard question categories). Unfortunately, presenting the questions in this order does not allow you to easily prepare for the theory test using existing books, such as the Highway Code, that contain the theory you need to learn to pass this test and become a safe driver. Consequently, with other books, the reader has to primarily rely upon the use of rote learning (i.e. memorising answers to questions without any form of structured pre-study). This approach is not only tedious it is also very ineffective.

Following a properly structured learning programme, as provided in this book, will enable the learning process to be far more productive and rewarding. With this book you could choose to read a section or two of the Highway Code while travelling to college or work and then undertake the quiz that relates to that study when you get home at night. If you have the CD-rom version of this product (entitled "LDC Theory Test") you could choose to use a computerised quiz, just like the real test, to check what you have learnt that day. By structuring the quizzes to match the study material (i.e. the Highway Code) you can learn the theory in small manageable chunks. The alternative, using other books, is to read the whole of the Highway Code and then answer all the questions in one big indigestible gulp.

Out of the official questions for car drivers 34 questions are excluded from the Northern Ireland test. Otherwise the test is identical.

Hazard perception

When the hazard perception test was first introduced into the theory test, in November 2002, the Driving Standards Agency (DSA) allowed professional driving instructors the opportunity to sit this particular test so that they could become familiar with it.

To our surprise on some hazard video clips driving instructors were actually scoring zero out of a possible 5 marks. This was not because the driving instructors were poor at seeing potential hazards, indeed it was just the opposite. On these occasions the driving instructors were clicking the mouse button (this is how you inform the computer that you have seen a hazard) too early, before the potential hazard had become what the DSA term a "developing hazard". Therefore to ensure you get a maximum score on the hazard perception test it helps to fully understand the DSA term "developing hazard" as opposed to "potential hazard" more commonly used by professional driving instructors.

It is also important to understand how the scoring mechanism works. This is why we cover these aspects of the hazard perception test in some detail as part of this book.

Finally, to aid the development of your hazard perception skills we have also included a lesson brief from the highly acclaimed Learner Driving tuition system. This explains what you need to know to start the development of this most important skill.

How to use this book

Once you have read the early sections of this book about the multiple choice test it is time to undertake the 12 quizzes that form the Highway Code quiz programme. However, before you undertake any quiz in this programme you will need to read the appropriate section or sections of the Highway Code as stated at the start of each quiz. Consequently, you will need to buy a copy of the Highway Code or visit www.learnerdriving.com to view an online copy of this publication. Unfortunately not all the theory necessary to pass this test can be found in the Highway Code. Consequently, we have included a set of supplementary notes for you to read before you embark upon quiz 12. Quiz 12 contains all the official questions not answered by the Highway Code.

To answer any quiz simply take a piece of paper and write down which of the answers to each question you think are correct. If you are unsure of any answer place an asterisk or question mark next to that answer for later review. You can then check your answers by referring to the quiz answers section of this book. Revise the appropriate Highway Code rule, sign, annex or supplementary note of those

questions incorrectly answered or that you were unsure about as denoted by the asterisk or question mark. Make a list of the question numbers and then use this list to revise the questions and correct answers just prior to the test. If you have difficulty remembering the answers to any particular question write out the question and correct answer or answers in full. The physical task of doing this will help you to memorise the correct answers to these final questions.

In regards to using this book to help you pass the hazard perception test make sure you study the appropriate sections carefully. This will give you a sound understanding of exactly how the test works, what to expect and what you need to know to start to develop this most important skill.

The only way to become proficient at identifying and dealing with hazards is to take practical lessons from a professional driving instructor. If you want to experience actual test conditions you can purchase the CD-rom version of this product entitled "LDC Theory Test" by ringing 01977 691810. However, you will need access to a suitably specified PC for at least a couple of hours to complete this task. See advert opposite Contents page for more details.

Applying for your provisional driving licence

Before you can book a theory test you need to apply for a provisional driving licence from the DVLA in Swansea. You can contact the DVLA direct on 0870 240 0009 to obtain an application form or visit any post office. Certain post offices can also partly process the application for you. Please contact the Post Office customer help line on 08457 223344 for information on participating post office branches.

How to arrange the theory test for your 17th birthday

You can apply for a provisional driving licence when you are sixteen but it will not be valid for learning to drive cars until you are seventeen. However, you can use it to book a theory test up to two months prior to your seventeenth birthday to take place on your birthday or shortly afterwards depending on whether your birthday falls on a normal working day.

Booking the test

You can obtain a theory test application form from your driving instructor, any driving or theory test centre or by telephoning the theory test enquiry line on 0870 0101 372 or 0845 600 6700 in Northern Ireland, between 8am and 6pm Monday to Friday and 8am to 4pm on Saturdays. Welsh speakers can also book on 0870 0100 372. If you are deaf and need a minicom machine telephone 0870 0106 372. If you are able to pay by credit or debit card you can book a theory test appointment direct on the same numbers without the need to complete an application form. You will however, need to quote your driver number from your provisional driving licence. Upon booking you will be given a booking number and sent an appointment letter as confirmation within 8 days.

You can also now book the theory test via the internet on www.driving-tests.co.uk or www.dsa.gov.uk.

Cancelling the test

You are required to give a minimum of three clear working days notice of your decision to cancel or postpone your test, otherwise you will lose your test fee.

Arranging a re-test

If you fail the test you will have to wait a minimum of three clear working days before you can take the test again.

Other languages supported

The test is not only available in English, the following languages are also supported:

Albanian	Hindi	Pushto
Arabic	Kashmiri	Spanish
Bengali	Kurdish	Tamil
Cantonese	Mirpuri	Turkish
Dari	Portuguese	Urdu
Farsi	Polish	Welsh
Gujarati	Punjabi	

Through a headset you will be able to listen to the test being read in any of the above languages. In Northern Ireland other language tests are only available in Cantonese, Bengali and Urdu.

Reading difficulties

The DSA are required to make every effort to ensure that the theory test can be taken by all candidates. However, it is important that you discuss your needs with them when booking the test.

To help candidates with dyslexia or other reading problems a headset can be provided with an English language voice-over. You can also ask for up to double the

normal time to complete the test. In such circumstances you will be required to provide a letter from an appropriately qualified individual such as a teacher, psychologist or doctor. If you have any queries please ring the booking number stated earlier and ask for the Special Needs section.

If you cannot read or write in any of the languages provided, you are allowed to bring a translator with you. However, it must be a DSA approved translator.

Hearing difficulties
Both parts of the test can also be delivered in British Sign Language (BSL) by an on-screen signer if you are deaf or have hearing difficulties.

A BSL interpreter or lip operator can be provided if requested at the time of booking.

Foreign licence holders
If your driving licence was issued outside of the EEA (European Economic Area) you will need to check with the Driver Vehicle Licensing Authority (telephone 01792 772151) to determine if your licence is valid in the UK.

At the test centre
You must take one of the following items with you to the test centre.

1. Both parts of your signed photocard driving licence or;

2. your signed driving licence and your Passport;

It would also be helpful if you take your appointment letter.

It is extremely important that you arrive in good time at the test centre so that the above documents can be checked. If you arrive after the start time you will not be allowed to sit the test and you will lose your test fee.

The result

At the end of the test you will be given the result for both the multiple choice test and the hazard perception test. To pass the multiple choice test you need to score 30 out of a possible 35 marks. To pass the hazard perception test you need to score 44 out of a possible 75 marks. If you fail either the multiple choice test or the hazard perception test you will need to take both tests again.

Theory test computer touch screens

Question and answer screen

Question Number

Your Name and Type of test

Time Remaining

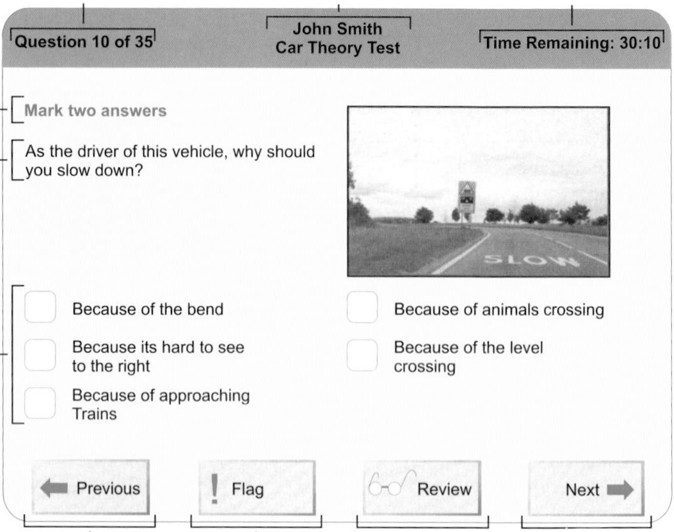

Question 10 of 35

John Smith
Car Theory Test

Time Remaining: 30:10

This red text indicates how many answers to select

Mark two answers

The question

As the driver of this vehicle, why should you slow down?

Touch the appropriate button or buttons to select the correct answer or answers. Press again to deselect if you change your mind

- Because of the bend
- Because its hard to see to the right
- Because of approaching Trains
- Because of animals crossing
- Because of the level crossing

SLOW

Previous

Flag

Review

Next

Go back to previous question

Flag question for later review

Move to review screen below

Go to next question

Review screen

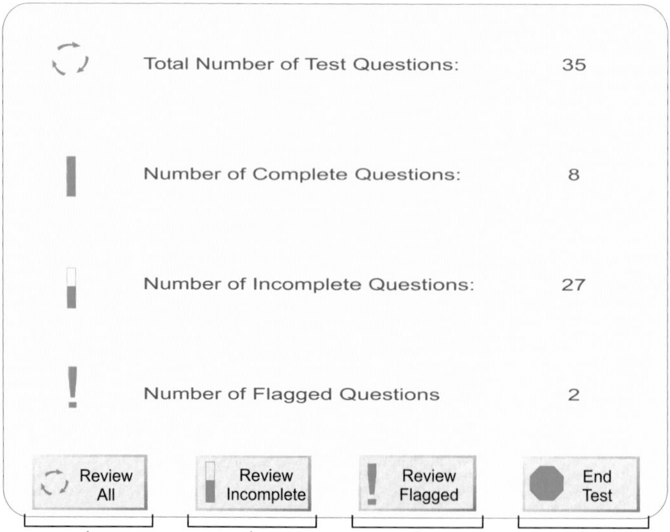

	Total Number of Test Questions:	35
	Number of Complete Questions:	8
	Number of Incomplete Questions:	27
	Number of Flagged Questions:	2

Review All

Review Incomplete

Review Flagged

End Test

Go back to question 1

Review questions not completed or wrong number of answers selected

Review questions flagged

End the test or go to start if pressed during practice session

Introduction

This part of the DSA theory test for car drivers consists of 35 multiple choice questions.

Associated with each question is a list of potential answers. You need to select the correct answer, or answers, by touching the appropriate area of the computer screen. Please see opposite for details. You will be given 40 minutes to complete the test. To pass you need to correctly answer 30 out of the 35 questions (i.e. 86%).

The examination process

Before you start the actual test a short video tutorial will explain how the test should be undertaken. You will be given the opportunity to complete some practice questions to make sure you are familiar with the computer screens.

As you can see from the layout of the theory test computer screens opposite, you move from one question to the next by touching the arrowed buttons at the bottom.

To select any particular answer press the button on the screen next to the answer you wish to select. The answer will then be highlighted with a blue background. To unselect an answer simply touch the answer button on the screen again. This will cause the highlighted blue background to disappear.

The red text in the top left hand corner will tell you how many answers to mark (i.e. to select). This text will flash if you have not selected sufficient answers and try to move onto another screen. If you press again it will let you move on even if you still haven't supplied sufficient answers. In this case the question will be recorded as incomplete.

If you wish to flag a question so that you can review it later you will need to press the flag button at the bottom of the screen. This will cause the flag button to turn red.

At any point you can call up the review screen. This screen enables you to check all the questions and your answers from the start. Alternatively you can just review those questions flagged or those questions incomplete (i.e. not fully answered or not attempted). You will also need to press the review button so that you can end the test. To end the test you press the end test button on the review screen.

The test will automatically end if you run out of time. The time you have left to finish answering the questions is shown at the top right hand side of the question and answer screen.

Hints and tips

Before you press on the end test button in the review screen make sure that the number of complete questions equals 35, the same as the total number of test questions.

If this is not the case review those questions not fully answered or not attempted (i.e. incomplete questions), and any that you have flagged. Incomplete questions require you to select one or more answers until you have marked the required number as indicated by the red text in the top left hand corner of the question and answer screen.

Even if you have completed all the questions, and provided you have the time, it is worth the effort of reviewing all your answers again before pressing the end test button.

Once you have completed the test you will be given the option of a 3 minute break before you move on to the next part of the test, hazard perception.

Analysing the results

At the end of the theory test you will be given your result for this part of the test and a list of those DSA categories where you answered a question incorrectly. Unfortunately, the DSA will not tell you which questions were wrongly answered only the category they relate to. To help you find the questions in this book that relate to any particular DSA category we have provided a cross reference to the DSA categories. This cross reference will help you should you fail an attempt at the multiple choice test and wish to revise those questions specific to any one of the 14 DSA categories.

Introduction

This part of the theory test requires you to view 14 hazard video clips on the computer screen of approximately one minute each. You are required to watch these clips as if you were the driver. There will be 15 hazards to find - at least one on each clip. However, one clip will have 2 hazards. The hazard clips will not contain any sound - just like the old silent movies.

You click the mouse button whenever you think you can see a hazard developing. The speed at which you click the mouse button as a hazard develops will determine your score for that particular hazard clip. You can score between 0 and 5 on each hazard. Therefore the maximum you can score is 75 (i.e. 15 hazards x 5). To pass you need a score of 44.

The examination process

The hazard perception part of the theory test will start with a short video tutorial played on the computer screen that will explain how the hazard perception test works and what you are required to do. At the end of this clip you have the option to go onto the test or play the tutorial again.

Each hazard clip will start with a freeze frame of the start of the video sequence and a count down from 10 will commence. At the end of the count down the clip will start to play and you will be required to click the mouse button each time you see a developing hazard.

To let you know that the program has registered your click a red flag will appear on a grey band across the bottom of the screen - one flag for each click you make in any particular clip. At the end of the clip all the flags will be removed before you start the next clip.

Although each clip contains several potential hazards only the one that materialises into a real hazard and involves other road users is marked . This is known as a "developing hazard". Therefore you will only receive a score if you spot a hazard before it fully materialises and is brought about by the action of another road user. You will know if the hazard materialises because the driver will have to take evasive action (e.g. slow down, stop or swerve out of the way).

The score you obtain will be dependant upon how quickly you spot the developing hazard. The time from when the developing hazard could be potentially seen on the screen to when the vehicle arrives at the hazard is the time frame or window used to determine your score.

Time

Potential Hazard

Actual Hazard

5 Points   4 Points   3 Points   2 Points   1 Points

Developing hazard window

This window of time is divided into 5 equal segments. If you click the mouse while in the first segment (i.e. just as the developing hazard appears) you will obtain the maximum score of 5 points. If you click in the second segment of this window of time you will score 4 points, then 3, then 2 and then in the last segment just 1. This is accurate to one twenty fifth of a second.

YOU RESPONDED TO THIS CLIP IN AN UNACCEPTABLE MANNER. YOU WILL SCORE ZERO FOR THIS CLIP.

If you click several times during this window of time the computer will always take your highest score and record that for that particular clip. If you don't click the mouse button in this window of time you will score nothing in respect to that hazard.

If you try to cheat the system by clicking the button repeatedly throughout the video clip the computer program will pick this up and a message will inform you that you have scored zero for that clip due to responding in an unacceptable manner.

The anti-cheat mechanism will also consider you have tried to cheat if you register too many clicks (although this figure is believed to be well over 20 per clip) or if you click the mouse button 4 or 5 times in quick succession.

When the clip ends the screen will turn black for a few seconds before the freeze frame for the next video clip appears and the count down commences again, warning you to get ready. This pattern is repeated until all 14 video clips have been shown.

At the end of the hazard perception part of the theory test you will be given the option to complete a customer care survey if you so wish.

You will then be directed to leave the room and collect your score for the two parts of the exam. The maximum score that can be obtained for the hazard perception part of the theory test is 75 (i.e. 15x5). To pass the hazard perception part of the car, moped and motorcycle theory test you must obtain a score of 44. To pass the theory test you

must pass both parts. If you fail either part you are required to take both parts of the test again.

Hints and tips

When watching the video clips do not be frightened to click the mouse button whenever you see a potential hazard involving another road user (i.e. anything that you think may cause the driver to change speed, position or direction). Watch the hazard and each time the situation changes click the mouse button again. However, avoid clicking rapidly or when nothing has changed. This will ensure that you click within the scoring window.

Some of these potential hazards will not materialise and therefore you will not receive a score for spotting them. For example, if the cyclist shown in the developing hazard sequence on the previous page stopped at the end of the side road (i.e. at the 4 point stage) the hazard would not have materialised (also see page 25 official hazard clip 3). In the actual clip the cyclist was travelling too fast to stop. This was the real clue to what was going to happen next.

In a few instances it is difficult to determine when a potential hazard becomes a developing hazard and therefore when the scoring window should start. This is why it is safer to click a few times as you see a hazard develop to make sure you don't click once too early and miss the opening of this window.

In this second example also supplied by the DSA you will notice a very young child riding a bike on the pavement (also see page 24 official hazard clip 2). This alone may be classified as a potential hazard, particularly as the child is unsupervised.

However, the scoring window on this clip doesn't open until the child starts to turn towards the road to cross it as shown below and highlighted by the red circle. This is the point at which the potential hazard becomes a developing hazard and the scoring window opens.

Therefore if you had only clicked your mouse button once as you saw the child riding her bike along the pavement you would have scored zero. Therefore, remember to click the button a couple of times as the hazard develops to avoid this problem.

The main type of hazards that you will need to look for in this test are:

1. pedestrians or cyclists crossing the road particularly at school crossing patrols and zebra crossings;
2. vehicles emerging from side roads, parking places or driveways;
3. large vehicles moving over to your side of the road as they negotiate bends, overtake or turn left or right;
4. meeting oncoming vehicles on narrow roads or where other obstructions or slow moving vehicles make the road narrow;
5. cyclists moving out to turn right, cyclists approaching traffic islands or other situations that result in the road narrowing thus making it unsafe to overtake;
6. vehicles turning left or right where the exit is blocked or where oncoming vehicles prevent the vehicle from turning;
7. vehicles pulling up or moving off from the side of the road;
8. animals wondering onto the road;
9. horse riders or horse driven vehicles on narrow roads and around bends;
10. emergency vehicles with flashing lights that require you to give them priority;
11. powered vehicles used by disabled people that may cross your path or make the road ahead narrow;
12. electric vehicles such as trams and milk floats that may move out or cross your path;

13. slow moving vehicles with flashing amber lights.

To further help you prepare for this part of the test we have included:

1. a section that contains the hazard perception and defensive driving lesson brief taken from the Learner Driving programme of driving tuition (see page opposite) and;

2. a section that shows you the scoring windows of each of the 14 official hazard perception practice video clips supplied by the Driving Standards Agency (DSA);

3. free access to an online forum at www.learnerdriving.com.

Introduction

In this section we have included the lesson brief on hazard perception and defensive driving taken from the Learner Driving programme of driving tuition. This represents lesson 11 in the programme. If you want to read all the lesson briefs in the Learner Driving programme please visit our website at www.learnerdriving.com under the section Training aids.

Lesson brief - introduction

During this lesson you will learn how to deal with much busier traffic situations. To do this effectively you will need to further develop your hazard perception skills (i.e. your ability to recognise potential hazards) and your defensive driving skills (i.e. your ability to deal with them).

You will recall from lesson 6 that a hazard may be defined as anything that may require you to change speed, position or direction of your vehicle. Basically hazards can be caused by static road features (e.g. junctions, bends, humps, dips, passing places, traffic lights, bridges, crossings, road works, parked vehicles, wet leaves, spilt oil, surface water etc) or by the actions of other road users or a combination of the two.

Although static road features can present a hazard the routine for dealing with them and the type of hazard they present is covered elsewhere in the Learner Driving programme. In this part of the programme we will be concentrating on those hazards that develop through the actions of other road users and those circumstances that can contribute to their hazardous behaviour.

Hazard Perception; a bit of detection work!

Perception in driving terms can be defined as: 'The art of being able to pick out the important details from all the information being supplied by your sensors.' A perceptive driver must look for clues and build up a mental picture of what they think may happen next.

While hazard perception skills can only truly be acquired through experience (preferably under the guidance of an appropriately qualified professional driving instructor) you can speed up the learning process by having a better understanding of the factors that an expert driver considers when building up this mental picture of what's likely to happen next. These are the main factors that an expert driver would consider:

Road signs

Road signs can provide you with a clear warning of what lies ahead. It is essential that you train yourself to take note of all road signs and act accordingly.

Your location

Are you in a busy town centre or on a country road? It would be unlikely that you would meet a flock of sheep in the High Street, but there may be one just around the next corner on a country road. Whatever your location you must always consider the type of hazard that you may expect to meet there, and be driving at such a speed that you can stop safely, if necessary.

The time of day

The time of day can give you a lot of information about what to expect on the road. If you see a warning sign for cattle, or mud on the road you should be especially vigilant at dawn or dusk because cows are often taken for milking at these times and may well be on the road ahead ... perhaps around the next bend.

Although children can be present in the road at any time, they are out in force just before and after school. Therefore, you should be keeping a special look out for children during the morning rush hour and mid-afternoon periods.

Other road users

It may seem fairly obvious that you should look out for other road users, but remember, you are not just looking for them, you are looking for clues about what they will do next?

Pedestrians: The Highway Code explains that those pedestrians most at risk on the road are over 60 or less than 15. Old people do not judge speed and distance very well and their reactions can be slow. Have they seen you? Can they hear you? Look for clues. Are they carrying a white stick? Are they looking your way? And so on.

Children have little time to consider road safety; they are more interested in the game that they are playing or the ice cream van that they are running after. Look for clues. Are they alone? If one child runs or cycles into the road there will often be at least one more following; footballs are followed by children; cycles, seemingly abandoned at the side of the road, will mean that children are not far away.

All pedestrians, not just the young and old, are at risk on the road. If there are pedestrians about, make sure that you know what they are going to do before they do it.

Animals: are frightened by noise and vehicles. Therefore, drive slowly, don't sound your horn or rev up the engine and keep you distance. Watch their behaviour carefully, particularly if it is a horse being ridden by a child.

Cyclists: A High Court judge once ruled that a cyclist is entitled to wobble. Drivers should have more control over their vehicles than cyclists who are dependent upon physical strength and effort to pilot their machines.

Always leave plenty of room when passing cyclists, look out for clues about their next move. For example, a cyclist who looks around over his or her right shoulder may be about to turn right; a puddle in the road will cause a cyclist to move out. Cyclists are not easy to see and they can easily get lost in the blind spots around your vehicle such as those caused by your windscreen and door pillars. Particularly watch out for them in slow moving traffic in built up areas – they may overtake you on either side when you least expect.

Motorcyclists: Like cyclists motorcyclists are not easy to see particularly at dusk and at night. Like cyclists they may also take up unusual road positions to avoid holes and bumps in the road surface. It is very easy to miss an approaching motorcyclist when emerging at junctions – so remember think once, think twice, think bike!

Drivers: If you are unsure about what a driver is going to do next, leave plenty of space between you and them. A sporty looking "custom-car" may be driven by someone more interested in "posing" than driving.

Look out for the actions of drivers: a driver who has just stopped may open his door without checking to see if it is safe; a driver who seems to be dithering about may be a stranger to the area and could, therefore, make a last minute turn without a signal when he or she sees the road they are looking for.

Large vehicles: Buses and large vehicles need more room and may take up unusual road positions to turn round corners at junctions etc. Hold back and give them plenty of room.

Inconsistent behaviour
Inconsistent behaviour is often a very good clue to what might happen next. Just because a bus is signalling left prior to the side road that you intend to emerge from doesn't mean that you should go on the assumption that the bus is turning left? Look to see if all the actions of the driver are consistent with the signal. Is the vehicle slowing down as you would expect to complete the proposed turn? Is the position of the vehicle consistent with the proposed manoeuvre? Is the driver looking in the direction they intend to turn? Could the driver be signalling left for any other reason? In this example the bus driver may be signalling left to pull up at a bus stop just after the side road. Make sure you look at all the evidence before you finally decide.

Train your mind to recognise inconsistency – that's not quite right – why's that?

What other drivers cannot see
Consider what you can see that other drivers cannot see. This may play an important part in determining what may happen next. Consider whether you can see something or someone that they cannot see that may cause them to alter their course or abort the manoeuvre at the last minute. Also consider whether other drivers need to see you and if so determine what you can do to make your presence know to them.

The weather and visibility
Bright sunlight, fog, rain and snow can severely affect visibility therefore remember to slow down and give yourself more space.

At dusk and at night the driver loses the ability to see any detail and dark objects easily merge into the background. Consider not only how this may affect your judgement but also how these conditions may affect other drivers. Is the other driver being blinded by bright sunlight or if at night by headlights on full beam? Are the windows of other vehicles misty - can the driver see you? Will the high-sided vehicle, in high wind, remain stable when it crosses a gap in the hedge or buildings that might line the side of the road?

Also remember the effects of water, ice and snow on the road surface – are the other drivers driving too fast for the weather conditions – are you driving too fast for these conditions?

Defensive driving
Driving defensively is all about giving yourself time to react and keeping your options open. Even someone with lightening fast reactions needs time to

react. The laws of physics simply prevent a car from stopping dead. Even if you are Superman or Superwoman, with supernatural reactions, you couldn't stop a car within fewer car lengths than those shown below:

Look well ahead and perceive potential problems early

See and be seen. Take up safe road positions that allow you to see and be seen. Be attentive; focus on the driving task - don't let your mind wander.

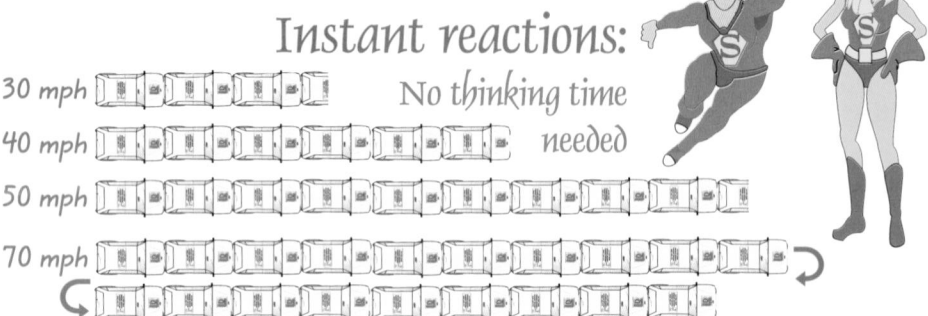

Instant reactions: No thinking time needed

30 mph
40 mph
50 mph
70 mph

Consequently, anything or anybody who is within the distances shown above of the front of your car will be hit! You could call this area to the front of your car the impact zone or if you are travelling at 40 MPH or more the killing zone as anyone hit at these speeds is unlikely to survive. This clearly demonstrates the importance of anticipating what might happen and acting upon that rather than waiting until it happens. To do this effectively you need to:

· **Look well ahead and perceive potential problems early.**

· **Apply your hazard drill in good time.**

· **Give yourself plenty of space.**

Keep your eyes moving and scan the road well ahead. Avoid staring at any single point ahead or to the side. Concentrate on the available space (i.e. the gaps), not the obstructions.

With experience and guidance from your instructor you will begin to recognise what feedback from your sensors are important and what is not. Ignore the superficial information you can see. For example don't concentrate on identifying individual drivers or pedestrians or the make, model or the colours of vehicles. Instead concentrate on the position, speed and potential course of other vehicles and/or pedestrians both to the front, rear and sides of your vehicle.

Look as far down the road as you can see for any potential hazards whether they are static road features or situations being caused by other road users. A gap in the tree line ahead may mean that there is a side road at that point or an upside down triangle sign in the distance may warn you

that you are approaching a T Junction and so on.

Initially you may perceive risks that aren't really there or indeed ignore risks that are. With experience you will begin to develop your own judgement in this regard.

Apply the hazard drill in good time

The hazard drill that we recommend and use is based on a simplified version of the police system of vehicle control. The manoeuvre part of the Mirror-Signal-Manoeuvre routine (MSM) is split into Position-Speed-Gear. See the diagram below.

Hazard drill (MSPSG)

Each time you are presented with a potential or actual hazard on the road (i.e. anything that may require you to have to change speed, position or direction) you will go through the following hazard drill one or more times. While each step of the drill needs to be considered in the order shown it need not necessarily be

the drill may be repeated at any point throughout the drill as required.

Signal: Give signals in good time. Use signals to help or warn other road users. Be careful not to give misleading signals.

Position: Determine the best position/course to negotiate the hazard. Think before you change position; be careful not to mislead others.

Speed: Adjust your speed so that you can negotiate the hazard ahead and stop within the distance you can see to be clear.

Gear: Select the gear to match your speed and the power you need. Make sure that the gear is selected before the hazard is negotiated.

As soon as you perceive a potential danger begin to employ this hazard drill and determine where you can go or how you can stop if the danger materialises.

Take observations as necessary throughout the drill

MIRRORS → SIGNAL → POSITION → SPEED → GEAR
(Must)   (Surely)   (Prevent)   (Some)   (Grief)

acted upon. Observations to the front, rear and sides are carried out at the start and as necessary throughout the application of the drill.

Mirrors: Use your interior mirror and side mirror(s) early. Glance into your right and left blind spots as appropriate. Because this forms part of your observations this part of

Remember you need to consider what's behind as well as what is in front when considering your options.

Give yourself plenty of space

You need to give yourself the time to recognise a potential problem and apply the hazard drill. We refer to this as "**driving in space**".

Driving in space is all about maintaining a buffer of 'safety space' or if you like a safety bubble all around you at all times. The higher your speed (or greater your stopping distance) the bigger the bubble needs to be.

- **Space to the front**

  Always allow yourself enough room to stop. On narrow country roads with a limited view, this may be as much as twice your overall stopping distance (to leave room for the idiot coming the other way!).

- **Space to the sides**

  Make sure that you leave enough room for pedestrians, cyclists, motorcyclists and other vehicles. If you are unsure whether or not you will fit through a gap, you won't! Give parked cars and pedestrians at the side of the road plenty of clearance. Remember pedestrians are far more vulnerable then vehicles. Allow for car doors opening or children appearing from between parked cars or pedestrians wandering onto the road particularly in crowded streets or joggers on country roads moving out to avoid puddles or mud on the road side. Position your car accordingly and reduce speed as the space to your sides is reduced.

- **Space to the rear**

  If other vehicles follow too close slow down and let them pass. Remember that it's your neck that will suffer if someone hits your car from the back! The less space you have at the back the more you need at the front.

Start of score 5 segment

Start of score 2 segment

Start of score 4 segment

Start of score 1 segment

Start of score 3 segment

Start of score zero

Start of score 5 segment

Start of score 2 segment

Start of score 4 segment

Start of score 1 segment

Start of score 3 segment

Start of score zero

Start of score 5 segment

Start of score 2 segment

Start of score 4 segment

Start of score 1 segment

Start of score 3 segment

Start of score zero

Start of score 5 segment

Start of score 2 segment

Start of score 4 segment

Start of score 1 segment

Start of score 3 segment

Start of score zero

Start of score 5 segment

Start of score 2 segment

Start of score 4 segment

Start of score 1 segment

Start of score 3 segment

Start of score zero

Start of score 5 segment

Start of score 2 segment

Start of score 4 segment

Start of score 1 segment

Start of score 3 segment

Start of score zero

Official hazard perception practice clip 7

Start of score 5 segment

Start of score 2 segment

Start of score 4 segment

Start of score 1 segment

Start of score 3 segment

Start of score zero

Start of score 5 segment

Start of score 2 segment

Start of score 4 segment

Start of score 1 segment

Start of score 3 segment

Start of score zero

Start of score 5 segment

Start of score 2 segment

Start of score 4 segment

Start of score 1 segment

Start of score 3 segment

Start of score zero

Start of score 5 segment

Start of score 2 segment

Start of score 4 segment

Start of score 1 segment

Start of score 3 segment

Start of score zero

Start of score 5 segment

Start of score 2 segment

Start of score 4 segment

Start of score 1 segment

Start of score 3 segment

Start of score zero

Start of score 5 segment

Start of score 2 segment

Start of score 4 segment

Start of score 1 segment

Start of score 3 segment

Start of score zero

Start of score 5 segment

Start of score 2 segment

Start of score 4 segment

Start of score 1 segment

Start of score 3 segment

Start of score zero

Start of score 5 segment

Start of score 2 segment

Start of score 4 segment

Start of score 1 segment

Start of score 3 segment

Start of score zero

Introduction

Unfortunately about 12% of the theory test questions cannot be answered by the Highway Code. Consequently, we have grouped these questions together and put them into quiz 12. Therefore before you undertake quiz 12 you will need to read the following supplementary notes.

1. Motor Insurance and Vehicle Excise Duty

It is a legal requirement that before you drive a vehicle on public roads you have the proper insurance cover. Indeed to obtain a vehicle excise licence (i.e. a tax disc) it is necessary for you to have insurance cover. There are three main types insurance cover. These are:

- Third Party Insurance
  This is the legal minimum cover and is also the cheapest. It covers anyone who you might injure or whose property you might damage. It does not cover your own property or injury to yourself.
- Third Party, Fire and Theft
  This offers the same benefits as third party insurance but also covers your own vehicle should it be damaged by fire or stolen.
- Fully Comprehensive
  This is the best and the most expensive. As well as the benefits of the two previous types it also covers damage to your own vehicle and injury to yourself.

The cost of insurance varies from company to company and also depends on certain factors. These include:

- Age of driver (e.g. people in the age group 17 - 25 years are the most likely to have an accident, therefore the younger the driver the more expensive the insurance).
- Make of vehicle.
- Size of engine.
- Number of years driving experience.
- Full or provisional licence holder.
- Court convictions, if any.
- Where you live.
- Where the vehicle is to be kept and if it has an alarm.
- Intended use of vehicle.
- No Claims Bonus (a discount given to drivers off their insurance premium for each year they do not make a claim).
- Amount of excess (the amount you are required to pay towards each claim the higher the excess the lower the premium).
- Completion of Pass Plus Scheme to reduce the risk of an accident (a scheme to give new drivers more experience by taking further training with an ADI after passing their test). Everyone who takes and passes the course will get reduced premiums with certain insurance companies.

When looking for insurance shop around to find the best policy for your requirements.

Buy the best policy you can afford. Do not just go for the cheapest as you may regret it later if you need to make a claim. Please remember you can be fined up to £5,000 and acquire 6-8 penalty points if you are caught driving without insurance.

Vehicle Excise Duty (Car Tax)

All vehicles using the road must display a valid vehicle licence (tax disc) in the bottom nearside corner of the windscreen. Any vehicle which is exempt from duty must display a 'nil' tax disc.

The registered keeper of a vehicle is responsible for taxing the vehicle or

making a SORN (Statutory Off Road Notification) until the vehicle is officially transferred to a new keeper.

Keepers who fail to declare SORN or re-licence will incur an automatic penalty.

A keeper can declare SORN if the vehicle is not going to be used or kept on a public road, this means that road tax does not have to be paid.

A SORN declaration is valid for 12 months provided the vehicle remains off the road.

2. The Environment

The car is no longer a luxury. It has now become an essential part of modern life. As more and more cars are using our roads they are unfortunately having a detrimental effect on the environment.

As fuel is burned in the engine it produces waste gases which are toxic and harmful. These pollutants are released into the air causing damage to plant life and human health problems such as asthma. Buildings are now showing the effects of these pollutants as stone and brickwork start to deteriorate.

The more cars that are being used means that we need to make more roads or widen the existing ones. This changes the landscape and disrupts wildlife. More fuel is also being used which depletes our natural resources.

As we are becoming more aware of the effects of pollution on the environment, motor manufacturers are researching and developing ways that these effects can be minimised. Smaller and more efficient vehicles for town use are being developed. Engines able to run on unleaded fuel are used more widely. All modern vehicles with a petrol engine are now fitted with a catalytic converter.

A catalytic converter is a honeycombed filter fitted to the exhaust system. The surface area of this honeycomb is coated with precious metals, usually platinum or palladium, which speed up the chemical reaction in the exhaust gases as the engine heats up and remove up to 75% of carbon monoxide, nitrogen oxide (the toxic and polluting gases) and hydrocarbons (the unburned fuel compounds).

The MOT test now includes a strict emissions test to ensure that car engines are properly tuned so that pollution is reduced.

The responsibility for looking after the environment cannot rest solely on the shoulders of the motor vehicle manufacturers. Drivers themselves can do a lot to reduce the effects of pollution, for example:
- Share a vehicle with someone who makes the same journey.
- Walk or cycle instead of using the car.
- Avoid using the car for very short journeys particularly when the engine is cold.
- Use public transport.
- Make sure your car is properly serviced and the engine is correctly tuned.
- Inflate your tyres to the correct pressure. Under inflated tyres increase fuel consumption.
- Travelling at a constant speed will not only reduce your fuel consumption but will also reduce your overall journey time. In fact driving smoothly can reduce fuel consumption by about 15%.
- Avoid rapid acceleration or harsh braking because this leads to increased fuel consumption.

- Slow down as the faster you go the more fuel you will use. At 70mph a vehicle will use up to 30% more fuel than at 50mph.
- Do not carry unnecessary weight in your car.
- Remove your roof rack when not in use.
- Have your vehicles engine converted to unleaded fuel.
- Plan well ahead when driving so as to avoid braking hard.
- Do not over rev the engine in the lower gears.
- If you service your own car dispose of the old engine oil safely by taking it to a local authority site. Do not pour it down the drain as it is harmful to the environment, illegal and could result in prosecution.
- If in a city use trams where available. They are environmentally friendly because they reduce noise pollution, use electricity and reduce town traffic.

Be careful about the way you dispose of the car battery or the cars oil as both pose potential hazards to the environment. In both cases take them to a local authority refuse site or garage who will have facilities to dispose of them safely. Remember, this is our world and we must do everything we can to protect it.

3. Tyres

It is vitally important that the tyres on your car are in good condition and inflated to the correct pressure. They are your only contact with the road and will not grip safely if they are in bad condition. Check the condition of your tyres regularly and replace them if necessary. The walls of the tyres should be free from cuts and bulges.

The tread depth should be a minimum of 1.6mm across the central three quarters of the breadth of the tyre and around the entire circumference. This is the minimum legal requirement.

If the tyres are worn unevenly this could be due to the wheels not being aligned or balanced correctly. Alternatively it may be a fault with the suspension or braking systems. Get it checked and put right. If the wheels are not balanced correctly this can cause a vibration on the steering wheel as you drive.

Tyre pressures should be checked weekly and before any long journey, particularly one which will include motorway driving. Always try to check pressures when the tyres are cold so as to get a more accurate reading. Do not forget the spare! Recommended tyre pressures for each vehicle can be found in the owner's handbook.

Tyres can be inflated to a higher pressure (but never more than the recommended maximum) when carrying a heavy load or driving at speed for long distances. Under-inflated tyres can reduce stability and cause the car to use more fuel. This will also have the effect of making the steering of the car heavy, as the tyres will not have enough air in them, which will cause the rubber to drag against the surface of the road.
It is an offence to drive a car with an incorrectly inflated tyre.

The penalties for using a car with defective tyres or a tread depth below the legal minimum are severe and will apply for every tyre on your vehicle. The most severe penalty of all is DEATH.

4. Fuel
Leaded Petrol
Becoming increasingly unpopular because of its high lead content and bad effect on the environment. Used mainly in older cars, it is gradually being phased out. It must not be used in cars fitted with a catalytic converter.

Unleaded Petrol
Most common type of petrol used today. When used in a car fitted with a catalytic converter the harmful emissions are greatly reduced.

Diesel
Only to be used in engines designed to be fuelled by diesel. Although these engines produce higher levels of some pollutants they are very fuel efficient. To improve emissions further low sulphur diesel could be used.

Spare fuel should be carried in a container specifically designed and approved for that purpose. It is illegal and dangerous to carry fuel in any other type of container.

5. Power Steering
Power steering is becoming increasingly common in modern cars. A motor assists the driver when he turns the steering wheel, making it easier to steer as the driver does not need as much strength to turn the wheel. The steering on a car fitted with power steering seems lighter than that on a car fitted with conventional steering. Because of this you need to be particularily careful not to steer while the vehicle is stationary as this may cause damage to the tyres and the steering mechanism.

6. Oil and electrics
Oil is a vital component needed to lubricate the engine of your car. It performs at high pressures and temperatures of up to 300oC. It helps to keep the engine cool, resists wear on the moving surfaces and also combats the corrosive acids formed whilst hydrocarbons in the fuel are burnt. It is therefore important that the oil is kept at the level recommended by your vehicles manufacturer. Check the oil level weekly, before any long journey and top up as required with the correct grade of oil. The engine oil and filter should be changed at regular intervals (see recommendations in owner's handbook).

How to check the oil level
- Oil should be checked when the engine is cold.
- Park your car on level ground.
- Raise bonnet and locate the dipstick on the engine block.
- Take the dipstick out and wipe clean with a dry cloth.
- Note the markings on the dipstick which indicate the lowest and highest levels.
- Push the dipstick fully back into the engine block.
- Take the dipstick out and see where the oil level has reached.
- If oil is below the minimum then top up as required, being careful not to overfill as this will cause excessive pressure that could damage the engine seals and gaskets and cause oil leaks. It can also result in the vehicles exhaust becoming very smoky. If oil is above the minimum then no oil is required.

How to check your battery fluid levels
The distilled water in your battery cells may occasionally need to be topped up. You do this by filling each cell until the distilled water is just above the cell plate.

7. Brakes
The foot brake operates the brakes on all four wheels. Typically, the braking system on a modern front wheel drive car comprises two hydraulic systems. Each is connected to a front and a rear wheel. This ensures that should there be a leak of hydraulic fluid from either system, at least half the braking force will still be available.

Note any variations in the braking efficiency. If the brakes feel spongy or the vehicle pulls to one side when braking, get them checked by a qualified mechanic. You can check the brake fluid level regularly and keep it topped up by following the instructions in the owner's handbook.

Excessive use of the foot brake makes the brakes hot. When this happens the brakes are liable to become less effective and are then said to 'fade'.

The handbrake is used to hold the car still after it has stopped. It operates on two wheels only (usually the back) and, unlike the other brakes, it is mechanically operated.

8. Cooling System
Most cars use water to take the heat away from the engine. The water flows through spaces around the cylinders and valves and out of the top of the engine to the radiator. Cooling air takes the heat from the water as it passes through the radiator before returning to the engine. The water is usually mixed with a dual purpose antifreeze/coolant which prevents the water from freezing in winter and so causing serious damage.

The level of water/coolant mix must not be allowed to drop below the minimum level marked on the bottle. Instructions on how to refill and keep it topped up can be found in the owner's handbook.

9. Distractions
When driving it is important that your attention is concentrated on the task of driving and that there are no unnecessary distractions.

Do not hang anything from the rear view mirror as it will restrict your view as well as distract your attention.

Playing loud music will prevent you from hearing anything else, particularly the sirens of emergency vehicles. You can gain a lot of information about your surroundings by listening as well as looking.

You need a good unrestricted view from all the windows of your car so do not cover them with stickers or block the view to the rear by piling things on the parcel shelf. If you have a mobile phone do not use it while you are driving, either to make or receive calls. Pull over into a safe and convenient place first. People who use mobile phones while driving are not only now breaking the law they are also 4 times as likely to have an accident.

Do not drive if you are angry or upset as this will seriously affect your concentration. If you are still feeling angry after an argument, you should always give yourself time to Calm Down, before attempting to set out on any journey.

10. Mirrors

There are three main mirrors fitted to your car: an interior mirror and two exterior mirrors. The surface of the exterior mirrors is usually convex which gives a wider field of vision but makes vehicles appear to be further away than they actually are. The surface of the interior mirror is flat, making it easier to judge the speed, distance and position of following vehicles than when looking in the exterior mirrors.

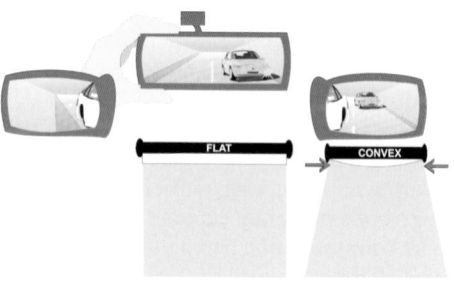

They should be used as part of the basic Mirror, Signal, Manoeuvre (MSM) routine and to keep up to date with what is behind and to the sides of your vehicle, thus enabling you to make safe and sensible decisions based on the position and speed of other road users.Always check your mirrors well before signalling, changing speed and changing direction. If you use the mirrors early as part of the MSM routine you can deal with hazards in plenty of time which will help other road users to know your intentions.If you are dazzled by the lights of following vehicles when driving at night set your interior mirror to 'antidazzle'. Just behind the lower edge of the mirror is a small lever pull this forward and you will still be able to see the lights of the vehicles behind but the dazzle will be greatly reduced. Always remember to reset the mirror by pushing the lever towards the windscreen.

If you are towing a caravan or a trailer it is difficult to see alongside your vehicle and almost impossible to use the rear view mirror. So, fit an exterior mirror on an extended arm to be able to see past the caravan or trailer.

Remember, a good driver always knows what is happening behind his vehicle as well as what is happening to the front.

11. The Dashboard

Directly in front of the driver is an instrument panel which gives the driver information as he drives along. Two of the main instruments are the speedometer and the fuel gauge.

The Speedometer

This tells the driver how fast the car is travelling in both miles per hour and kilometres per hour. It is usually a dial with a needle but it can also be digital. It must not be obscured from the drivers view.

The Fuel Gauge

This indicates the amount of fuel in the tank. Some show a reading all the time, others will only show a reading when the ignition is switched on. Before setting off on a journey always make sure you have enough fuel to reach your destination or to get you to the next petrol station.

WARNING LIGHTS
There are also several warning lights which come on to warn the driver of any problems or to give information about the functions selected. Details of all the warning lights on your car can be found in the owner's handbook. They will include the Oil Warning Light, the Brake Warning Light and the Parking Brake Light.

Oil Warning Light

This light with a small oil can warns of low oil pressure which could mean there is little or no oil in the engine. If this light comes on when you are driving, stop as soon as you can and check the oil level. If it stays on after checking and correcting the oil level do not drive your car as serious damage may occur. Have your car checked by a qualified mechanic.

Brake Warning Light "!"

If this light with an exclaimation mark in a circle comes on when you are driving it could indicate that there is a fault within the braking system. This could be dangerous and so you should stop as soon as you can, trying not to rely on the brakes too much, and get the braking system checked by a qualified mechanic. This light may also come on when the hand brake is applied so make sure you release the handbrake fully and the light goes out.

Parking Brake Light "P"

Some cars have this light with the letter "P" in a circle. This light which comes on when the handbrake is applied. If the hand-brake is not released properly the light will stay on.

Headlight/Fog light indicator lights "=D"

This light with a side view of a headlight with a series of vertical lines in front indicates that your lights are on full beam.

This light with a side view of a headlight with a series of downward pointing lines in front indicates that your lights are on dipped beam.

This light with a side view of a headlight with a series of short vertical lines and two horizontal wavy lines in front indicates that your fog lights are on.

Indicator lights ">" and "<"

There are two of these lights, one with an arrow pointing to the right and one with an arrow pointing to the left. When you use the flashing indicators to signal your intentions to other road users, one of these lights will flash and you will hear a clicking noise. Always check that your signal has cancelled when it is no longer required.

Hazard light indicator

This light with a triangle will flash when the hazard warning lights are on. If you have access to a vehicle owner's manual read the section on warning lights.

12. Stopping in an Emergency

The cause of most accidents is driver error. When an accident happens it is usually blamed on the weather (fog, rain, bright sunshine etc.), the road surface (ice, snow, gravel, water etc.), the pedestrian who ran out from 'nowhere' and numerous other causes, when in fact it was the driver who was not driving appropriately for the road and weather conditions. If he had been then the accident may never have happened.

However there are the rare occasions when even the most alert and careful driver can do little to prevent an accident occurring. The best he can do is know how to stop as quickly and as safely as possible and to try to do so.

If you need to stop in an emergency quick reactions can save vital seconds and even a life.

The quicker you apply the foot brake the sooner the car will stop. Be careful though. If you press the brake too hard or 'slam' the brakes on your car is likely to skid. Always use the brake pedal progressively i.e. pushing the brake pedal harder as the car slows down.

Harsh braking throws the weight of the car forwards rapidly, making it very difficult to keep the vehicle straight, and makes the rear lighter. The wheels may lock (stop turning) but the car will keep going, skidding along the road surface. If this happens release the foot brake so as to allow the wheels to turn again. Then reapply so the brakes can continue to slow the car. Keep both hands on the steering wheel and depress the clutch just before the car comes to a halt. This will allow the engine and the brakes to work together so stopping the car quicker.

Some modern cars are fitted with an antilocking brake system (ABS) which senses when the wheels are about to lock and very quickly releases the braking pressure such that the wheels are allowed to turn very slowly spreading the frictional force over more of the tyre. This allows optimum braking to be achieved on a normal road surface while allowing the driver to steer the car at the same time. ABS is slightly less effective on icy, wet or loose surfaces and the brakes are only as good as the tyre grip on the road.

So try to avoid having to stop quickly and brake harshly by always driving at a speed that is appropriate for the road and traffic conditions and that allows you to stop safely within the distance you can see to be clear. If it is not clear SLOW DOWN.

13. First Aid

It may happen that one day you come across the scene of, or are involved in, an accident so it may be helpful to be familiar with a few basic first aid procedures. Firstly there is the ABC procedure for dealing with unconscious accident victims. It is essential that you follow this procedure immediately if the casualty is unconscious and permanent injury is to be avoided.

A - Clear the airway of any obstructions including false teeth, chewing gum etc. Breathing should begin and colour improve.

B - If breathing does not begin, lift the chin and tilt the head gently backwards. Pinch the casualty's nose and blow gently (particularly if it is a child) into the mouth until the chest rises. Repeat this every four seconds until the casualty can breathe unaided.

C - Circulation must be maintained by preventing blood loss. If the casualty is bleeding apply firm pressure over the wound, using clean material if possible, taking care not to press on any foreign body which may be in the wound. If the limb is not broken it should be raised to lessen the bleeding.

Back Injury
Any casualty you suspect has a back or neck injury should not be moved unless they are in danger. Movement could add to the injury. Do not remove the safety helmet of an injured motorcyclist unless it is absolutely essential as serious injury could result.

Burns

If any casualty is suffering from burns, no matter how severe, it is possible that they could go into immediate nervous shock. This will cause them to go pale, confused, anxious, frightened or they may even faint. Douse the burns with a cold, clean, nontoxic liquid unless they are very severe, in which case the burn should be lightly covered with a clean cloth and professional medical attention sought immediately.

Never try to remove anything which is stuck to the burn. Leave that to the experts. You should always carry a first aid kit in your car.

You could also learn first aid by attending a course run by the St. John's Ambulance Brigade or the British Red Cross Society. Hopefully you will never need to use either, but it might just help to save a life!

14. Hills

When going uphill it is more difficult to maintain or increase speed as the engine has to work harder to make the car go faster. You may find you will need to change to a lower gear to give you more power. This should be done fairly quickly as the car will loose speed when the gas pedal is released and the clutch pedal pressed down. Ideally you should change down before you start to climb the hill. The brakes will slow the car down quicker when going uphill. Remember to apply the handbrake once you have stopped otherwise the car will roll back.

When going downhill the engine is helped along by the weight of the car and so it will travel faster, making it more difficult to slow down, as the brakes have less effect. Select a lower gear before you start

to go down a hill. Using a lower gear in this manner to reduce the speed of the car is known as engine braking. Use the foot brake carefully to keep control of the speed. Try to avoid depressing the clutch as the car will go faster until the clutch is reengaged. If you need to change gear when going downhill do so with your foot on the foot brake to prevent the car from speeding up.

Always be on the lookout for signs warning you of hills. Assess the gradient early, whether uphill or downhill, and decide on what action, if any, you need to take to negotiate the hill. Then take that action before you start to climb or descend. Driving downhill or uphill can have an effect on your control of the car.

15. Fuel Spillage

Fuel is a precious commodity and all precautions to avoid wasting it should be taken. If you suspect that the fuel tank of your vehicle is leaking have it checked and, if necessary, replaced. Your leaking fuel tank may result in a fire or an explosion. While leaking diesel might not ignite it will make the road surface extremely slippery. When refuelling make sure you do not overfill the tank and ensure that the filler cap is securely fastened.

16. Manoeuvring

You can legally remove your seat belt when performing any manoeuvre that includes reversing.

This allows you greater freedom to move around and turn your head for better observation.

Always check all around before you start to reverse. If you are not sure whether or

not it is clear behind your vehicle, get out and have a look. If you cannot see clearly as you reverse get someone to guide you. There are many dangers as you reverse, mainly from approaching traffic and pedestrians. Keep your speed down and give yourself time to take good observations. Before you steer check for other road users as the front of your vehicle may swing out into the path of another vehicle.

Always be prepared to give way to other traffic when reversing. It is much easier for other drivers to go round your car when it is stood still than when it is moving. Remember it is illegal to reverse for longer than necessary so once you have completed the manoeuvre, stop.

17. Vehicle Loading

As a driver it is your responsibility to ensure that your vehicle is loaded properly and safely. If you have to carry a load it must be fastened securely and not stick out dangerously. A heavy load on a roof rack will reduce the stability of your vehicle and make it more difficult to handle.

18. Signs and Markings

The majority of road signs and road markings are explained in The Highway Code. However there are a few less common ones, which are not included. Some of these are explained below. This sign with a "P" over a car on a raised verge on a blue background means that you may legally park your car fully on the verge or footpath.

This arrow sign with a "P +" and a silhouette of a bus on a blue background is becoming more common. It indicates an area where a Park and Ride system is in operation.

You can park your car in an out-of-town car park and a bus service is provided to take you into the town. This system is successful in keeping traffic out of busy town centres.

You will find this sign with an "R" on a green background at intervals alongside the road, indicating that you are travelling on the Ring Road.

This sign with a silhouette of a man running towards an open door on a green background is found in tunnels, indicating the Emergency Exit For Pedestrians.

This sign with a man walking on a white circle with a red band is sometimes seen on dual carriageways, ring roads and places where it would be dangerous for pedestrians to walk. It means No Pedestrians.

On the approach to a concealed railway crossing you might see countdown markings denoting the distance to the stop line. Red diagonal strips on a white background. Three strips means three hundred feet, two strips two hundred feet and one strip one hundred feet.

Drivers sometimes ignore "zz SCHOOL KEEP CLEAR zz" road makings that are used to mark where school children cross the road. The markings are there to inform drivers not to wait or park in this area. To do so would cause danger by potentially blocking the view of children crossing the road or drivers driving up or down the road.

Yellow lines are sometimes painted across the road surface on the approach to a hazard, such as a roundabout. Their function is to make the driver aware of his speed and direct him to slow down.

Some road markings, such as the white lines between the motorway carriageway and the hard shoulder, have raised areas at regular intervals, which make a noise as you drive over them. These rumble devices are there to alert the driver to a hazard, in this case the edge of the carriageway, or to encourage the driver to slow down as would be the case if the yellow lines illustrated above were slightly raised.

To separate traffic flowing in opposite directions, particularly on bends, you may see an area in the middle of the road painted red enclosed with broken or unbroken white lines with white diagonal strips. This area is designed to discourage drivers from moving too close to the centre of the road and therefore present a hazard to oncoming vehicles that may do the same.

When driving through a tunnel make sure you look out for variable message signs. These signs will provide warnings and orders as necessary.

19. Lane Discipline

Lane discipline is vital when travelling along multil-ane roads. You should always follow the lane markings and road signs. They are there to guide the traffic and make the best use of road space.
When driving in lanes, position yourself in the centre of your lane, keeping to the left hand lane wherever possible.

If you find that you are in the wrong lane do not move across immediately. Carry on in that lane until you can change lanes safely or, if it is not possible to change lanes, continue in your lane and find another way back to your route.

The same applies to a oneway street. If you find yourself travelling down a oneway street but you need to go in the opposite direction, you must not turn round.

Continue to the end of the road and then find an alternative route to your destination.

20. Towing

If you passed your driving test before 1st January 1997 you are allowed to drive a vehicle towing a trailer provided their combined weight is under 8.25 tonnes and you are over 21 years old (7.5 tonnes if you are under 21 years old).

If you passed your driving test on or after 1st January 1997 then you may have to take a further test if you want to tow a large trailer. Details can be obtained from DVLA leaflet INF30 'Towing Trailers in Great Britain'.

When towing a caravan or trailer there are a few basic principles you need to follow. These include:

- Never exceed the manufacturer's recommended maximum weight that can be towed by your car or the maximum noseweight that can be applied to the tow ball (details can be found in owner's handbook). It is usually safest for the loaded weight of the trailer not to exceed 85% of the kerbside (empty) weight of the towing vehicle.

- Fit exterior mirrors with extending arms so you can see clearly along both sides of the trailer.
- Fit a stabiliser to help reduce the effects of cross winds. It can also help to make the combination (i.e. the towing vehicle and trailer) easier to handle but will not compensate for a poorly loaded combination. Heavy items should be loaded as low as possible, mainly over the axle. Any lighter items should be distributed to give a suitable noseweight at the front. The overall stability of the towing vehicle and the trailer depends on correct weight distribution.
- Passengers must never be allowed to travel in a caravan when it is being towed.
- Before starting on a journey ensure that the trailer is correctly hitched and that the breakaway cable is properly connected. Should the trailer and the towing vehicle become separated this will break and apply the brakes to the trailer. Check that all the lights, indicators and brakes are working properly, that windows, roof light and doors are closed and that the tyre pressures on both the trailer and the towing vehicle are correct.
- Before towing for the first time take professional instruction from one of the larger caravanning organisations. You will then feel more confident in your ability to handle the combination and deal with difficult traffic situations.

21. Automatic Transmission
A car fitted with automatic transmission will change gear automatically as it detects the need for a different gear according to the road speed and the load on the engine. It will change to a higher gear as the road speed increases and to a lower gear as the road speed decreases.

Sometimes the driver may need quick acceleration, for example to overtake. This can be achieved by pressing the accelerator pedal all the way to the floor, causing a quick change to a lower gear, so speed can be increased quickly. A higher gear will then be selected as the pressure on the accelerator is eased off. This technique is known as 'kick down'.

22. Four Wheel Drive
Most cars are two wheel drive which means that either the front or rear wheels are driven by the engine, the other two are either pushed or pulled along. However some vehicles are fitted with four wheel drive which means that all four wheels are driven by the engine. One of the main benefits of this system is that road holding is improved.

23. Emergency Vehicles
When driving along always be on the look out for emergency vehicles. You can recognise them by their flashing blue lights and loud sirens. They include police, fire brigade, ambulance, coastguard, blood transfusion service, bomb disposal and mountain rescue vehicles. Check where they are coming from and watch to see where they are going. Keep out of their way and take any action you can to help them get through but do not endanger other road users. If all you need to do is pull in on the left, signal left as you do so. The driver then knows you have seen him and he can drive past safely.

If you see a vehicle with a green flashing light treat it just the same as this is a doctor on an emergency call out.

24. Junctions and bends

Special care must be taken when emerging from a junction (going from the side road into the main road).

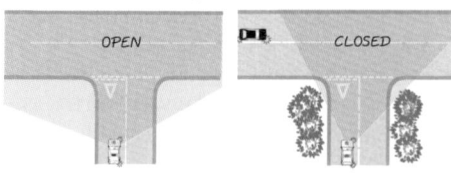

Make good, early observations as you approach. This will help you to decide if you can see clearly enough to determine whether it is safe to go or not. This decision will be influenced by your zone of vision (the amount of the new road you can see to either the left or the right as you approach the junction). Your zone of vision can be limited by parked vehicles, buildings, bends, hills, traffic on the main road, trees, hedges, walls and fences.

As you approach the junction your zone of vision usually improves, but it can be blocked by parked cars. In cases where there is reduced visibility you can only decide when it is safe to emerge by edging forward very slowly, looking both ways, into a position where your zone of vision is improved. If you are near shops or other buildings or objects with reflective surfaces you may be able to use this to help you determine if it is safe to emerge.

Do not emerge unless you are absolutely certain it is clear and safe to do so. Similarly any vehicles turning left into the side road, particularly large vehicles, can hide other vehicles travelling behind or alongside them. Always take extra care at junctions where visibility is reduced. If parked vehicles obscure your view of the junction continue to creep forward slowly until you can obtain a view as in the example shown.

Emerging at Y junctions

The procedure for approaching and emerging from Y junctions is basically the same as T-junctions. However, the position of the vehicle may need to be slightly different just prior to emerging to make emerging safer and extra observations must be taken as the windscreen pillars of the car may obscure your view and may cause you to miss something small like a motorcycle. Therefore, make sure to look around your windscreen pillars by moving your head backwards and forwards to minimise this risk. The windscreen pillars can also obscure you view when negotiating bends.

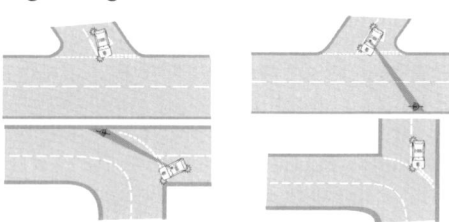

Emerging at unmarked crossroads

Neither road is the major road and therefore no one has priority. Consequently you must slow down on approach and be prepared to stop. Anticipating other driver's actions and driving at a speed that enables you to stop is critical. Priority regarding oncoming vehicles is not changed, if you are turning right you would need to give way to oncoming traffic turning left or going straight ahead. If you come across a crossroad where the traffic lights have failed you should treat this as a unmarked

crossroad, slow down on approach, look both ways and be prepared to stop.

When you want to pull up on the left just after a junction on the left is very careful not to mislead anyone with your signal. You should indicate left just as you pass the junction and not before it.

25. Motorcyclists
Motorbikes and pedal cycles are not as large or as wide as a car and as such are much more difficult to see. Many accidents happen because drivers do not notice them, particularly at junctions. So always be on the look out for them. When driving in slow moving queues of traffic motorcyclists sometimes ride between the lanes. Before you change lanes make sure you have checked for bikes filtering through the traffic.

THINK ONCE, THINK TWICE, THINK BIKE.

26. Following Other Vehicles
When following any vehicle always leave a safe gap between your vehicle and the one in front.

This gap should not be less than the overall stopping distance for the speed you are travelling. If you are travelling very slowly in heavy urban traffic then this distance can be reduced to no less than your thinking distance. As a rough guide leave a gap equal to 1 metre for every mile per hour you are travelling e.g. a speed of 50mph = a distance of 50 metres.

When following a large vehicle, such as a lorry or double decker bus, always keep well back, even when travelling slowly. This will allow you a better view of what is happening in front of the lorry and you

will be able to judge when or if you can overtake it safely. Keeping well back also allows the driver of the lorry to see you in his mirrors. If you cannot see the mirrors on the lorry then the driver cannot see you. It may be that you find yourself being followed very closely by another vehicle (tailgating). This can make you feel uneasy and pressured into going faster in an effort to get away from it. If this happens try to stay calm and do not speed up as the following driver will only speed up as well. If you can do so safely allow him to overtake. Sometimes this is not possible so the safest thing you can do is to gradually allow the gap between your vehicle and the one in front to increase to double what it should be by gradually slowing down. This will then give you more time to slow down or stop, should the need arise, without putting yourself in too much danger.

27. Dead Ground
Dead ground is a section of road that

is hidden in a dip. Vehicles in this dip cannot be seen so care must be taken before overtaking to ensure there are no areas of dead ground hiding the oncoming traffic.

28. Humpback Bridge
This type of bridge is found mainly on rural roads where the road goes over a stream or a river. The 'hump' can be

quite high and will sometimes hide an oncoming vehicle from view. Consider using the horn to warn any other road users of your presence before you start to go over the bridge particularily if the road is narrow. Also listen out for the horns of other vehicles warning you and watch for pedestrians using the bridge.

29. Priorities

The Highway Code says that where there is an obstruction on your side of the road, such as a parked car, you should give way to oncoming traffic. However sometimes common sense and courtesy should prevail and the advice of the Highway Code altered to suit the situation. For example, if you are travelling downhill and a large heavy vehicle is travelling uphill with an obstruction on his side of the road, you should give way to the lorry allowing him to continue up the hill without stopping. It is far easier for you to restart downhill than it is for the lorry going uphill.

30. Bad Weather

Fog

If you have to travel in foggy conditions always allow extra time for your journey as you will have to drive slower and so it will take you longer to reach your destination.

Use dipped headlights, even in daytime fog, and if visibility is reduced to less than 100 metres use your fog lamps.
Do not follow the lights of the vehicle in front as you could be too close. Try to leave as large a gap as possible between your vehicle and the one in front.
Give signals earlier than you would do normally to allow other drivers time to see your signal and react accordingly.
Keep a check on your speed; you may be travelling faster than you think.
Use the wipers to keep the windscreen clear.

Remember to turn your fog lamps off when they are no longer needed or they will dazzle other drivers.

If it is foggy and your journey is not essential, stay in.

Snow

In deep snow special wheel chains can be fitted to help prevent skidding.

Heavy Rain

When driving in heavy rain use your dipped headlights so that other drivers will be able to see your car easier. Do not use fog lights as this will dazzle other drivers and give the false impression that you are braking.

Increase the distance between you and the car in front. It should be at least double on a wet than on a dry road surface.
Keep your speed down to reduce the risk of aquaplaning. This is where a build up of water between the tyre and the road surface causes the vehicle to slide as the tyres loose contact with the road. You can tell when this happens as the steering suddenly becomes very light. To correct it ease off the accelerator and try to keep the vehicle in a straight line. Do not try to steer. Once the car has slowed down the tyres will grip again.

31. Security

If possible you should always park your car in the garage if you have one. This is the safest place for it. Failing this you should look to park your car in a secure car park. If you do have to park your car on the street try to look for a prominent position where the car is very visible. At night make sure the area is also well lit. If you have a local vehicle watch scheme in operation join this so that you can help to protect your car when parked near your home.

If you install a car radio/CD/DVD make sure it is a security coded radio.

32. Pedestrian Crossings

There are four main types of pedestrian crossing. These are the zebra crossing, pelican crossing, puffin crossing and the toucan crossing. Pelican, puffin and toucan crossings are controlled by traffic lights. Even if a traffic light is on green you should always be prepared to stop, particularily, if pedestrians have been waiting for sometime and as a consequence you suspect that the green light may shortly change to red. You should also pay special attention to certain types of pedestrian who are particularily at risk when crossing the road. For example, pedstrians over 60 and those under 15.

Pedstrians who have disabilities or who may be deaf and/or blind. If you see a pedestrian with a dog who has a bright orange collar and lead then this informs you that the pedestrian is deaf. If the person is carrying a white stick they are blind and if they are carrying a white stick with a red band they are blind and deaf.

Types of crossing

Although each of the 4 types of pedestran crossing are different certain rules and advice apply to them all:-
- You must not park on a crossing or in the area within the zigzag lines.
- You must not overtake the vehicle nearest the crossing.
- Never beckon pedestrians to cross; let them decide when they feel it is safe to cross.
- In a queue of traffic keep the crossing clear.
- Do not harass pedestrians when they are crossing by revving the engine or inching forward. Give them plenty of time to cross.

Some rules and advice apply to certain types of crossing:

Zebra Crossing
- You must give way to anyone who has stepped onto the crossing, so be on the lookout as you approach for people who are waiting to cross or who are approaching from the side and be prepared to stop.
- A zebra crossing with a central island is two crossings. If it goes straight across the road with no island it is one crossing.

Pelican Crossing
These are signal controlled crossings. The sequence of the lights is:
Red
Flashing Amber
Green
Amber
Red.

The lights are operated by pedestrians using a push button when they want to cross. If the amber light is flashing you must give way to pedestrians who are still on the crossing. If there are no pedestrians on the crossing when the amber light is flashing you may proceed but with caution in case anyone runs onto the crossing in an attempt to beat the lights.

Pelican crossings which go straight across the road with an island in the centre are one crossing. If the crossing is staggered it is two crossings.

You must give way to pedestrians who are still crossing even when the signal for traffic changes to green. Remember green means you can proceed only if it is clear and safe to do so.

Puffin Crossing

A puffin crossing is signal controlled. The sequence of the lights is the same as normal traffic lights. They are also operated using a push button. However they also have a sensor which detects when someone is within the crossing area. Once activated the lights will not go back to green until the crossing area is clear of people as detected by the sensor.

Toucan Crossing

A toucan crossing is signal controlled and has the same sequence as traffic lights. This type of crossing is shared by pedestrians and cyclists ('two can cross'). Cyclists can ride across the crossing but at other crossings they should dismount and walk. The signals are push button operated and there is a separate light to indicate when cyclists can cross.

33. Night-time Driving

At night you will not be able to see as far as you can in daylight and so the way you drive must change to allow for the conditions.

When you first go out into the darkness give your eyes a minute or two to adjust before you start to drive.

Make sure you switch on your vehicle lights so you can see and be seen. Only use main beam headlights on roads without street lamps. These lights are very bright and can dazzle the drivers of oncoming vehicles or vehicles in front so switch to dipped headlights if another vehicle approaches you or overtakes you. If a vehicle is overtaking (and there is no oncoming traffic) do not dip your headlights until the vehicle passes you. Your main beam will help the overtaking vehicle to see if there are any hazards up ahead that would make the manoeuvre unsafe.

When waiting at a junction do not keep your foot on the brake pedal as the lights can dazzle the driver behind.

Beware of bends if you overtake anything. It is difficult to see as far in the dark and it is not easy to judge distances.

Pedestrians are more difficult to see and can seem to appear from 'nowhere'. You need to be more alert. Never drive so fast that you cannot stop within the distance you can see to be clear. At night that distance is within the range of your lights.

34. Motorways

Once you have passed your driving test you are allowed to drive on the motorway. The traffic travels faster which means that conditions change rapidly. You need to be alert and have total concentration. Continuous high speeds may increase the risk of your vehicle breaking down so remember to particularily check your vehicle carefully before you embark on a long motorway journey.

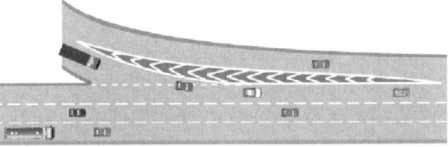

As you join the motorway the slip road may be divided into lanes or separated from the main carriageway by chevron road marking. You must not cross the solid white line; it is there to keep the lanes of traffic separate. Stay in lane. If you are travelling along the left hand lane of a motorway and you see vehicles ahead joining from a slip road be prepared to

move into another lane to help the merging traffic.

You must not stop on the motorway except in an emergency, in which case use the hard shoulder. Emergency telephones are located along the edge of the motorway approximately 1 mile apart. They are connected to police control or the highways agency control centre who can locate you from the number on the box. If you break down use the emergency telephone not a mobile telephone as you may not know exactly where you are. To find the nearest emergency telephone look for the small marker posts which will have an arrow on them pointing in the direction of the closest one. When using an emergency telephone always face the oncoming traffic.

If you see a car on the hard shoulder displaying a HELP pennant this means the driver is disabled and may need assistance in calling for the breakdown services. If you need to stop for a break to relieve tiredness and fatigue use the closest service area or leave the motorway at the next exit.

Motorways are statistically safer than other roads in so far as the number of accidents which occur is concerned. However when accidents do happen, because the traffic is travelling at high speed, the injuries are usually more serious and there is a greater loss of life.

So if you are a new driver, before you use the motorway make sure you know all the rules and advice as laid down in the Highway Code, ensure you know the meaning of all the road signs and markings, and, most importantly, take further training from an ADI so you are

fully prepared and can drive safely on these fast moving roads. Your forward planning and rear observation skills need to be well honed.

35. Active Traffic Management

Active Traffic Management is a new pilot scheme being introduced in an effort to reduce congestion.

When driving in an actively managed area you must obey all signals displayed on the overhead gantries. In addition to the normal signals found on motorways there may also be a single red X which is applicable to the hard shoulder only. This red X does not have flashing beacons and when you see this sign do not use this lane except in an emergency. If you see a mandatory speed limit sign displayed above the hard shoulder this means the hard shoulder can be used as a running lane.

You may also see Emergency Refuge Areas these are designed to be used in cases of emergency or breakdown. They are wider than the hard shoulder, approximately 100 metres long and located about every 500 metres along the carriageway. Features include:
-   CCTV – allowing assistance to be sent as needed
-   sensors to alert the control centre when a vehicle has entered
-   additional distance from the main carriageway
-   emergency roadside telephones containing additional support for the hard of hearing and foreign visitors.

They can also pinpoint your location.

Highway Agency Traffic Officers

These officers are working in partnership with the police and are extra eyes and ears on the motorway. They wear a full uniform including a high visibility orange and yellow jacket and drive a high visibility vehicle with yellow and black chequered markings. A traffic officers duties include:
- offering safety advice for motorists
- helping broken down motorists
- clearing debris from the carriageway
- supporting police and emergency services
- managing diversion routes
- undertaking high visibility patrols
- providing mobile/temporary road closures

Traffic officers do not have any enforcement powers but are able to stop and direct anyone travelling on the motorway. It is an offence not to comply with the directions given by a traffic officer.

36. Journey Planning

To help ease and avoid congestion and stress plan your journey so as to avoid busy times of day wherever possible. This will help you to have a shorter and more pleasant journey. Make sure that you know where you are going by looking on a map or contact one of the major motoring organisations who offer a route planning service. This can also be done on the internet using one of the widely available route planners. You may find it useful to plan an alternative route just in case you encounter road works or an accident.

37. Urban Congestion

A congestion charge scheme was introduced into London to ease congestion in the City. Not all drivers have to pay the charge, some of those who are exempt include
- residents living within the zone
- disabled people who hold a blue badge
- drivers of electrically propelled or alternative fuel vehicles
- riders of two wheelers

38. Eco-safe driving

Transport is an essential part of our lives and most of us appreciate this does not come without certain environmental consequences. In particular, the emissions produced by vehicles cause significant air pollution and are a major contributor to global warming. Eco-safe driving is a style of driving that will help to reduce this damage to our planet and the air we breath whilst improving road safety. Transport currently accounts for 20% of all air pollution emissions in the world. Eco-safe driving is not about driving at lower speeds (although this would undoubtedly help to reduce fuel consumption and accidents) it is more about avoiding senseless wastage of fuel through unnecessary acceleration or braking, inefficient use of the gears and speeding (i.e. exceeding permitted limits or driving at speeds unsafe for the prevailing conditions).

When you accelerate quickly or rapidly you disproportionately use more fuel. Accelerating rapidly allows you to gain speed in a shorter space of time, however, that saving in time costs you dearly in fuel. The accelerator can be compared to a tap handle in that it controls the flow of fuel to the engine. The harder you depress the pedal the faster the fuel will flow. If the accelerator can be compared to a tap

handle then each gear can be compared to a different tap size. First gear is a very large wide tap and fifth gear is a very small narrow tap. Therefore the more you need to use the big wide taps (i.e. the lower gears) the more fuel you will use when you turn the handle (i.e. depress the accelerator). You particularly use more fuel when you accelerate from a standstill because more energy is needed to move a static object than one that is already moving and has momentum. This is why first gear is required to move a stationary vehicle.

The skills required for hazard perception, defensive driving and progressive driving play a big part in Eco-safe driving as they will help you to avoid inefficient use of the accelerator, brake and gears through better awareness, anticipation and planning. In particular to be Eco friendly you need to: Minimise harsh or rapid acceleration. Whenever it is safe to do so, gradually increase speed by gently depressing the accelerator. Look well ahead to see what is happening, to ensure that any acceleration now, will not be wasted a little later on because you have to brake. Let gravity aid you so that if you are going down hill you may find you can fully release pressure on the accelerator and still maintain a safe speed. With your foot fully off the accelerator the engine needs very little fuel, so take advantage of engine braking wherever possible. Avoid using acceleration to exceed legal speed limits or driving faster than it is safe for the prevailing road, traffic or weather conditions as this may not only cost you more fuel it may cost you your life. Vehicles travelling at 70 mph use up to 30% more fuel to cover the same distance as those travelling at 50 mph.

Minimise harsh braking or unnecessary stopping. Look well ahead and if you see that you will need to reduce speed, do it gradually using engine braking rather than applying the brake at the last minute. Gradually adjust your speed to time your arrival at meet situations or when turning right such that you can potentially maintain progress and avoid having to stop. Similarly, you can do this when emerging from a give way junction provided you have a good view of the road you intend to emerge into as you approach the junction.

Engage higher gears as soon as possible without labouring the engine. Avoid engaging unnecessary intermediate gear changes so that you can more quickly engage higher gears or delay engaging lower gears. Modern cars are designed to deliver power even when engine revs are quite low and provided you haven't lost momentum as you slow down you will be surprised how late you can leave a downward gear change without risking an engine stall.

Cold engines use more fuel; therefore avoid manoeuvring whilst the engine is cold if at all possible. Do any manoeuvring before you get out of the vehicle rather then when you return to the vehicle (for example by reversing into parking places or driveways rather than reversing out). Not only does this save fuel, it is also a much safer way to emerge onto a road. Finally, if you need to use a manual choke to start the vehicle, always remember to press it back in once the engine is sufficiently warm. When driving remember, safety is paramount, so never sacrifice safety for fuel saving.

Other ways you can save fuel include making sure your vehicle is properly maintained, that tyre pressures are correct and that no objects are fastened to the vehicle that will cause drag. Before making any journey carefully plan your route to avoid any known hold ups or road works. This will help you save fuel by avoiding slow moving queuing traffic.

Therefore Eco-safe drivers do not:
- Rev-up the engine whilst waiting to move off.
- Use excessive acceleration to move off at speed as if competing in a race.
- Tailgate vehicles resulting in continual harsh braking and acceleration.
- Wait until the last minute to react to hazards including junctions ahead by braking harshly.
- Peak the revs in each gear to obtain maximum acceleration.
- Rush to overtake at each and every opportunity even on congested roads where little benefit will be gained.
- Eco-safe driving is the exact opposite of rally, drag or formula one racing driving.

When done properly Eco-safe driving can save up to 15% on your fuel bill while helping road safety. So save money, save lives, save our planet - adopt an Eco-safe style of driving.

39. Tunnels

The following is an extract from the official DSA guide to Driving the essential skills:

"If you break down or have an accident in a tunnel
- switch on your hazard warning lights
- switch off the engine
- leave your vehicle
- give first aid to any injured people, if you are able
- call for help from an emergency point.

If your vehicle is on fire and you can drive it out of the tunnel, do so. If not
- pull over to the side and switch off the engine
- leave the vehicle immediately
- put out the fire using the vehicle's extinguisher or the one available in the tunnel
- move without delay to an emergency exit if you cannot put out the fire
- call for help from the nearest emergency point.

If the vehicle in front is on fire switch on your warning lights, then follow the above procedure, giving first aid to the injured if possible."

1. Rules for motorcyclists and drivers

Before completing quiz 1 read Highway Code rules 5, 25, 33, 65, 69, 72-84.

Question: 1.1
At night you see a pedestrian wearing reflective clothing and carrying a bright red light. What does this mean?
Mark one answer
a) You are approaching roadworks
b) You are approaching an organised walk
c) You are approaching a slow-moving vehicle
d) You are approaching an accident black spot
HC rule 5

Question: 1.2
At toucan crossings
Mark two answers
a) there is no flashing amber light
b) cyclists are not permitted
c) there is a continuously flashing amber beacon
d) pedestrians and cyclists may cross
e) you only stop if someone is waiting to cross
HC rules 25 65 175

Question: 1.3
The left-hand pavement is closed due to street repairs. What should you do?
Mark one answer
a) Watch out for pedestrians walking in the road
b) Use your right hand mirror more often
c) Speed up to get past the road works quicker
d) Position close to the left hand kerb
HC rule 33

Question: 1.4
At toucan crossings, apart from pedestrians you should be aware of
Mark one answer
a) emergency vehicles emerging
b) buses pulling out
c) trams crossing in front
d) cyclists riding across
HC rule 65

Question: 1.5
A toucan crossing is different from other crossings because
Mark one answer
a) moped riders can use it
b) it is controlled by a traffic warden
c) it is controlled by two flashing lights
d) cyclists can use it
HC rule 65

Question: 1.6
At which type of crossing are cyclists allowed to ride across with pedestrians?
Mark one answer
a) Toucan
b) Puffin
c) Pelican
d) Zebra
HC rule 65

Question: 1.7
Who can use a toucan crossing?
Mark two answers
a) Trains
b) Cyclists
c) Buses
d) Pedestrians
e) Trams
HC rule 65

Question: 1.8
In daylight, an approaching motorcyclist is using a dipped headlight. Why?
Mark one answer
a) So that the rider can be seen more easily
b) To stop the battery overcharging
c) To improve the rider's vision
d) The rider is inviting you to proceed
HC rule 69

Question: 1.9
Motorcyclists should wear bright clothing mainly because
Mark one answer
a) they must do so by law
b) it helps keep them cool in summer
c) the colours are popular
d) drivers often do not see them
HC rule 69

Question: 1.10
The most important reason for having a properly adjusted head restraint is to
Mark one answer
a) make you more comfortable
b) help you to avoid neck injury
c) help you to relax
d) help you to maintain your driving position
HC rule 73

Question: 1.11
It is important to wear suitable shoes when you are driving. Why is this?
Mark one answer
a) To prevent wear on the pedals
b) To maintain control of the pedals
c) To enable you to adjust your seat
d) To enable you to walk for assistance if you break down
HC rule 73

Question: 1.12
What will reduce the risk of neck injury resulting from a collision?
Mark one answer
a) An air-sprung seat
b) Anti-lock brakes
c) A collapsible steering wheel
d) A properly adjusted head restraint
HC rule 73

Question: 1.13
If a trailer swerves or snakes when you are towing it you should
Mark one answer
a) ease off the accelerator and reduce your speed
b) let go of the steering wheel and let it correct itself
c) brake hard and hold the pedal down
d) increase your speed as quickly as possible
HC rule 74

Question: 1.14
Any load that is carried on a roof rack should be
Mark one answer
a) securely fastened when driving
b) loaded towards the rear of the vehicle
c) visible in your exterior mirror
d) covered with plastic sheeting
HC rule 74

Question: 1.15
You are towing a caravan along a motorway. The caravan begins to swerve from side to side. What should you do?
Mark one answer
a) Ease off the accelerator slowly
b) Steer sharply from side to side
c) Do an emergency stop
d) Speed up very quickly
HC rule 74

Question: 1.16
Who is responsible for making sure that a vehicle is not overloaded?
Mark one answer
a) The driver of the vehicle
b) The owner of the items being carried
c) The person who loaded the vehicle
d) The licensing authority
HC rule 74

Question: 1.17
Overloading your vehicle can seriously affect the
Mark two answers
a) gearbox
b) steering
c) handling
d) battery life
e) journey time
HC rule 74

Question: 1.18
How can you stop a caravan snaking from side to side?
Mark one answer
a) Turn the steering wheel slowly to each side
b) Accelerate to increase your speed
c) Stop as quickly as you can
d) Slow down very gradually
HC rule 74

Question: 1.19
A child under three years is being carried in your vehicle. They should be secured in a restraint. Which of these is suitable?
Mark one answer
a) An adult holding a child
b) A lap belt
c) A baby carrier
d) An adult seat belt
HC rule 75

Question: 1.20
Car passengers MUST wear a seat belt if one is available, unless they are
Mark one answer
a) under 14 years old
b) under 1.5 metres (5 feet) in height
c) sitting in the rear seat
d) exempt for medical reasons
HC rule 75

Question: 1.21
You are carrying two 13 year old children and their parents in your car. Who is responsible for seeing that the children wear seat belts?
Mark one answer
a) The children's parents
b) You, the driver
c) The front-seat passenger
d) The children
HC rule 76

Question: 1.22
You are driving the children of a friend home from school. They are both under 14 years old. Who is responsible for making sure they wear a seat belt?
Mark one answer
a) An adult passenger
b) The children
c) You, the driver
d) Your friend
HC rule 76

Question: 1.23
Which of these is a suitable restraint for a child under three years?
Mark one answer
a) A child seat
b) An adult holding a child
c) An adult seat belt
d) A lap belt
HC rule 78

Question: 1.24
Rear-facing baby seats should NEVER be used on a seat protected with
Mark one answer
a) an airbag
b) seat belts
c) head restraints
d) seat covers
HC rule 78

Question: 1.25
After passing your driving test, you suffer from ill health. This affects your driving. You MUST
Mark one answer
a) inform your local police station
b) avoid using motorways
c) always drive accompanied
d) inform the licensing authority
HC rule 79

Question: 1.26
You must notify the licensing authority when
Mark three answers
a) your health affects your driving
b) your eyesight does not meet a set standard
c) you intend lending your vehicle
d) your vehicle requires an MOT certificate
e) you change your vehicle
HC rules 79 81

Question: 1.27
During periods of illness your ability to drive may be impaired. You MUST
Mark two answers
a) see your doctor each time before you drive
b) only take smaller doses of any medicines
c) be medically fit to drive
d) not drive after taking certain medicines
e) take all your medicines with you when you drive
HC rules 79 84

Question: 1.28
As a driver you find that your eyesight has become very poor. Your optician says they cannot help you. The law says that you should tell
Mark one answer
a) the licensing authority
b) your own doctor
c) the local police station
d) another optician
HC rules 79 81 83

Question: 1.29
You are on a motorway. You feel tired.
You should
Mark one answer
a) carry on but go slowly
b) leave the motorway at the next exit
c) complete your journey as quickly as possible
d) stop on the hard shoulder
HC rules 80 236

Question: 1.30
You feel drowsy when driving. You should
Mark two answers
a) stop and rest as soon as possible
b) turn the heater up to keep you warm and comfortable
c) make sure you have a good supply of fresh air
d) continue with your journey but drive more slowly
e) close the car windows to help you concentrate
HC rule 80

Question: 1.31
What else can seriously affect your concentration, other than alcoholic drinks?
Mark three answers
a) Drugs
b) Tiredness
c) Tinted windows
d) Contact lenses
e) Loud music
HC rules 80 84 126

Question: 1.32
You start to feel tired while driving.
What should you do?
Mark one answer
a) Increase your speed slightly
b) Decrease your speed slightly
c) Find a less busy route
d) Pull over at a safe place to rest
HC rule 80

Question: 1.33
Which TWO things would help to keep you alert during a long journey?
Mark two answers
a) Finishing your journey as fast as you can
b) Keeping off the motorways and using country roads
c) Making sure that you get plenty of fresh air
d) Making regular stops for refreshments
HC rules 80 236

Question: 1.34
Driving long distances can be tiring.
You can prevent this by
Mark three answers
a) stopping every so often for a walk
b) opening a window for some fresh air
c) ensuring plenty of refreshment breaks
d) completing the journey without stopping
e) eating a large meal before driving
HC rule 80

Question: 1.35
If your motorway journey seems boring and you feel drowsy while driving, you should
Mark one answer
a) open a window and drive to the next service area
b) stop on the hard shoulder for a sleep
c) speed up to arrive at your destination sooner
d) slow down and let other drivers overtake
HC rules 80 236

Question: 1.36
If you are feeling tired it is best to stop as soon as you can. Until then you should
Mark one answer
a) increase your speed to find a stopping place quickly
b) ensure a supply of fresh air
c) gently tap the steering wheel
d) keep changing speed to improve concentration
HC rule 80

Question: 1.37
You are planning a long journey. Do you need to plan rest stops?
Mark one answer
a) Yes, you should plan to stop every half an hour
b) Yes, regular stops help concentration
c) No, you will be less tired if you get there as soon as possible
d) No, only fuel stops will be needed
HC rule 80

Question: 1.38
You are about to drive home. You feel very tired and have a severe headache. You should
Mark one answer
a) wait until you are fit and well before driving
b) drive home, but take a tablet for headaches
c) drive home if you can stay awake for the journey
d) wait for a short time, then drive home slowly
HC rule 80

Question: 1.39
On a long motorway journey boredom can cause you to feel sleepy. You should
Mark two answers
a) leave the motorway and find a safe place to stop
b) keep looking around at the surrounding landscape
c) drive faster to complete your journey sooner
d) ensure a supply of fresh air into your vehicle
e) stop on the hard shoulder for a rest
HC rules 80 236

Question: 1.40
You are driving along a motorway and become tired. You should
Mark two answers
a) stop at the next service area and rest
b) leave the motorway at the next exit and rest
c) increase your speed and turn up the radio volume
d) close all your windows and set heating to warm
e) pull up on the hard shoulder and change drivers
HC rules 80 236

Question: 1.41
You are travelling on a motorway. You decide you need a rest. You should
Mark two answers
a) stop on the hard shoulder
b) go to a service area
c) park on the slip road
d) park on the central reservation
e) leave at the next exit
HC rules 80 236

Question: 1.42
You find that you need glasses to read vehicle number plates at the required distance. When MUST you wear them?
Mark one answer
a) Only in bad weather conditions
b) At all times when driving
c) Only when you think it necessary
d) Only in bad light or at night time
HC rule 81

Question: 1.43
You are about to drive home. You cannot find the glasses you need to wear. You should
Mark one answer
a) drive home slowly, keeping to quiet roads
b) borrow a friend's glasses and use those
c) drive home at night, so that the lights will help you
d) find a way of getting home without driving
HC rule 81

Question: 1.44
Before entering a tunnel it is good advice to
Mark one answer
a) put on your sunglasses
b) check tyre pressures
c) change to a lower gear
d) tune your radio to a local channel
HC rule 82

Question: 1.45
Before driving through a tunnel what should you do?
Mark one answer
a) Switch your radio off
b) Remove any sunglasses
c) Close your sunroof
d) Switch on windscreen wipers
HC rule 82

Question: 1.46
Which of the following types of glasses should NOT be worn when driving at night?
Mark one answer
a) Half-moon
b) Round
c) Bi-focal
d) Tinted
HC rule 82

Question: 1.47
You go to a social event and need to drive a short time after. What precaution should you take?
Mark one answer
a) Avoid drinking alcohol on an empty stomach
b) Drink plenty of coffee after drinking alcohol
c) Avoid drinking alcohol completely
d) Drink plenty of milk before drinking alcohol
HC rule 83

Question: 1.48
Which THREE result from drinking alcohol?
Mark three answers
a) Less control
b) A false sense of confidence
c) Faster reactions
d) Poor judgement of speed
e) Greater awareness of danger
HC rule 83

Question: 1.49
Drinking any amount of alcohol is likely to
Mark three answers
a) slow down your reactions to hazards
b) increase the speed of your reactions
c) worsen your judgement of speed
d) improve your awareness of danger
e) give a false sense of confidence
HC rule 83

Question: 1.50
Which THREE of these are likely effects of drinking alcohol?
Mark three answers
a) Reduced co-ordination
b) Increased confidence
c) Poor judgement
d) Increased concentration
e) Faster reactions
f) Colour blindness
HC rule 83

Question: 1.51
What advice should you give to a driver who has had a few alcoholic drinks at a party?
Mark one answer
a) Have a strong cup of coffee and then drive home
b) Drive home carefully and slowly
c) Go home by public transport
d) Wait a short while and then drive home
HC rule 83

The Highway Code quiz programme

Question: 1.52
You are invited to a pub lunch. You know that you will have to drive in the evening. What is your best course of action?

Mark one answer
a) Avoid mixing your alcoholic drinks
b) Not drink any alcohol at all
c) Have some milk before drinking alcohol
d) Eat a hot meal with your alcoholic drinks
HC rule 83

Question: 1.53
How does alcohol affect you?
Mark one answer
a) It speeds up your reactions
b) It increases your awareness
c) It improves your co-ordination
d) It reduces your concentration
HC rule 83

Question: 1.54
You are about to return home from holiday when you become ill. A doctor prescribes drugs which are likely to affect your driving. You should
Mark one answer
a) drive only if someone is with you
b) avoid driving on motorways
c) not drive yourself
d) never drive at more than 30 mph
HC rule 84

Question: 1.55
You have been taking medicine for a few days which made you feel drowsy. Today you feel better but still need to take the medicine. You should only drive
Mark one answer
a) if your journey is necessary
b) at night on quiet roads
c) if someone goes with you
d) after checking with your doctor
HC rule 84

Question: 1.56
You take some cough medicine given to you by a friend. What should you do before driving?
Mark one answer
a) Ask your friend if taking the medicine affected their driving
b) Drink some strong coffee one hour before driving
c) Check the label to see if the medicine will affect your driving
d) Drive a short distance to see if the medicine is affecting your driving
HC rule 84

Question: 1.57
Your doctor has given you a course of medicine. Why should you ask how it will affect you?
Mark one answer
a) Drugs make you a better driver by quickening your reactions
b) You will have to let your insurance company know about the medicine
c) Some types of medicine can cause your reactions to slow down
d) The medicine you take may affect your hearing
HC rule 84

Question: 1.58
You are taking drugs that are likely to affect your driving. What should you do?
Mark one answer
a) Seek medical advice before driving
b) Limit your driving to essential journeys
c) Only drive if accompanied by a full licence-holder
d) Drive only for short distances
HC rule 84

Question: 1.59
You are not sure if your cough medicine will affect you. What TWO things should you do?
Mark two answers
a) Ask your doctor
b) Check the medicine label
c) Drive if you feel alright
d) Ask a friend or relative for advice
HC rule 84

2. General rules part 1
Before completing quiz 2 read Highway Code rules 85 - 105.

Question: 2.1
Signals are normally given by direction indicators and
Mark one answer
a) brake lights
b) side lights
c) fog lights
d) interior lights
HC rule 85

Question: 2.2
Your indicators may be difficult to see in bright sunlight. What should you do?
Mark one answer
a) Put your indicator on earlier
b) Give an arm signal as well as using your indicator
c) Touch the brake several times to show the stop lights
d) Turn as quickly as you can
HC rule 85

Question: 2.3
You are signalling to turn right in busy traffic. How would you confirm your intention safely?
Mark one answer
a) Sound the horn
b) Give an arm signal
c) Flash your headlights
d) Position over the centre line
HC rule 85

Question: 2.4
Why should you make sure that your indicators have been cancelled after turning?
Mark one answer
a) To avoid flattening the battery
b) To avoid misleading other road users
c) To avoid dazzling other road users
d) To avoid damage to the indicator relay
HC rule 85

Question: 2.5
You think the driver of the vehicle in front has forgotten to cancel their right indicator. You should
Mark one answer
a) flash your lights to alert the driver
b) sound your horn before overtaking
c) overtake on the left if there is room
d) stay behind and not overtake
HC rules 86 143

Question: 2.6
You are waiting at a T-junction. A vehicle is coming from the right with the left signal flashing. What should you do?

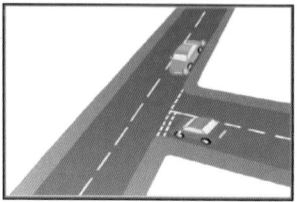

Mark one answer
a) Move out and accelerate hard
b) Wait until the vehicle starts to turn in
c) Pull out before the vehicle reaches the junction
d) Move out slowly
HC rule 86

Question: 2.7
You MUST stop when signalled to do so by which THREE of these?
Mark three answers
a) A police officer
b) A pedestrian
c) A school crossing patrol
d) A bus driver
e) A red traffic light
HC rules 87 89 151

Question: 2.8
On which THREE occasions MUST you stop your vehicle?
Mark three answers
a) When involved in an accident
b) At a red traffic light
c) When signalled to do so by a police officer
d) At a junction with double broken white lines
e) At a pelican crossing when the amber light is flashing and no pedestrians are crossing
HC rules 89 151 260

Question: 2.9
There is a police car following you. The police officer flashes the headlights and points to the left. What should you do?
Mark one answer
a) Turn at the next left
b) Pull up on the left
c) Stop immediately
d) Move over to the left
HC rule 89

Question: 2.10
How will a police officer in a patrol vehicle normally get you to stop?
Mark one answer
a) Flash the headlights, indicate left and point to the left
b) Wait until you stop, then approach you
c) Use the siren, overtake, cut in front and stop
d) Pull alongside you, use the siren and wave you to stop
HC rule 89

Question: 2.11
Other drivers may sometimes flash their headlights at you. In which situation are they allowed to do this?
Mark one answer
a) To warn of a radar speed trap ahead
b) To show that they are giving way to you
c) To warn you of their presence
d) To let you know there is a fault with your vehicle
HC rule 90

Question: 2.12
You should ONLY flash your headlights to other road users
Mark one answer
a) to show that you are giving way
b) to show that you are about to turn
c) to tell them that you have right of way
d) to let them know that you are there
HC rule 90

Question: 2.13
You are travelling at the legal speed limit. A vehicle comes up quickly behind, flashing its headlights. You should
Mark one answer
a) accelerate to make a gap behind you
b) our brake lights
c) maintain your speed to prevent the vehicle from overtaking
d) allow the vehicle to overtake
HC rule 91

Question: 2.14
You must NOT sound your horn
Mark one answer
a) between 10 pm and 6 am in a built-up area
b) at any time in a built-up area
c) between 11.30 pm and 7 am in a built-up area
d) between 11.30 pm and 6 am on any road
HC rule 92

Question: 2.15
When may you sound the horn?
Mark one answer
a) To give you right of way
b) To attract a friend's attention
c) To warn others of your presence
d) To make slower drivers move over
HC rule 92

Question: 2.16
When should you NOT use your horn in a built-up area?
Mark one answer
a) Between 8 pm and 8 am
b) Between 9 pm and dawn
c) Between dusk and 8 am
d) Between 11.30 pm and 7 am
HC rule 92

Question: 2.17
You must not use your horn when you are stationary
Mark one answer
a) unless a moving vehicle may cause you danger
b) at any time whatsoever
c) unless it is used only briefly
d) except for signalling that you have just arrived
HC rule 92

Question: 2.18
What should you use your horn for?
Mark one answer
a) To alert others to your presence
b) To allow you right of way
c) To greet other road users
d) To signal your annoyance
HC rule 92

Question: 2.19
You are driving along this road. The driver on the left is reversing from a driveway. You should

Mark one answer
a) move to the opposite side of the road
b) drive through as you have priority
c) sound your horn and be prepared to stop
d) speed up and drive through quickly
HC rule 92

Question: 2.20
You are driving on a clear night. There is a steady stream of oncoming traffic. The national speed limit applies. Which lights should you use?
Mark one answer
a) Full beam headlights
b) Sidelights
c) Dipped headlights
d) Fog lights
HC rules 93 95

Question: 2.21
You are on a motorway at night with other vehicles just ahead of you. Which lights should you have on?
Mark one answer
a) Front fog lights
b) Main beam headlights
c) Sidelights only
d) Dipped headlights
HC rules 93 95

Question: 2.22
You are on a well-lit motorway at night. You must
Mark one answer
a) use only your sidelights
b) always use your headlights
c) always use rear fog lights
d) use headlights only in bad weather
HC rule 93

Question: 2.23
Daytime visibility is poor but not seriously reduced. You should switch on
Mark one answer
a) headlights and fog lights
b) front fog lights
c) dipped headlights
d) rear fog lights
HC rules 93 95

Question: 2.24
You are driving with your front fog lights switched on. Earlier fog has now cleared. What should you do?

Mark one answer
a) Leave them on if other drivers have their lights on
b) Switch them off as long as visibility remains good
c) Flash them to warn oncoming traffic that it is foggy
d) Drive with them on instead of your headlights
HC rule 94

Question: 2.25
You are travelling on a well-lit road at night in a built-up area. By using dipped headlights you will be able to
Mark one answer
a) see further along the road
b) go at a much faster speed
c) switch to main beam quickly
d) be easily seen by others
HC rule 95

Question: 2.26
You are overtaking a car at night. You must be sure that
Mark one answer
a) you flash your headlights before overtaking
b) you select a higher gear
c) you have switched your lights to full beam before overtaking
d) you do not dazzle other road users
HC rule 95

Question: 2.27
You are driving at night on an unlit road behind another vehicle. You should
Mark one answer
a) flash your headlights
b) use dipped beam headlights
c) switch off your headlights
d) use full beam headlights
HC rule 95

Question: 2.28
When MUST you use dipped headlights during the day?
Mark one answer
a) All the time
b) Along narrow streets
c) In poor visibility
d) When parking
HC rule 95

Question: 2.29
You are travelling at night. You are dazzled by headlights coming towards you. You should
Mark one answer
a) pull down your sun visor
b) slow down or stop
c) switch on your main beam headlights
d) put your hand over your eyes
HC rule 95

Question: 2.30
You are driving on a motorway. You have to slow down quickly due to a hazard. You should
Mark one answer
a) switch on your hazard lights
b) switch on your headlights
c) sound your horn
d) flash your headlights
HC rule 96

Question: 2.31
Your vehicle breaks down in a tunnel. What should you do?
Mark one answer
a) Stay in your vehicle and wait for the Police
b) Stand in the lane behind your vehicle to warn others
c) Stand in front of your vehicle to warn oncoming drivers
d) Switch on hazard lights then go and call for help immediately
HC rules 96 248

Question: 2.32
You are driving on a motorway. The traffic ahead is braking sharply because of an accident. How could you warn traffic behind you?
Mark one answer
a) Briefly use the hazard warning lights
b) Switch on the hazard warning lights continuously
c) Briefly use the rear fog lights
d) Switch on the headlights continuously
HC rule 96

Question: 2.33
When may you use hazard warning lights?
Mark one answer
a) To park alongside another car
b) To park on double yellow lines
c) When you are being towed
d) When you have broken down
HC rule 96

Question: 2.34
Hazard warning lights should be used when vehicles are
Mark one answer
a) broken down and causing an obstruction
b) faulty and moving slowly
c) being towed along a road
d) reversing into a side road
HC rule 96

Question: 2.35
For which TWO should you use hazard warning lights?
Mark two answers
a) When you slow down quickly on a motorway because of a hazard ahead
b) When you have broken down
c) When you wish to stop on double yellow lines
d) When you need to park on the pavement
HC rule 96

Question: 2.36
When may you use hazard warning lights when driving?
Mark one answer
a) Instead of sounding the horn in a built-up area between 11.30 pm and 7 am
b) On a motorway or unrestricted dual carriageway, to warn of a hazard ahead
c) On rural routes, after a warning sign of animals
d) On the approach to toucan crossings where cyclists are waiting to cross
HC rule 96

Question: 2.37
You are driving on a motorway. The car ahead shows its hazard lights for a short time. This tells you that
Mark one answer
a) the driver wants you to overtake
b) the other car is going to change lanes
c) traffic ahead is slowing or stopping suddenly
d) there is a police speed check ahead
HC rule 96

Question: 2.38
When are you allowed to use hazard warning lights?
Mark one answer
a) When stopped and temporarily obstructing traffic
b) When travelling during darkness without headlights
c) When parked for shopping on double yellow lines
d) When travelling slowly because you are lost
HC rule 96

Question: 2.39
For which of these may you use hazard warning lights?
Mark one answers
a) When driving on a motorway to warn traffic behind of a hazard ahead
b) When you are double-parked on a two way road
c) When your direction indicators are not working
d) When warning oncoming traffic that you intend to stop
HC rule 96

Question: 2.40
When should you use hazard warning lights?
Mark one answer
a) When you are double-parked on a two way road
b) When your direction indicators are not working
c) When warning oncoming traffic that you intend to stop
d) When your vehicle has broken down and is causing an obstruction
HC rules 96 248

Question: 2.41
You are driving through a tunnel. Your vehicle breaks down. What should you do?
Mark one answer
a) Switch on hazard warning lights
b) Remain in your vehicle
c) Wait for the police to find you
d) Rely on CCTV cameras seeing you
HC rules 96 148

Question: 2.42
You are turning left on a slippery road. The back of your vehicle slides to the right. You should
Mark one answer
a) brake firmly and not turn the steering wheel
b) steer carefully to the left
c) steer carefully to the right
d) brake firmly and steer to the left
HC rule 99

Question: 2.43
You are braking on a wet road. Your vehicle begins to skid. It does not have anti-lock brakes. What is the FIRST thing you should do?
Mark one answer
a) Quickly pull up the handbrake
b) Release the footbrake fully
c) Push harder on the brake pedal
d) Gently use the accelerator
HC rule 99

Question: 2.44
What is the most common cause of skidding?
Mark one answer
a) Worn tyres
b) Driver error
c) Other vehicles
d) Pedestrians
HC rule 99

Question: 2.45
To correct a rear-wheel skid you should
Mark one answer
a) not steer at all
b) steer away from it
c) steer into it
d) apply your handbrake
HC rule 99

Question: 2.46
Skidding is mainly caused by
Mark one answer
a) the weather
b) the driver
c) the vehicle
d) the road
HC rule 99

Question: 2.47
Anti-lock brakes prevent wheels from locking. This means the tyres are less likely to
Mark one answer
a) aquaplane
b) skid
c) puncture
d) wear
HC rules 99 100

Question: 2.48
Your vehicle has anti-lock brakes, but they may not always prevent skidding. This is most likely to happen when driving
Mark two answers
a) in foggy conditions
b) on surface water
c) on loose road surfaces
d) on dry tarmac
e) at night on unlit roads
HC rules 99 100 202

Question: 2.49
You are driving a vehicle fitted with anti-lock brakes. You need to stop in an emergency. You should apply the footbrake
Mark one answer
a) slowly and gently
b) slowly but firmly
c) rapidly and gently
d) rapidly and firmly
HC rule 100

Question: 2.50
Anti-lock brakes reduce the chances of a skid occurring particularly when
Mark one answer
a) driving down steep hills
b) braking during normal driving
c) braking in an emergency
d) driving on good road surfaces
HC rule 100

Question: 2.51
Your vehicle is fitted with anti-lock brakes. To stop quickly in an emergency you should
Mark one answer
a) brake firmly and pump the brake pedal on and off
b) brake rapidly and firmly without releasing the brake pedal
c) brake gently and pump the brake pedal on and off
d) brake rapidly once, and immediately release the brake pedal
HC rule 100

Question: 2.52
Your anti-lock brakes warning light stays on. You should
Mark one answer
a) check the brake fluid level
b) check the footbrake free play
c) check that the handbrake is released
d) have the brakes checked immediately
HC rule 100

Question: 2.53
Your car is fitted with anti-lock brakes. You need to stop in an emergency. You should
Mark one answer
a) brake normally and avoid turning the steering wheel
b) press the brake pedal rapidly and firmly until you have stopped
c) keep pushing and releasing the foot brake quickly to prevent skidding
d) apply the handbrake to reduce the stopping distance
HC rule 100

Question: 2.54
Anti-lock brakes are most effective when you
Mark one answer
a) keep pumping the foot brake to prevent skidding
b) brake normally, but grip the steering wheel tightly
c) brake rapidly and firmly until you have slowed down
d) apply the handbrake to reduce the stopping distance
HC rule 100

Question: 2.55
Anti-lock brakes will take effect when
Mark one answer
a) you do not brake quickly enough
b) excessive brake pressure has been applied
c) you have not seen a hazard ahead
d) speeding on slippery road surfaces
HC rule 100

Question: 2.56
Vehicles fitted with anti-lock brakes
Mark one answer
a) are impossible to skid
b) can be steered while you are braking
c) accelerate much faster
d) are not fitted with a handbrake
HC rule 100

Question: 2.57
Anti-lock brakes are of most use when you are
Mark one answer
a) braking gently
b) driving on worn tyres
c) braking excessively
d) driving normally
HC rule 100

Question: 2.58
Driving a vehicle fitted with anti-lock brakes allows you to
Mark one answer
a) brake harder because it is impossible to skid
b) drive at higher speeds
c) steer and brake at the same time
d) pay less attention to the road ahead
HC rule 100

Question: 2.59
Anti-lock brakes can greatly assist with
Mark one answer
a) a higher cruising speed
b) steering control when braking
c) control when accelerating
d) motorway driving
HC rule 100

Question: 2.60
When would an anti-lock braking system start to work?
Mark one answer
a) After the parking brake has been applied
b) When ever pressure on the brake pedal is applied
c) Just as the wheels are about to lock
d) When the normal braking system fails to operate
HC rule 100

Question: 2.61
You have driven through a flood. What is the first thing you should do?
Mark one answer
a) Stop and check the tyres
b) Stop and dry the brakes
c) Check your exhaust
d) Test your brakes
HC rule 101

Question: 2.62
You are driving along a country road. You see this sign. AFTER dealing safely with the hazard you should always

Mark one answer
a) check your tyre pressures
b) switch on your hazard warning lights
c) accelerate briskly
d) test your brakes
HC rule 101

Question: 2.63
You have just gone through deep water. To dry off the brakes you should
Mark one answer
a) accelerate and keep to a high speed for a short time
b) go slowly while gently applying the brakes
c) avoid using the brakes at all for a few miles
d) stop for at least an hour to allow them time to dry
HC rule 101

Question: 2.64
What does this sign mean?

Mark one answer
a) Uneven road surface
b) Bridge over the road
c) Road ahead ends
d) Water across the road
HC rule 101

Question: 2.65
Which FOUR of the following may apply when dealing with this hazard?

Mark four answers
a) It could be more difficult in winter
b) Use a low gear and drive slowly
c) Use a high gear to prevent wheelspin
d) Test your brakes afterwards
e) Always switch on fog lamps
f) There may be a depth gauge
HC rule 101

The Highway Code quiz programme

Question: 2.66
Why should you test your brakes after this hazard?

Mark one answer
a) Because you will be on a slippery road
b) Because your brakes will be soaking wet
c) Because you will have gone down a long hill
d) Because you will have just crossed a long bridge
HC rule 101

Question: 2.67
After this hazard you should test your brakes. Why is this?

Mark one answer
a) You will be on a slippery road
b) Your brakes will be soaking wet
c) You will be going down a long hill
d) You will have just crossed a long bridge
HC rule 101

Question: 2.68
Why is travelling in neutral for long distances (known as coasting) wrong?
Mark one answer
a) It will cause the car to skid
b) It will make the engine stall
c) The engine will run faster
d) There is no engine braking
HC rule 102

Question: 2.69
What are TWO main reasons why coasting downhill is wrong?
Mark two answers
a) Fuel consumption will be higher
b) The vehicle will get faster
c) It puts more wear and tear on the tyres
d) You have less braking and steering control
e) It damages the engine
HC rule 102

Question: 2.70
Travelling for long distances in neutral (known as coasting)
Mark one answer
a) improves the driver's control
b) makes steering easier
c) reduces the driver's control
d) uses more fuel
HC rule 102

Question: 2.71
You are driving down a steep hill. Why could keeping the clutch down or rolling in neutral for too long be dangerous?
Mark one answer
a) Fuel consumption will be higher
b) Your vehicle will pick up speed
c) It will damage the engine
d) It will wear tyres out more quickly
HC rule 102

Question: 2.72
Holding the clutch pedal down or rolling in neutral for too long while driving will
Mark one answer
a) use more fuel
b) cause the engine to overheat
c) reduce your control
d) improve tyre wear
HC rule 102

Question: 2.73
Why could keeping the clutch down or selecting neutral for long periods of time be dangerous?
Mark one answer
a) Fuel spillage will occur
b) Engine damage may be caused
c) You will have less steering and braking control
d) It will wear tyres out more quickly
HC rule 102

Question: 2.74
A single carriageway road has this sign. What is the maximum permitted speed for a car towing a trailer?

Mark one answer
a) 30 mph
b) 40 mph
c) 50 mph
d) 60 mph
HC rule 103

Question: 2.75
You are towing a small caravan on a dual carriageway. You must not exceed

Mark one answer
a) 50 mph
b) 40 mph
c) 70 mph
d) 60 mph
HC rule 103

Question: 2.76
You are on a road that has no traffic signs. There are street lights. What is the speed limit?
Mark one answer
a) 20 mph
b) 30 mph
c) 40 mph
d) 60 mph
HC rule 103

Question: 2.77
What is the national speed limit for cars and motorcycles in the centre lane of a three-lane motorway?
Mark one answer
a) 40 mph
b) 50 mph
c) 60 mph
d) 70 mph
HC rule 103

Question: 2.78
What is the national speed limit for cars and motorcycles on a dual carriageway?
Mark one answer
a) 30 mph
b) 50 mph
c) 60 mph
d) 70 mph
HC rule 103

Question: 2.79
There are no speed limit signs on the road. How is a 30 mph limit indicated?
Mark one answer
a) By hazard warning lines
b) By street lighting
c) By pedestrian islands
d) By double or single yellow lines
HC rule 103

Question: 2.80
Where you see street lights but no speed limit signs the limit is usually
Mark one answer
a) 30 mph
b) 40 mph
c) 50 mph
d) 60 mph
HC rule 103

Question: 2.81
You are driving a car on a motorway. Unless signs show otherwise you must NOT exceed
Mark one answer
a) 50 mph
b) 60 mph
c) 70 mph
d) 80 mph
HC rule 103

Question: 2.82
You are towing a trailer on a motorway. What is your maximum speed limit?
Mark one answer
a) 40 mph
b) 50 mph
c) 60 mph
d) 70 mph
HC rule 103

Question: 2.83
You are towing a small trailer on a busy three-lane motorway. All the lanes are open. You must
Mark two answers
a) not exceed 60 mph
b) not overtake
c) have a stabiliser fitted
d) use only the left and centre lanes
HC rules 103 239

Question: 2.84
What is the maximum speed on a single carriageway road?
Mark one answer
a) 50 mph
b) 60 mph
c) 40 mph
d) 70 mph
HC rule 103

Question: 2.85
What is the national speed limit on a single carriageway road for cars and motorcycles?
Mark one answer
a) 70 mph
b) 60 mph
c) 50 mph
d) 30 mph
HC rule 103

Question: 2.86
While driving, you see this sign ahead. You should

Mark one answer
a) stop at the sign
b) slow, but continue around the bend
c) slow to a crawl and continue
d) stop and look for open farm gates
HC rules 104 124

Question: 2.87
When approaching this hazard why should you slow down?

Mark two answers
a) Because of the bend
b) Because its hard to see to the right
c) Because of approaching traffic
d) Because of animals crossing
e) Because of the level crossing
HC rule 104

Question: 2.88
In good conditions, what is the typical stopping distance at 70 mph?
Mark one answer
a) 53 metres (175 feet)
b) 60 metres (197 feet)
c) 73 metres (240 feet)
d) 96 metres (315 feet)
HC rule 105

Question: 2.89
You are following a vehicle on a wet road. You should leave a time gap of at least
Mark one answer
a) one second
b) two seconds
c) three seconds
d) four seconds
HC rule 105

Question: 2.90
You are on a fast, open road in good conditions. For safety, the distance between you and the vehicle in front should be

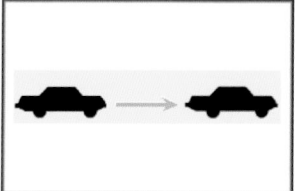

Mark one answer
a) a two-second time gap
b) one car length
c) 2 metres (6feet 6inches)
d) two car lengths
HC rule 105

Question: 2.91
Following this vehicle too closely is unwise because

Mark one answer
a) your brakes will overheat
b) your view ahead is increased
c) your engine will overheat
d) your view ahead is reduced
HC rules 105 140

Question: 2.92
You are on a good, dry road surface. Your vehicle has good brakes and tyres. What is the BRAKING distance at 50 mph?
Mark one answer
a) 38 metres (125 feet)
b) 14 metres (46 feet)
c) 24 metres (79 feet)
d) 55 metres (180 feet)
HC rule 105

Question: 2.93
The conditions are good and dry. You could use the 'two-second rule'
Mark one answer
a) before restarting the engine after it has stalled
b) to keep a safe gap from the vehicle in front
c) before using the 'Mirror-Signal-Manoeuvre' routine
d) when emerging on wet roads
HC rule 105

Question: 2.94
The traffic ahead of you in the left-hand lane is slowing. You should

Mark two answers
a) be wary of cars on your right cutting in
b) accelerate past the vehicles in the left lane
c) pull up on the left hand verge
d) move across and continue in the right hand lane
e) slow down keeping a safe separation distance
HC rule 105

Question: 2.95
What is the shortest overall stopping distance on a dry road at 60 mph?
Mark one answer
a) 53 metres (175 feet)
b) 58 metres (190 feet)
c) 73 metres (240 feet)
d) 96 metres (315 feet)
HC rule 105

Question: 2.96
You are on a good, dry, road surface and your vehicle has good brakes and tyres. What is the typical overall stopping distance at 40 mph?
Mark one answer
a) 23 metres (75 feet)
b) 36 metres (120 feet)
c) 53 metres (175 feet)
d) 96 metres (315 feet)
HC rule 105

Question: 2.97
You should leave at least a two-second gap between your vehicle and the one in front when conditions are

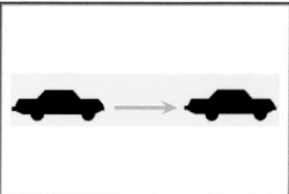

Mark one answer
a) wet
b) good
c) damp
d) foggy
HC rule 105

Question: 2.98
Which THREE of the following will affect your stopping distance?
Mark three answers
a) How fast you are going
b) The tyres on your vehicle
c) The time of day
d) The weather
e) The street lighting
HC rule 105

Question: 2.99
You are travelling at 50 mph on a good, dry road. What is your shortest overall stopping distance?
Mark one answer
a) 36 metres (120 feet)
b) 53 metres (175 feet)
c) 75 metres (245 feet)
d) 96 metres (315 feet)
HC rule 105

3. General rules part 2
Before completing quiz 3 read Highway Code rules 106 - 134.

Question: 3.1
This broken white line painted in the centre of the road means

Mark one answer
a) oncoming vehicles have priority over you
b) you should give priority to oncoming vehicles
c) there is a hazard ahead of you
d) the area is a national speed limit zone
HC rule 106

Question: 3.2
A white line like this along the centre of the road is a

Mark one answer
a) bus lane marking
b) hazard warning
c) give way marking
d) lane marking
HC rule 106

Question: 3.3
What does this road marking mean?

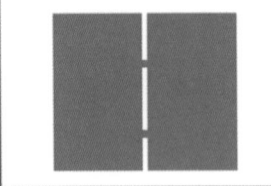

Mark one answer
a) Do not cross the line
b) No stopping allowed
c) You are approaching a hazard
d) No overtaking allowed
HC rule 106

Question: 3.4
Which is a hazard warning line?

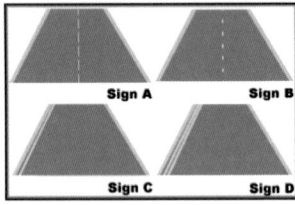

Mark one answer
a) Sign A
b) Sign B
c) Sign C
d) Sign D
HC rule 106

Question: 3.5
When may you cross a double solid white line in the middle of the road?

Mark one answer
a) To pass traffic that is queuing back at a junction
b) To pass a car signalling to turn left ahead
c) To pass a road maintenance vehicle travelling at 10 mph or less
d) To pass a vehicle that is towing a trailer
HC rules 107 108

Question: 3.6
Where on a motorway would you find green reflective studs?
Mark one answer
a) Separating driving lanes
b) Between the hard shoulder and the carriageway
c) At slip road entrances and exits
d) Between the carriageway and the central reservation
HC rule 111

Question: 3.7
You are on a motorway in fog. The left-hand edge of the motorway can be identified by reflective studs. What colour are they?

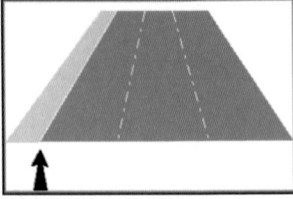

Mark one answer
a) Green
b) Amber
c) Red
d) White
HC rule 111

The Highway Code quiz programme

Question: 3.8
On a motorway the amber reflective studs can be found between
Mark one answer
a) the hard shoulder and the carriageway
b) the acceleration lane and the carriageway
c) the central reservation and the carriageway
d) each pair of the lanes
HC rule 111

Question: 3.9
What colour are the reflective studs between the lanes on a motorway?

Mark one answer
a) Green
b) Amber
c) White
d) Red
HC rule 111

Question: 3.10
What colour are the reflective studs between a motorway and its slip road?
Mark one answer
a) Amber
b) White
c) Green
d) Red
HC rule 111

Question: 3.11
Where can you find reflective amber studs on a motorway?
Mark one answer
a) Separating the slip road from the motorway
b) On the left-hand edge of the road
c) On the right-hand edge of the road
d) Separating the lanes
HC rule 111

Question: 3.12
You are on a motorway. What colour are the reflective studs on the left of the carriageway?
Mark one answer
a) Green
b) Red
c) White
d) Amber
HC rule 111

Question: 3.13
You are on a three-lane motorway. There are red reflective studs on your left and white ones to your right. Where are you?

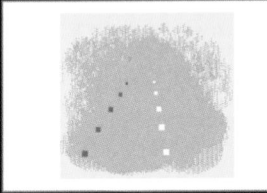

Mark one answer
a) In the right-hand lane
b) In the middle lane
c) On the hard shoulder
d) In the left-hand lane
HC rule 111

Question: 3.14
Why are place names painted on the road surface?
Mark one answer
a) To restrict the flow of traffic
b) To warn you of oncoming traffic
c) To enable you to change lanes early
d) To prevent you changing lanes
HC rules 113 121

Question: 3.15
Some two-way roads are divided into three lanes. Why are these particularly dangerous?
Mark one answer
a) Traffic in both directions can use the middle lane to overtake
b) Traffic can travel faster in poor weather conditions
c) Traffic can overtake on the left
d) Traffic uses the middle lane for emergencies only
HC rule 114

Question: 3.16
When may you NOT overtake on the left?
Mark one answer
a) On a free-flowing motorway or dual carriageway
b) When the traffic is moving slowly in queues
c) On a one-way street
d) When the car in front is signalling to turn right
HC rules 116 121 139

Question: 3.17
You are on a two-lane dual carriageway. For which TWO of the following would you use the right-hand lane?
Mark one answer
a) Turning right
b) Normal progress
c) Staying at the minimum allowed speed
d) Constant high speed
e) Overtaking slower traffic
f) Mending punctures
HC rule 116

Question: 3.18
On a three-lane dual carriageway the right-hand lane can be used for

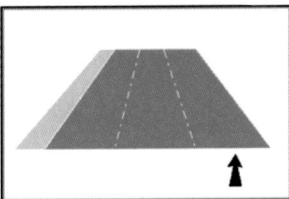

Mark one answer
a) overtaking only, never turning right
b) overtaking or turning right
c) fast-moving traffic only
d) turning right only, never overtaking
HC rule 117

Question: 3.19

A crawler lane on a motorway is found

Mark one answer
a) on a steep gradient
b) before a service area
c) before a junction
d) along the hard shoulder
HC rule 118

Question: 3.20

What does this sign mean?

Mark one answer
a) Leave motorway at next exit
b) Lane for heavy and slow vehicles
c) All lorries use the hard shoulder
d) Rest area for lorries
HC rule 118

Question: 3.21

A cycle lane is marked by a solid white line. You must not drive or park in it
Mark one answer
a) at any time
b) during the rush hour
c) if a cyclist is using it
d) during its period of operation
HC rule 119

Question: 3.22

You are driving along a road that has a cycle lane. The lane is marked by a solid white line. This means that during its period of operation
Mark one answer
a) the lane may be used for parking your car
b) you may drive in that lane at any time
c) the lane may be used when necessary
d) you must not drive in that lane
HC rule 119

Question: 3.23

As a car driver, which THREE lanes are you NOT normally allowed to use?
Mark three answers
a) Crawler lane
b) Bus lane
c) Overtaking lane
d) Acceleration lane
e) Cycle lane
f) Tram lane
HC rules 119 120

Question: 3.24

You are driving on a road that has a cycle lane. The lane is marked by a broken white line. This means that
Mark two answers
a) you should not drive in the lane unless it is unavoidable
b) you should not park in the lane unless it is unavoidable
c) cyclists can travel in both directions in that lane
d) the lane must be used by motorcyclists in heavy traffic
HC rule 119

Question: 3.25

When may you drive a motor car in this bus lane?

Mark one answer
a) Outside its hours of operation
b) To get to the front of a traffic queue
c) You may not use it at any time
d) To overtake slow-moving traffic
HC rule 120

Question: 3.26

A bus lane on your left shows no times of operation. This means it is

Mark one answer
a) not in operation at all
b) only in operation at peak times
c) in operation 24 hours a day
d) only in operation in daylight hours
HC rule 120

Question: 3.27

Where may you overtake on a one-way street?
Mark one answer
a) Only on the left-hand side
b) Overtaking is not allowed
c) Only on the right-hand side
d) Either on the right or the left
HC rule 121

Question: 3.28

You are in a one-way street and want to turn right. You should position yourself

Mark one answer

a) in the right-hand lane
b) in the left-hand lane
c) in either lane, depending on the traffic
d) just left of the centre line

HC rule 121

Question: 3.29

Where would you see a contraflow bus and cycle lane?

Mark one answer

a) On a dual carriageway
b) On a roundabout
c) On an urban motorway
d) On a one-way street

HC rule 121

Question: 3.30

You lose your way on a busy road. What is the best action to take?

Mark one answer

a) Stop at traffic lights and ask pedestrians
b) Shout to other drivers to ask them the way
c) Turn into a side road, stop and check a map
d) Check a map, and keep going with the traffic flow

HC rule 122

Question: 3.31

You may drive over a footpath

Mark one answer

a) to overtake slow-moving traffic
b) when the pavement is very wide
c) if no pedestrians are near
d) to get into a property

HC rule 123

Question: 3.32

You are driving at 60 mph. As you approach this hazard you should

Mark one answer

a) maintain your speed
b) reduce your speed
c) take the next right turn
d) take the next left turn

HC rule 124

Question: 3.33

Who has priority at an unmarked crossroads?

Mark one answer

a) The larger vehicle
b) No one has priority
c) The faster vehicle
d) The smaller vehicle

HC rule 124

Question: 3.34

At a crossroads there are no signs or road markings. Two vehicles approach. Which has priority?

Mark one answer

a) Neither of the vehicle
b) The vehicle travelling the fastest
c) Oncoming vehicles turning right
d) Vehicles approaching from the right

HC rule 124

Question: 3.35

A driver's behaviour has upset you. It may help if you

Mark one answer

a) stop and take a break
b) shout abusive language
c) gesture to them with your hand
d) follow their car, flashing the headlights

HC rule 125

Question: 3.36

A vehicle pulls out in front of you at a junction. What should you do?

Mark one answer

a) Swerve past it and sound your horn
b) Flash your headlights and drive up close behind
c) Slow down and be ready to stop
d) Accelerate past it immediately

HC rule 125

Question: 3.37

A driver pulls out of a side road in front of you. You have to brake hard. You should

Mark one answer

a) ignore the error and stay calm
b) flash your lights to show your annoyance
c) sound your horn to show your annoyance
d) overtake as soon as possible

HC rule 125

Question: 3.38

A driver does something that upsets you. You should

Mark one answer

a) try not to react
b) let them know how you feel
c) flash your headlights several times
d) sound your horn

HC rule 125

Question: 3.39

Which THREE are likely to make you lose concentration while driving?

Mark three answers

a) Looking at road maps
b) Listening to loud music
c) Using your windscreen washers
d) Looking in your wing mirror
e) Using a mobile phone

HC rules 126 127

Question: 3.40

You are most likely to lose concentration when driving if you

Mark two answers

a) use a mobile phone
b) listen to very loud music
c) switch on the heated rear window
d) look at the door mirrors

HC rules 126 127

Question: 3.41
Which FOUR are most likely to cause you to lose concentration while you are driving?
Mark four answers
a) Using a mobile phone
b) Talking into a microphone
c) Tuning your car radio
d) Looking at a map
e) Checking the mirrors
f) Using the demisters
HC rules 126 127

Question: 3.42
Which of the following may cause loss of concentration on a long journey?
Mark four answers
a) Loud music
b) Arguing with a passenger
c) Using a mobile phone
d) Putting in a cassette tape
e) Stopping regularly to rest
f) Pulling up to tune the radio
HC rules 126 127

Question: 3.43
Your vehicle is fitted with a hands-free phone system. Using this equipment whilst driving
Mark one answer
a) is quite safe as long as you slow down
b) could distract your attention from the road
c) is recommended by The Highway Code
d) could be very good for road safety
HC rule 127

Question: 3.44
What is the safest way to use a mobile phone in your vehicle?
Mark one answer
a) Use hands free equipment
b) Find a suitable place to stop
c) Drive slowly on a quiet road
d) Direct your call through the operator
HC rule 127

Question: 3.45
You should ONLY use a mobile phone when
Mark one answer
a) receiving a call
b) suitably parked
c) driving at less than 30 mph
d) driving an automatic vehicle
HC rule 127

Question: 3.46
Using a mobile phone while you are driving
Mark one answer
a) is acceptable in a vehicle with power steering
b) will reduce your field of vision
c) could distract your attention from the road
d) will affect your vehicle's electronic systems
HC rule 127

Question: 3.47
Your mobile phone rings while you are on the motorway. Before answering you should
Mark one answer
a) reduce your speed to 50 mph
b) pull up on the hard shoulder
c) move into the left hand lane
d) stop in a safe place
HC rule 127

Question: 3.48
To answer a call on your mobile phone while travelling you should
Mark one answer
a) reduce your speed wherever you are
b) stop in a proper and convenient place
c) keep the call time to a minimum
d) slow down and allow others to overtake
HC rule 127

Question: 3.49
Your vehicle is fitted with a hand-held telephone. To use the telephone you should
Mark one answer
a) reduce your speed
b) find a safe place to stop
c) steer the vehicle with one hand
d) be particularly careful at junctions
HC rule 127

Question: 3.50
You should not use a mobile phone while driving
Mark one answer
a) until you are satisfied that no other traffic is near
b) unless you are able to drive one handed
c) because it might distract your attention from the road ahead
d) because reception is poor when the engine is running
HC rule 127

Question: 3.51
Your mobile phone rings while you are travelling. You should
Mark one answer
a) stop immediately
b) answer it immediately
c) pull up in a suitable place
d) pull up at the nearest kerb
HC rule 127

Question: 3.52
Using a hands-free phone is likely to
Mark one answer
a) improve your safety
b) increase your concentration
c) reduce your view
d) divert your attention
HC rule 127

Question: 3.53
Your vehicle is fitted with a navigation system. How should you avoid letting this distract you while driving?
Mark one answer
a) Keep going and input your destination into the system
b) Keep going as the system will adjust to your route
c) Stop immediately to view and use the system
d) Stop in a safe place before using the system
HC rule 128

The Highway Code quiz programme

Question: 3.54
You are going through a congested tunnel and have to stop. What should you do?
Mark one answer
a) Pull up very close to the vehicle in front to save space
b) Ignore any message signs as they are never up to date
c) Keep a safe distance from the vehicle in front
d) Make a U-turn and find another route
HC rule 129

Question: 3.55
Why should the junction on the left be kept clear?

Mark one answer
a) To allow vehicles to enter and emerge
b) To allow the bus to reverse
c) To allow vehicles to make a U-turn
d) To allow vehicles to park
HC rule 129

Question: 3.56
What THREE things should the driver of the grey car (arrowed) be especially aware of?

Mark three answers
a) Pedestrians stepping out between cars
b) Other cars behind the grey car
c) Doors opening on parked cars
d) The bumpy road surface
e) Cars leaving parking spaces
f) Empty parking spaces
HC rule 130

Question: 3.57
You are going along a street with parked vehicles on the left-hand side. For which THREE reasons should you keep your speed down?
Mark three answers
a) So that oncoming traffic can see you more clearly
b) You may set off car alarms
c) Vehicles may be pulling out
d) Drivers' doors may open
e) Children may run out from between the vehicles
HC rule 130

Question: 3.58
In some narrow residential streets you may find a speed limit of
Mark one answer
a) 20 mph
b) 25 mph
c) 35 mph
d) 40 mph
HC rule 130

Question: 3.59
What TWO main hazards should you be aware of when going along this street?

Mark two answers
a) Glare from the sun
b) Car doors opening suddenly
c) Lack of road markings
d) The headlights on parked cars being switched on
e) Large goods vehicles
f) Children running out from between vehicles
HC rule 130

Question: 3.60
You are driving past parked cars. You notice a bicycle wheel sticking out between them. What should you do?
Mark one answer
a) Accelerate past quickly and sound your horn
b) Slow down and wave the cyclist across
c) Brake sharply and flash your headlights
d) Slow down and be prepared to stop for a cyclist
HC rule 130

Question: 3.61
Which of these plates normally appear with this road sign?

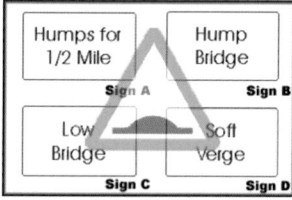

Mark one answer
a) Sign A
b) Sign B
c) Sign C
d) Sign D
HC rule 131

Question: 3.62
Traffic calming measures are used to
Mark one answer
a) stop road rage
b) help overtaking
c) slow traffic down
d) help parking
HC rule 131

Question: 3.63
You enter a road where there are road humps. What should you do?

Mark one answer
a) Maintain a reduced speed throughout
b) Accelerate quickly between each one
c) Always keep to the maximum legal speed
d) Drive slowly at school times only
HC rule 131

Question: 3.64
What does this sign mean?

Mark one answer
a) Maximum speed limit with traffic calming
b) Minimum speed limit with traffic calming
c) '20 cars only' parking zone
d) Only 20 cars allowed at any one time
HC rule 131

Question: 3.65
What does this sign mean?

Mark one answer
a) New speed limit 20 mph
b) No vehicles over 30 tonnes
c) Minimum speed limit 30 mph
d) End of 20 mph zone
HC rule 131

Question: 3.66
What does this sign mean?

Mark one answer
a) Humpback bridge
b) Humps in the road
c) Entrance to tunnel
d) Soft verges
HC rule 131

Question: 3.67
Where would you see this road marking?

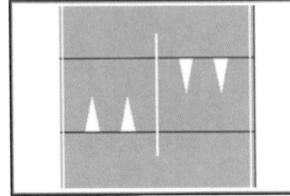

Mark one answer
a) At traffic lights
b) On road humps
c) Near a level crossing
d) At a box junction
HC rule 131   D

Question: 3.68
In areas where there are 'traffic calming' measures you should
Mark one answer
a) drive at a reduced speed
b) always drive at the speed limit
c) position in the centre of the road
d) only slow down if pedestrians are near
HC rule 131

Question: 3.69
You are driving in a built-up area. You approach a speed hump. You should

Mark one answer
a) move across to the left-hand side of the road
b) wait for any pedestrians to cross
c) slow your vehicle right down
d) stop and check both pavements
HC rule 131

Question: 3.70
Road humps, chicanes, and narrowings are
Mark one answer
a) always at major road works
b) used to increase traffic speed
c) at toll-bridge approaches only
d) traffic calming measures
HC rule 131

Question: 3.71
You are on a country road. What should you expect to see coming towards you on YOUR side of the road?
Mark one answer
a) Motorcycles
b) Bicycles
c) Pedestrians
d) Horse riders
HC rules 132 2

78

Question: 3.72
You are driving towards this left-hand bend. What dangers should you be aware of?

Mark one answer
a) A vehicle overtaking you
b) No white lines in the centre of the road
c) No sign to warn you of the bend
d) Pedestrians walking towards you
HC rules 132 2

Question: 3.73
You are driving a slow-moving vehicle on a narrow winding road. In order to let other vehicles overtake you should
Mark one answer
a) wave to them to pass
b) pull in when you can
c) show a left turn signal
d) keep left and hold your speed
HC rules 133 145

Question: 3.74
You are driving a slow moving vehicle on a narrow road. When traffic wishes to overtake you should
Mark one answer
a) take no action
b) put your hazard warning lights on
c) stop immediately and wave it on
d) pull in safely as soon as you can do so
HC rules 133 145

Question: 3.75
You are driving a slow moving vehicle on a narrow winding road. You should
Mark one answer
a) keep well out to stop vehicles overtaking dangerously
b) wave following vehicles past you if you think they can overtake quickly
c) pull in safely when you can, to let following vehicles overtake
d) give a left signal when it is safe for vehicles to overtake you
HC rules 133 145

Question: 3.76
You see a vehicle coming towards you on a single-track road. You should
Mark one answer
a) go back to the main road
b) do an emergency stop
c) stop at a passing place
d) put on your hazard warning lights
HC rule 133

Question: 3.77
You are on a road that is only wide enough for one vehicle. There is a car coming towards you. What should you do?
Mark one answer
a) Pull into a passing place on your right
b) Force the other driver to reverse
c) Pull into a passing place if your vehicle is wider
d) Pull into a passing place on your left
HC rule 133

4. Using the road
Before completing quiz 4 read Highway Code rules 135 - 179.

Question: 4.1
Before you make a U-turn in the road, you should
Mark one answer
a) give an arm signal as well as using your indicators
b) signal so that other drivers can slow down for you
c) look over your shoulder for a final check
d) select a higher gear than normal
HC rule 135

Question: 4.2
When you are moving off from behind a parked car you should
Mark three answers
a) look round before you move off
b) use all the mirrors on the vehicle
c) look round after moving off
d) use the exterior mirrors only
e) give a signal if necessary
f) give a signal after moving off
HC rule 135

Question: 4.3
What does the term 'Blind Spot' mean for a driver?
Mark one answer
a) An area covered by your right hand mirror
b) An area not covered by your headlights
c) An area covered by your left hand mirror
d) An area not seen in your mirrors
HC rule 135

Question: 4.4
You are on a long, downhill slope. What should you do to help control the speed of your vehicle?
Mark one answer
a) Select neutral
b) Select a lower gear
c) Grip the handbrake firmly
d) Apply the parking brake gently
HC rule 136

Question: 4.5
When approaching a right-hand bend you should keep well to the left. Why is this?

Mark one answer
a) To improve your view of the road
b) To overcome the effect of the road's slope
c) To let faster traffic from behind overtake
d) To be positioned safely if you skid
HC rule 136

Question: 4.6
How can you use your vehicle's engine as a brake?
Mark one answer
a) By changing to a lower gear
b) By selecting reverse gear
c) By changing to a higher gear
d) By selecting neutral gear
HC rule 136

Question: 4.7
You are about to go down a steep hill. To control the speed of your vehicle you should
Mark one answer
a) select a high gear and use the brakes carefully
b) select a high gear and use the brakes firmly
c) select a low gear and use the brakes carefully
d) select a low gear and avoid using the brakes
HC rule 136

Question: 4.8
Which of the following should you do before stopping?
Mark one answer
a) Sound the horn
b) Use the mirrors
c) Select a higher gear
d) Flash your headlights
HC rule 137

Question: 4.9
Which TWO should you allow extra room when overtaking?
Mark two answers
a) Motorcycles
b) Tractors
c) Bicycles
d) Road-sweeping vehicles
HC rules 139 189

Question: 4.10
When you are overtaking a cyclist you should leave as much room as you would give to a car. What is the main reason for this?
Mark one answer
a) The cyclist might change lanes
b) The cyclist might get off the bike
c) The cyclist might swerve
d) The cyclist might have to make a right turn
HC rules 139 189

Question: 4.11
You should never attempt to overtake a cyclist
Mark one answer
a) just before you turn left
b) on a left hand bend
c) on a one-way street
d) on a dual carriageway
HC rules 139 158 188

Question: 4.12
It is very windy. You are about to overtake a motorcyclist. You should
Mark one answer
a) overtake slowly
b) allow extra room
c) sound your horn
d) keep close as you pass
HC rules 139 207

Question: 4.13
In which THREE of these situations may you overtake another vehicle on the left?
Mark three answers
a) When you are in a one-way street
b) When approaching a motorway slip road where you will be turning off
c) When the vehicle in front is signalling to turn right
d) When a slower vehicle is travelling in the right-hand lane of a dual carriageway
e) In slow-moving traffic queues when traffic in the right-hand lane is moving more slowly
HC rules 139 121

Question: 4.14
You are travelling along this narrow country road. When passing the cyclist you should go

Mark one answer
a) slowly, sounding the horn as you pass
b) quickly, leaving plenty of room
c) slowly, leaving plenty of room
d) quickly, sounding the horn as you pass
HC rules 139 188

Question: 4.15
You meet an obstruction on your side of the road. You should
Mark one answer
a) carry on, you have priority
b) give way to oncoming traffic
c) wave oncoming vehicles through
d) accelerate to get past first
HC rule 139

Question: 4.16
Why should you allow extra room when overtaking a motorcyclist on a windy day?
Mark one answer
a) The rider may turn off suddenly to get out of the wind
b) The rider may be blown across in front of you
c) The rider may stop suddenly
d) The rider may be travelling faster than normal
HC rules 139 207

Question: 4.17
Why is passing a lorry more risky than passing a car?
Mark one answer
a) Lorries are longer than cars
b) Lorries may suddenly pull up
c) The brakes of lorries are not as good
d) Lorries climb hills more slowly
HC rule 140

Question: 4.18
Before overtaking a large vehicle you should keep well back. Why is this?
Mark one answer
a) To give acceleration space to overtake quickly on blind bends
b) To get the best view of the road ahead
c) To leave a gap in case the vehicle stops and rolls back
d) To offer other drivers a safe gap if they want to overtake you
HC rule 140

Question: 4.19
You wish to overtake a long, slow-moving vehicle on a busy road. You should
Mark one answer
a) follow it closely and keep moving out to see the road ahead
b) flash your headlights for the oncoming traffic to give way
c) stay behind until the driver waves you past
d) keep well back until you can see that it is clear
HC rule 140

Question: 4.20
You see this white arrow on the road ahead. It means

Mark one answer
a) entrance on the left
b) all vehicles turn left
c) keep left of the hatched markings
d) road bending to the left
HC rules 141 109

Question: 4.21
This road marking warns

Mark one answer
a) drivers to use the hard shoulder
b) overtaking drivers there is a bend to the left
c) overtaking drivers to move back to the left
d) drivers that it is safe to overtake
HC rule 141

Question: 4.22
There is a tractor ahead of you. You wish to overtake but you are NOT sure if it is safe to do so. You should
Mark one answer
a) follow another overtaking vehicle through
b) sound your horn to the slow vehicle to pull over
c) speed through but flash your lights to oncoming traffic
d) not overtake if you are in doubt
HC rule 142

Question: 4.23
You should not overtake when
Mark three answers
a) intending to turn left shortly afterwards
b) in a one-way street
c) approaching a junction
d) going up a long hill
e) the view ahead is blocked
HC rules 142 143 158

Question: 4.24
You are on a narrow road at night. A slower-moving vehicle ahead has been signalling right for some time. What should you do?
Mark one answer
a) Overtake on the left
b) Flash your headlights before overtaking
c) Signal right and sound your horn
d) Wait for the signal to be cancelled before overtaking
HC rule 143

Question: 4.25
You are following a slower-moving vehicle on a narrow country road. There is a junction just ahead on the right. What should you do?
Mark one answer
a) Overtake after checking your mirrors and signalling
b) Stay behind until you are past the junction
c) Accelerate quickly to pass before the junction
d) Slow down and prepare to overtake on the left
HC rule 143

Question: 4.26
You are following a long lorry. The driver signals to turn left into a narrow road. What should you do?
Mark one answer
a) Overtake on the left before the lorry reaches the junction
b) Overtake on the right as soon as the lorry slows down
c) Do not overtake unless you can see there is no oncoming traffic
d) Do not overtake, stay well back and be prepared to stop.
HC rule 143

Question: 4.27

You are following a large vehicle approaching crossroads. The driver signals to turn left. What should you do?

Mark one answer

a) Overtake if you can leave plenty of room.
b) Overtake only if there are no oncoming vehicles.
c) Do not overtake until the vehicle begins to turn.
d) Do not overtake when at or approaching a junction.

HC rule 143

Question: 4.28

You are driving in traffic at the speed limit for the road. The driver behind is trying to overtake. You should

Mark one answer

a) move closer to the car ahead, so the driver behind has no room to overtake
b) wave the driver behind to overtake when it is safe
c) keep a steady course and allow the driver behind to overtake
d) accelerate to get away from the driver behind

HC rule 144

Question: 4.29

You are following a vehicle at a safe distance on a wet road. Another driver overtakes you and pulls into the gap you have left. What should you do?

Mark one answer

a) Flash your headlights as a warning
b) Try to overtake safely as soon as you can
c) Drop back to regain a safe distance
d) Stay close to the other vehicle until it moves on

HC rule 144

Question: 4.30

A long, heavily-laden lorry is taking a long time to overtake you. What should you do?

Mark one answer

a) Speed up
b) Slow down
c) Hold your speed
d) Change direction

HC rule 144

Question: 4.31

You have just been overtaken by this motorcyclist who is cutting in sharply. You should

Mark one answer

a) sound the horn
b) brake firmly
c) keep a safe gap
d) flash your lights

HC rule 144

Question: 4.32

You are driving along this road. The red van cuts in close in front of you. What should you do?

Mark one answer

a) Accelerate to get closer to the red van
b) Give a long blast on the horn
c) Drop back to leave the correct separation distance
d) Flash your headlights several times

HC rule 144

Question: 4.33

You keep well back while waiting to overtake a large vehicle. A car fills the gap. You should

Mark one answer

a) sound your horn
b) drop back further
c) flash your headlights
d) start to overtake

HC rule 144

Question: 4.34

Where in particular should you look out for motorcyclists?

Mark one answer

a) In a filling station
b) At a road junction
c) Near a service area
d) When entering a car park

HC rules 146 187

Question: 4.35

You are about to reverse into a side road. A pedestrian wishes to cross behind you. You should

Mark one answer

a) wave to the pedestrian to stop
b) give way to the pedestrian
c) wave to the pedestrian to cross
d) reverse before the pedestrian starts to cross

HC rules 146 178

Question: 4.36

Why should you look particularly for motorcyclists and cyclists at junctions?

Mark one answer

a) They may want to turn into the side road
b) They may slow down to let you turn
c) They are harder to see
d) They might not see you turn

HC rules 146 187

Question: 4.37

You are turning left into a side road. What hazards should you be especially aware of?

Mark one answer

a) One way street
b) Pedestrians
c) Traffic congestion
d) Parked vehicles

HC rules 146 158

Question: 4.38
You are reversing around a corner when you notice a pedestrian walking behind you. What should you do?

Mark one answer
a) Slow down and wave the pedestrian across
b) Continue reversing and steer round the pedestrian
c) Stop and give way
d) Continue reversing and sound your horn

HC rules 146 178

Question: 4.39
Where should you take particular care to look out for motorcyclists and cyclists?

Mark one answer
a) On dual carriageways
b) At junctions
c) At zebra crossings
d) On one-way streets

HC rules 146 187

Question: 4.40
What MUST you do when you see this sign?

Mark one answer
a) Stop, ONLY if traffic is approaching
b) Stop, even if the road is clear
c) Stop, ONLY if children are waiting to cross
d) Stop, ONLY if a red light is showing

HC rule 147

Question: 4.41
At this blind junction you must stop

Mark one answer
a) behind the line, then edge forward to see clearly
b) beyond the line at a point where you can see clearly
c) only if there is traffic on the main road
d) only if you are turning to the right

HC rule 147

Question: 4.42
This marking appears on the road just before a

Mark one answer
a) no entry sign
b) give way sign
c) stop sign
d) no through road sign

HC rule 148

Question: 4.43
The dual carriageway you are turning right onto has a very narrow central reservation. What should you do?

Mark one answer
a) Proceed to central reserve and wait
b) Wait until the road is clear in both directions
c) Stop in first lane so that other vehicles give way
d) Emerge slightly to show your intentions

HC rule 149

Question: 4.44
You are turning right onto a dual carriageway. What should you do before emerging?

Mark one answer
a) Stop, apply the handbrake and then select a low gear
b) Position your vehicle well to the left of the side road
c) Check that the central reserve is wide enough for your vehicle
d) Make sure that you leave enough room for a following vehicle

HC rule 149

Question: 4.45
You want to turn right at a box junction. There is oncoming traffic. You should

Mark one answer
a) wait in the box junction if your exit is clear
b) wait before the junction until it is clear of all traffic
c) drive on, you cannot turn right at a box junction
d) drive slowly into the box junction when signalled by oncoming traffic

HC rule 150

Question: 4.46
You may only enter a box junction when

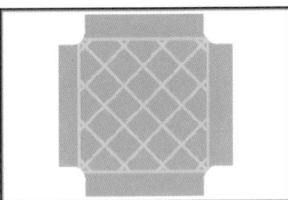

Mark one answer
a) there are less than two vehicles in front of you
b) the traffic lights show green
c) your exit road is clear
d) you need to turn left

HC rule 150

Question: 4.47

You may wait in a yellow box junction when

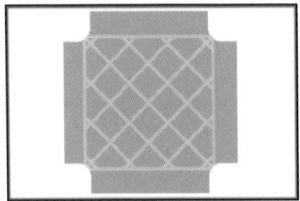

Mark one answer
a) oncoming traffic is preventing you from turning right
b) you are in a queue of traffic turning left
c) you are in a queue of traffic to go ahead
d) you are on a roundabout
HC rule 150

Question: 4.48

What is the purpose of these yellow criss-cross lines on the road?

Mark one answer
a) To make you more aware of the traffic lights
b) To guide you into position as you turn
c) To prevent the junction from becoming blocked
d) To show you where to stop when the lights change
HC rule 150

Question: 4.49

What is the reason for the yellow criss-cross lines painted on the road here?

Mark one answer
a) To mark out an area for trams only
b) To prevent queuing traffic from blocking the junction on the left
c) To mark the entrance lane to a car park
d) To warn you of the tram lines crossing the road
HC rule 150

Question: 4.50

When may you wait in a box junction?

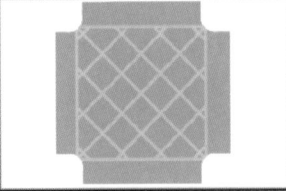

Mark one answer
a) When you are stationary in a queue of traffic
b) When approaching a pelican crossing
c) When approaching a zebra crossing
d) When oncoming traffic prevents you turning right
HC rule 150

Question: 4.51

A red traffic light means

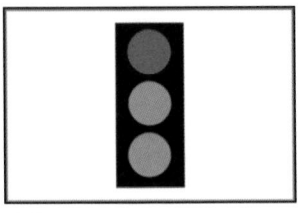

Mark one answer
a) you must stop behind the white stop line
b) you may go straight on if there is no other traffic
c) you may turn left if it is safe to do so
d) you must slow down and prepare to stop if traffic has started to cross
HC rule 151

Question: 4.52

A red traffic light means

Mark one answer
a) you should stop unless turning left
b) stop, if you are able to brake safely
c) you must stop and wait behind the stop line
d) proceed with caution
HC rule 151

Question: 4.53

At traffic lights, amber on its own means

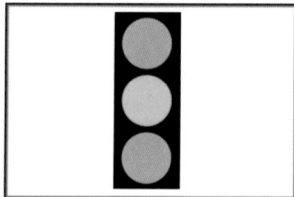

Mark one answer
a) prepare to go
b) go if the way is clear
c) go if no pedestrians are crossing
d) stop at the stop line
HC rule 151

Question: 4.54

You are approaching traffic lights. Red and amber are showing. This means

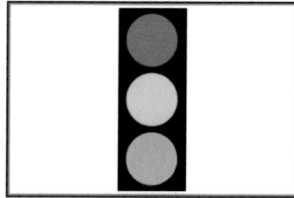

Mark one answer
a) pass the lights if the road is clear
b) there is a fault with the lights – take care
c) wait for the green light before you pass the lights
d) the lights are about to change to red
HC rule 151

Question: 4.55

When traffic lights are out of order, who has priority?
Mark one answer
a) Traffic going straight on
b) Traffic turning right
c) Nobody
d) Traffic turning left
HC rule 152

Question: 4.56

You are at a junction controlled by traffic lights. When should you NOT proceed at green?

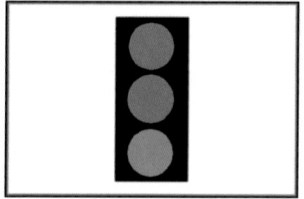

Mark one answer
a) When pedestrians are waiting to cross
b) When your exit from the junction is blocked
c) When you think the lights may be about to change
d) When you intend to turn right
HC rule 152

Question: 4.57

You are in the left-hand lane at traffic lights. You are waiting to turn left. At which of these traffic lights must you NOT move on?

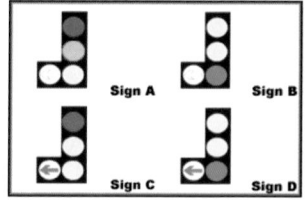

Mark one answer
a) Sign A
b) Sign B
c) Sign C
d) Sign D
HC rule 153

Question: 4.58

When the traffic lights change to green the white car should

Mark one answer
a) wait for the cyclist to pull away
b) move off quickly and turn in front of the cyclist
c) move close up to the cyclist to beat the lights
d) sound the horn to warn the cyclist
HC rule 154

Question: 4.59

You wish to turn right ahead. Why should you take up the correct position in good time?
Mark one answer
a) To allow other drivers to pull out in front of you
b) To give a better view into the road that you're joining
c) To help other road users know what you intend to do
d) To allow drivers to pass you on the right
HC rule 155

Question: 4.60

You are driving on a main road. You intend to turn right into a side road. Just before turning you should
Mark one answer
a) adjust your interior mirror
b) flash your headlamps
c) steer over to the left
d) check for traffic overtaking on your right
HC rule 156

Question: 4.61
You want to turn right from a main road into a side road. Just before turning you should
Mark one answer
a) cancel your right-turn signal
b) select first gear
c) check for traffic overtaking on your right
d) stop and set the handbrake
HC rule 156

Question: 4.62
You are at the front of a queue of traffic waiting to turn right into a side road. Why is it important to check your right mirror just before turning?
Mark one answer
a) To look for pedestrians about to cross
b) To check for overtaking vehicles
c) To make sure the side road is clear
d) To check for emerging traffic
HC rule 156

Question: 4.63
You intend to turn right into a side road. Just before turning you should check for motorcyclists who might be
Mark one answer
a) overtaking on your left
b) following you closely
c) emerging from the side road
d) overtaking on your right
HC rule 156

Question: 4.64
You are intending to turn right at a crossroads. An oncoming driver is also turning right. It will normally be safer to
Mark one answer
a) keep the other vehicle to your RIGHT and turn behind it (offside to offside)
b) keep the other vehicle to your LEFT and turn in front of it (nearside to nearside)
c) carry on and turn at the next junction instead
d) hold back and wait for the other driver to turn first
HC rule 157

Question: 4.65
You intend to turn left at the traffic lights. Just before turning you should

Mark one answer
a) check your right mirror
b) move close up to the white car
c) straddle the lanes
d) check for bicycles on your left
HC rule 158

Question: 4.66
You are following a cyclist. You wish to turn left just ahead. You should

Mark one answer
a) overtake the cyclist before the junction
b) pull alongside the cyclist and stay level until after the junction
c) hold back until the cyclist has passed the junction
d) go around the cyclist on the junction
HC rules 158 188

Question: 4.67
You are travelling behind a moped. You want to turn left just ahead. You should
Mark one answer
a) overtake the moped before the junction
b) pull alongside the moped and stay level until just before the junction
c) sound your horn as a warning and pull in front of the moped
d) stay behind until the moped has passed the junction
HC rules 158 188

Question: 4.68
While driving, you intend to turn left into a minor road. On the approach you should
Mark one answer
a) keep just left of the middle of the road
b) keep in the middle of the road
c) swing out wide just before turning
d) keep well to the left of the road
HC rule 159

Question: 4.69
You are going straight ahead at a roundabout. How should you signal?
Mark one answer
a) Signal right on the approach and then left to leave the roundabout
b) Signal left as you leave the roundabout
c) Signal left on the approach to the roundabout and keep the signal on until you leave
d) Signal left just after you pass the exit before the one you will take
HC rule 162

Question: 4.70
When going straight ahead at a roundabout you should
Mark one answer
a) indicate left before leaving the roundabout
b) not indicate at any time
c) indicate right when approaching the roundabout
d) indicate left when approaching the roundabout
HC rule 162

Question: 4.71
Which three of the following are most likely to take an unusual course at roundabouts?
Mark three answers
a) Horse riders
b) Milk floats
c) Delivery vans
d) Long vehicles
e) Estate cars
f) Cyclists
HC rule 163

Question: 4.72
Which vehicle might have to use a different course to normal at roundabouts?
Mark one answer
a) Sports car
b) Van
c) Estate car
d) Long vehicle
HC rule 163

Question: 4.73
You see a horse rider as you approach a roundabout. They are signalling right but keeping well to the left. You should

Mark one answer
a) proceed as normal
b) keep close to them
c) cut in front of them
d) stay well back
HC rule 163

Question: 4.74
A horse rider is in the left-hand lane approaching a roundabout. You should expect the rider to
Mark one answer
a) go in any direction
b) turn right
c) turn left
d) go ahead
HC rule 163

Question: 4.75
You are coming up to a roundabout. A cyclist is signalling to turn right. What should you do?
Mark one answer
a) Overtake on the right
b) Give a horn warning
c) Signal the cyclist to move across
d) Give the cyclist plenty of room
HC rule 163

Question: 4.76
You are following two cyclists. They approach a roundabout in the left-hand lane. In which direction should you expect the cyclists to go?
Mark one answer
a) Left
b) Right
c) Any direction
d) Straight ahead
HC rules 163 62

Question: 4.77
You are approaching a roundabout. There are horses just ahead of you. You should
Mark two answers
a) be prepared to stop
b) treat them like any other vehicle
c) give them plenty of room
d) accelerate past as quickly as possible
e) sound your horn as a warning
HC rule 163

Question: 4.78
You are approaching this roundabout and see the cyclist signal right. Why is the cyclist keeping to the left?

Mark one answer
a) It is a quicker route for the cyclist
b) The cyclist is going to turn left instead
c) The cyclist thinks The Highway Code does not apply to bicycles
d) The cyclist is slower and more vulnerable
HC rules 163 62

Question: 4.79
Where would you find these road marking?

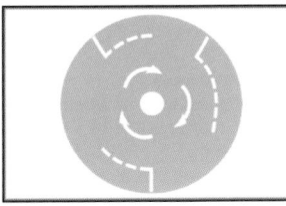

Mark one answer
a) At a railway crossing
b) At a junction
c) On a motorway
d) On a pedestrian crossing
HC rule 164

Question: 4.80
What do these zigzag lines at pedestrian crossings mean?

Mark one answer
a) No parking at any time
b) Parking allowed only for a short time
c) Slow down to 20 mph
d) Sounding horns is not allowed
HC rule 167

Question: 4.81
Which road user has caused a hazard?

Mark one answer
a) The parked car (arrowed A)
b) The pedestrian waiting to cross (arrowed B)
c) The moving car (arrowed C)
d) The car turning (arrowed D)
HC rules 167 215

Question: 4.82
You are having difficulty finding a parking space in a busy town. You can see there is space on the zigzag lines of a zebra crossing. Can you park there?
Mark one answer
a) No, unless you stay with your car
b) Yes, in order to drop off a passenger
c) Yes, if you do not block people from crossing
d) No, not in any circumstances
HC rule 167

Question: 4.83
You stop for pedestrians waiting to cross at a zebra crossing. They do not start to cross. What should you do?
Mark one answer
a) Be patient and wait
b) Sound your horn
c) Carry on
d) Wave them to cross
HC rules 170 171

Question: 4.84
You are approaching this crossing. You should

Mark one answer
a) prepare to slow down and stop
b) stop and wave the pedestrians across
c) speed up and pass by quickly
d) continue unless the pedestrians step out
HC rule 171

Question: 4.85
You should never wave people across at pedestrian crossings because
Mark one answer
a) there may be another vehicle coming
b) they may not be looking
c) it is safer for you to carry on
d) they may not be ready to cross
HC rule 171

Question: 4.86
Someone is waiting to cross at a zebra crossing. They are standing on the pavement. You should normally
Mark one answer
a) go on quickly before they step onto the crossing
b) stop before you reach the zigzag lines and let them cross
c) stop, let them cross, wait patiently
d) ignore them as they are still on the pavement
HC rule 171

Question: 4.87
What should the driver of the car approaching the crossing do?

Mark one answer
a) Continue at the same speed
b) Sound the horn
c) Drive through quickly
d) Slow down and get ready to stop
HC rule 171

Question: 4.88
You are approaching a zebra crossing. Pedestrians are waiting to cross. You should
Mark one answer
a) give way to the elderly and infirm only
b) slow down and prepare to stop
c) use your headlights to indicate they can cross
d) wave at them to cross the road
HC rule 171

Question: 4.89
You are driving towards a zebra crossing. A person in a wheelchair is waiting to cross. What should you do?
Mark one answer
a) continue on your way
b) wave to the person to cross
c) wave to the person to wait
d) be prepared to stop
HC rules 171 183

Question: 4.90
You are approaching a pelican crossing. The amber light is flashing. You must
Mark one answer
a) give way to pedestrians who are crossing
b) encourage pedestrians to cross
c) not move until the green light appears
d) stop even if the crossing is clear
HC rule 172

Question: 4.91
At a pelican crossing, what does a flashing amber light mean?
Mark one answer
a) You must not move off until the lights stop flashing
b) You must give way to pedestrians still on the crossing
c) You can move off, even if pedestrians are still on the crossing
d) You must stop because the lights are about to change to red
HC rule 172

Question: 4.92
At a pelican crossing the flashing amber light means you MUST
Mark one answer
a) stop and wait for the green light
b) stop and wait for the red light
c) give way to pedestrians waiting to cross
d) give way to pedestrians already on the crossing
HC rule 172

The Highway Code quiz programme

Question: 4.93
What must a driver do at a pelican crossing when the amber light is flashing?
Mark one answer
a) Signal the pedestrian to cross
b) Always wait for the green light before proceeding
c) Give way to any pedestrians on the crossing
d) Wait for the red-and-amber light before proceeding
HC rule 172

Question: 4.94
You are waiting at a pelican crossing. The red light changes to flashing amber. This means you must
Mark one answer
a) wait for pedestrians on the crossing to clear
b) move off immediately without any hesitation
c) wait for the green light before moving off
d) get ready and go when the continuous amber light shows
HC rule 172

Question: 4.95
As you approach a pelican crossing the lights change to green. Elderly people are halfway across. You should
Mark one answer
a) wave them to cross as quickly as they can
b) rev your engine to make them hurry
c) flash your lights in case they have not heard you
d) wait because they will take longer to cross
HC rules 174 170 183

Question: 4.96
You have stopped at a pelican crossing. A disabled person is crossing slowly in front of you. The lights have now changed to green. You should
Mark two answers
a) allow the person to cross
b) drive in front of the person
c) drive behind the person
d) sound your horn
e) be patient
f) edge forward slowly
HC rules 174 170 183

Question: 4.97
At puffin crossings, which light will not show to a driver?
Mark one answer
a) Flashing amber
b) Red
c) steady amber
d) green
HC rule 175

Question: 4.98
At a puffin crossing, which colour follows the green signal?
Mark one answer
a) Steady red
b) Flashing amber
c) Steady amber
d) Flashing green
HC rule 175

Question: 4.99
You are parked in a busy high street. What is the safest way to turn your vehicle around so you can go the opposite way?
Mark one answer
a) Find a quiet side road to turn round in
b) Drive into a side road and reverse into the main road
c) Get someone to stop the traffic
d) Do a U-turn
HC rule 176

Question: 4.100
You are on a busy main road and find that you are travelling in the wrong direction. What should you do?
Mark one answer
a) Turn into a side road on the right and reverse into the main road
b) Make a U-turn in the main road
c) Make a 'three-point' turn in the main road
d) Turn round in a side road
HC rule 176

Question: 4.101
When may you reverse from a side road into a main road?
Mark one answer
a) Only if both roads are clear of traffic
b) Not at any time
c) At any time
d) Only if the main road is clear of traffic
HC rule 177

Question: 4.102
You want to reverse into a side road. You are not sure that the area behind your car is clear. What should you do?
Mark one answer
a) Look through the rear window only
b) Get out and check
c) Check the mirrors only
d) Carry on, assuming it is clear
HC rule 178

Question: 4.103
You cannot see clearly behind when reversing. What should you do?
Mark one answer
a) Open your window to look behind
b) Open the door and look behind
c) Look in the nearside mirror
d) Ask someone to guide you
HC rule 178

Question: 4.104
Who is especially in danger of not being seen as you reverse your car?
Mark one answer
a) Motorcyclists
b) Car drivers
c) Cyclists
d) Children
HC rule 178

Question: 4.105
You must not reverse
Mark one answer
a) for longer than necessary
b) for more than a car's length
c) into a side road
d) in a built-up area
HC rule 179

5. Road users requiring extra care

Before completing quiz 5 read Highway Code rules 180 - 200.

Question: 5.1
At road junctions which of the following are most vulnerable?
Mark three answers
a) Cyclists
b) Motorcyclists
c) Pedestrians
d) Car drivers
e) Lorry drivers
HC rule 180

Question: 5.2
You are at a road junction, turning into a minor road. There are pedestrians crossing the minor road. You should

Mark one answer
a) stop and wave the pedestrians across
b) sound your horn to let the pedestrians know that you are there
c) give way to the pedestrians who are already crossing
d) carry on; the pedestrians should give way to you
HC rule 182

Question: 5.3
You are turning left into a side road. Pedestrians are crossing the road near the junction. You must

Mark one answer
a) wave them on
b) sound your horn
c) switch on your hazard lights
d) wait for them to cross
HC rule 182

Question: 5.4
You are driving past a line of parked cars. You notice a ball bouncing out into the road ahead. What should you do?

Mark one answer
a) Continue driving at the same speed and sound your horn
b) Continue driving at the same speed and flash your headlights
c) Slow down and be prepared to stop for children
d) Stop and wave the children across to fetch their ball
HC rule 182

Question: 5.5
You are driving in town. There is a bus at the bus stop on the other side of the road. Why should you be careful?
Mark one answer
a) The bus may have broken down
b) Pedestrians may come from behind the bus
c) The bus may move off suddenly
d) The bus may remain stationary
HC rule 182

Question: 5.6
You are turning left from a main road into a side road. People are already crossing the road into which you are turning. You should

Mark one answer
a) continue, as it is your right of way
b) signal to them to continue crossing
c) wait and allow them to cross
d) sound your horn to warn them of your presence
HC rule 182

Question: 5.7
You are turning left at a junction. Pedestrians have started to cross the road. You should

Mark one answer
a) go on, giving them plenty of room
b) stop and wave at them to cross
c) blow your horn and proceed
d) give way to them
HC rule 182

Question: 5.8

What should the driver of the red car (arrowed) do?

Mark one answer
a) Wave the pedestrians who are waiting to cross
b) Wait for the pedestrian in the road to cross
c) Quickly drive behind the pedestrian in the road
d) Tell the pedestrian in the road she should not have crossed
HC rule 182

Question: 5.9

You see a pedestrian with a white stick and red band. This means that the person is
Mark one answer
a) physically disabled
b) deaf only
c) blind only
d) deaf and blind
HC rule 183

Question: 5.10

What action would you take when elderly people are crossing the road?

Mark one answer
a) Wave them across so they know that you have seen them
b) Be patient and allow them to cross in their own time
c) Rev the engine to let them know that you are waiting
d) Tap the horn in case they are hard of hearing
HC rule 183

Question: 5.11

You see two elderly pedestrians about to cross the road ahead. You should
Mark one answer
a) expect them to wait for you to pass
b) speed up to get past them quickly
c) stop and wave them across the road
d) be careful, they may misjudge your speed
HC rule 183

Question: 5.12

You have just passed these warning lights. What hazard would you expect to see next?

Mark one answer
a) A level crossing with no barrier
b) An ambulance station
c) A school crossing patrol
d) An opening bridge
HC rule 184

Question: 5.13

There are flashing amber lights under a school warning sign. What action should you take?
Mark one answer
a) Reduce speed until you are clear of the area
b) Keep up your speed and sound the horn
c) Increase your speed to clear the area quickly
d) Wait at the lights until they change to green
HC rule 184

Question: 5.14

This yellow sign on a vehicle indicates this is

Mark one answer
a) a vehicle broken down
b) a school bus
c) an ice cream van
d) a private ambulance
HC rule 185

Question: 5.15

Where would you see this sign?

Mark one answer
a) Near a school crossing
b) At a playground entrance
c) On a school bus
d) At a 'pedestrians only' area
HC rule 185

Question: 5.16

Where would you see this sign?

Mark one answer
a) In the window of a car taking children to school
b) At the side of the road
c) At playground areas
d) On the rear of a school bus or coach
HC rule 185

Question: 5.17
How will a school crossing patrol signal you to stop?
Mark one answer
a) By pointing to children on the opposite pavement
b) By displaying a red light
c) By displaying a stop sign
d) By giving you an arm signal
HC rule 186

Question: 5.18
What is the main hazard shown in this picture?

Mark one answer
a) Vehicles turning right
b) Vehicles doing U-turns
c) The cyclist crossing the road
d) Parked cars around the corner
HC rule 187

Question: 5.19
You are waiting to come out of a side road. Why should you watch carefully for motorcycles?
Mark one answer
a) Motorcycles are usually faster than cars
b) Police patrols often use motorcycles
c) Motorcycles are small and hard to see
d) Motorcycles have right of way
HC rule 187

Question: 5.20
Motorcyclists are particularly vulnerable
Mark one answer
a) when moving off
b) on dual carriageways
c) when approaching junctions
d) on motorways
HC rule 187

Question: 5.21
Which THREE of the following are hazards motorcyclists present in queues of traffic?
Mark three answers
a) Cutting in just in front of you
b) Riding in single file
c) Passing very close to you
d) Riding with their headlight on dipped beam
e) Filtering between the lanes
HC rule 187

Question: 5.22
You are behind this cyclist. When the traffic lights change, what should you do?

Mark one answer
a) Try to move off before the cyclist
b) Allow the cyclist time and room
c) Turn right but give the cyclist room
d) Tap your horn and drive through first
HC rules 188 154

Question: 5.23
You are approaching this cyclist. You should

Mark one answer
a) overtake before the cyclist gets to the junction
b) flash your headlights at the cyclist
c) slow down and allow the cyclist to turn
d) overtake the cyclist on the left-hand side
HC rule 188

Question: 5.24
There is a slow-moving motorcyclist ahead of you. You are unsure what the rider is going to do. You should
Mark one answer
a) pass on the left
b) pass on the right
c) stay behind
d) move closer
HC rule 188

Question: 5.25
Motorcyclists will often look round over their right shoulder just before turning right. This is because
Mark one answer
a) they need to listen for following traffic
b) motorcycles do not have mirrors
c) looking around helps them balance as they turn
d) they need to check for traffic in their blind area
HC rule 188

Question: 5.26
What is the main hazard you should be aware of when following this cyclist?

Mark one answer
a) The cyclist may move into the left and dismount
b) The cyclist may swerve out into the road
c) The contents of the cyclist's carrier may fall onto the road
d) The cyclist may wish to turn right at the end of the road
HC rule 189

Question: 5.27

The road is wet. Why might a motorcyclist steer round drain covers on a bend?

Mark one answer

a) To avoid puncturing the tyres on the edge of the drain covers
b) To prevent the motorcycle sliding on the metal drain covers
c) To help judge the bend using the drain covers as marker points
d) To avoid splashing pedestrians on the pavement

HC rule 189

Question: 5.28

You are following a motorcyclist on an uneven road. You should

Mark one answer

a) allow less room so you can be seen in their mirrors
b) overtake immediately
c) allow extra room in case they swerve to avoid pot-holes
d) allow the same room as normal because road surfaces do not affect motorcyclists

HC rule 189

Question: 5.29

A person herding sheep asks you to stop. You should

Mark one answer

a) ignore them as they have no authority
b) stop and switch off your engine
c) continue on but drive slowly
d) try and get past quickly

HC rule 190

Question: 5.30

Which THREE should you do when passing sheep on a road?

Mark three answers

a) Allow plenty of room
b) Go very slowly
c) Pass quickly but quietly
d) Be ready to stop
e) Briefly sound your horn

HC rule 190

Question: 5.31

When overtaking a horse and rider you should

Mark one answer

a) sound your horn as a warning
b) go past as quickly as possible
c) flash your headlights as a warning
d) go past slowly and carefully

HC rule 191

Question: 5.32

You notice horse riders in front. What should you do FIRST?

Mark one answer

a) Pull out to the middle of the road
b) Be prepared to slow down
c) Accelerate around them
d) Signal right

HC rule 191

Question: 5.33

You are driving along a country road. A horse and rider are approaching. What should you do?

Mark two answers

a) Increase your speed
b) Sound your horn
c) Flash your headlights
d) Drive slowly past
e) Give plenty of room
f) Rev your engine

HC rule 191

Question: 5.34

How should you overtake horse riders?

Mark one answer

a) Drive up close and overtake as soon as possible
b) Speed is not important but allow plenty of room
c) Use your horn just once to warn them
d) Drive slowly and leave plenty of room

HC rule 191

Question: 5.35

An elderly person's driving ability could be affected because they may be unable to

Mark one answer

a) obtain car insurance
b) understand road signs
c) react very quickly
d) give signals correctly

HC rule 192

Question: 5.36

You are following a car driven by an elderly driver. You should

Mark one answer

a) expect the driver to drive badly
b) flash your lights and overtake
c) be aware that the driver's reactions may not be as fast as yours
d) stay very close behind but be careful

HC rule 192

Question: 5.37

You are following a learner driver who stalls at a junction. You should

Mark one answer

a) be patient as you expect them to make mistakes
b) stay very close behind and flash your headlights
c) start to rev your engine if they take too long to restart
d) immediately steer around them and drive on

HC rule 193

Question: 5.38

How would you react to drivers who appear to be inexperienced?

Mark one answer

a) Sound your horn to warn them of your presence
b) Be patient and prepare for them to react more slowly
c) Flash your headlights to indicate that it is safe for them to proceed
d) Overtake them as soon as possible

HC rule 193

Question: 5.39
When being followed by an ambulance showing a flashing blue beacon you should
Mark one answer
a) pull over as soon as safely possible to let it pass
b) accelerate hard to get away from it
c) maintain your speed and course
d) brake harshly and immediately stop in the road
HC rule 194

Question: 5.40
You are on a dual carriageway. Ahead you see a vehicle with an amber flashing light. What could this be?
Mark one answer
a) An ambulance
b) A fire engine
c) A doctor on call
d) A disabled person's vehicle
HC rule 195

Question: 5.41
Powered vehicles used by disabled people are small and hard to see. How do they give early warning when on a dual carriageway?
Mark one answer
a) They will have a flashing red light
b) They will have a flashing green light
c) They will have a flashing blue light
d) They will have a flashing amber light.
HC rule 195

Question: 5.42
In front of you is a powered vehicle (powered wheelchair) driven by a disabled person. These vehicles have a maximum speed of
Mark one answer
a) 8 mph
b) 18 mph
c) 28 mph
d) 38 mph
HC rule 195

Question: 5.43
Powered vehicles, such as wheelchairs or scooters, used by disabled people have a maximum speed of
Mark one answer
a) 8 mph
b) 12 mph
c) 16 mph
d) 20 mph
HC rule 195

Question: 5.44
You are following a large articulated vehicle. It is going to turn left into a narrow road. What action should you take?

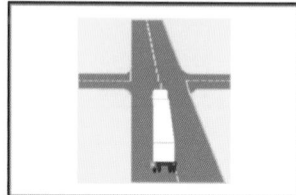

Mark one answer
a) Move out and overtake on the right
b) Pass on the left as the vehicle moves out
c) Be prepared to stop behind
d) Overtake quickly before the lorry moves out
HC rule 196

Question: 5.45
You are driving along this road. What should you be prepared to do?

Mark one answer
a) Sound your horn and continue
b) Slow down and give way
c) Report the driver to the police
d) Squeeze through the gap
HC rule 196

Question: 5.46
When approaching this bridge you should give way to

Mark one answer
a) bicycles
b) buses
c) motorcycles
d) cars
HC rule 196

Question: 5.47
What type of vehicle could you expect to meet in the middle of the road?

Mark one answer
a) Lorry
b) Bicycle
c) Car
d) Motorcycle
HC rule 196

Question: 5.48

What should you do as you approach this overhead bridge?

Mark one answer

a) Move out to the centre of the road before going through

b) Find another route, this is only for high vehicles

c) Be prepared to give way to large vehicles in the middle of the road

d) Move across to the right hand side before going through

HC rule 196

Question: 5.49

You are following a long vehicle. It approaches a crossroads and signals left, but moves out to the right. You should

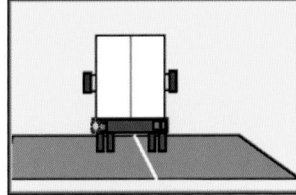

Mark one answer

a) get closer in order to pass it quickly

b) stay well back and give it room

c) assume the signal is wrong and it is really turning right

d) overtake as it starts to slow down

HC rule 196

Question: 5.50

You are driving behind a large goods vehicle. It signals left but steers to the right. You should

Mark one answer

a) slow down and let the vehicle turn

b) drive on, keeping to the left

c) overtake on the right of it

d) hold your speed and sound your horn

HC rule 196

Question: 5.51

You are approaching a mini-roundabout. The long vehicle in front is signalling left but positioned over to the right. You should

Mark one answer

a) sound your horn

b) overtake on the left

c) follow the same course as the lorry

d) keep well back

HC rules 196 163

Question: 5.52

What should you do as you approach this lorry?

Mark one answer

a) Slow down and be prepared to wait

b) Make the lorry wait for you

c) Flash your lights at the lorry

d) Move to the right hand side of the road

HC rule 196

Question: 5.53

You are following a long vehicle approaching a crossroads. The driver signals right but moves close to the left-hand kerb. What should you do?

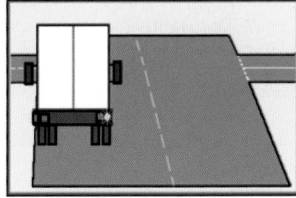

Mark one answer

a) Warn the driver of the wrong signal

b) Wait behind the long vehicle

c) Report the driver to the police

d) Overtake on the right-hand side

HC rule 196

Question: 5.54

You are following this lorry. You should keep well back from it to

Mark one answer

a) give you a good view of the road ahead

b) stop following traffic from rushing through the junction

c) prevent traffic behind you from overtaking

d) allow you to hurry through the traffic lights if they change

HC rule 197

Question: 5.55

Why should you be especially cautious when going past this stationary bus?

Mark two answers

a) There is traffic approaching in the distance
b) The driver may open the door
c) It may suddenly move off
d) People may cross the road in front of it
e) There are bicycles parked on the pavement
HC rule 198

Question: 5.56

You are driving in town. Ahead of you a bus is at a bus stop. Which TWO of the following should you do?

Mark two answers

a) Be prepared to give way if the bus suddenly moves off
b) Continue at the same speed but sound your horn as a warning
c) Watch carefully for the sudden appearance of pedestrians
d) Pass the bus as quickly as you possibly can
HC rule 198

Question: 5.57

A bus has stopped at a bus stop ahead of you. Its right-hand indicator is flashing. You should

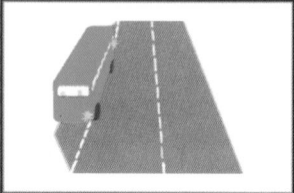

Mark one answer

a) flash your headlights and slow down
b) slow down and give way if it is safe to do so
c) sound your horn and keep going
d) slow down and then sound your horn
HC rule 198

Question: 5.58

What is the main hazard the driver of the red car (arrowed) should be aware of?

Mark one answer

a) Glare from the sun may affect the driver's vision
b) The black car may stop suddenly
c) The bus may move out into the road
d) Oncoming vehicles will assume the driver is turning right
HC rule 198

Question: 5.59

When you approach a bus signalling to move off from a bus stop you should

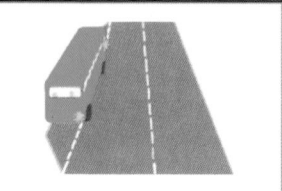

Mark one answer

a) get past before it moves
b) allow it to pull away, if it is safe to do so
c) flash your headlights as you approach
d) signal left and wave the bus on
HC rule 198

Question: 5.60

You are travelling behind a bus that pulls up at a bus stop. What should you do?

Mark two answers

a) Accelerate past the bus sounding your horn
b) Watch carefully for pedestrians
c) Be ready to give way to the bus
d) Pull in closely behind the bus
HC rule 198

Question: 5.61

As a driver why should you be more careful where trams operate?

Mark one answers

a) Because they do not have a horn
b) Because they do not stop for cars
c) Because they do not have lights
d) Because they cannot steer to avoid you
HC rule 199

Question: 5.62

Ahead of you there is a moving vehicle with a flashing amber beacon. This means it is

Mark one answer

a) slow moving
b) broken down
c) a doctor's car
d) a school crossing patrol
HC rule 200

6. Driving in adverse weather conditions and parking

Before completing quiz 6 read Highway Code rules 201 - 226.

Question: 6.1
You are on a wet motorway with surface spray. You should use
Mark one answer
a) hazard flashers
b) dipped headlights
c) rear fog lights
d) sidelights
HC rules 201 202

Question: 6.2
You should switch your rear fog lights on when visibility drops below
Mark one answer
a) your overall stopping distance
b) ten car lengths
c) 200metres (656feet)
d) 100 metres (328 feet)
HC rule 201

Question: 6.3
You may use front fog lights with headlights ONLY when visibility is reduced to less than
Mark one answer
a) 100 metres (328 feet)
b) 200 metres (656 feet)
c) 300 metres (984 feet)
d) 400 metres (1312 feet)
HC rules 201 211

Question: 6.4
Front fog lights should be used
Mark one answer
a) when visibility is reduced to 100 metres (328 feet)
b) as a warning to oncoming traffic
c) when driving during the hours of darkness
d) in any conditions and at any time
HC rule 201

Question: 6.5
Front fog lights should be used ONLY when
Mark one answer
a) travelling in very light rain
b) visibility is seriously reduced
c) daylight is fading
d) driving after midnight
HC rule 201

Question: 6.6
You may drive with front fog lights switched on

Mark one answer
a) when visibility is less than 100 metres (328 feet)
b) at any time to be noticed
c) instead of headlights on high speed roads
d) when dazzled by the lights of oncoming vehicles
HC rule 201

Question: 6.7
Front fog lights may be used ONLY if
Mark one answer
a) your headlights are not working
b) they are operated with rear fog lights
c) they were fitted by the vehicle manufacturer
d) visibility is seriously reduced
HC rule 201

Question: 6.8
Whilst driving, the fog clears and you can see more clearly. You must remember to
Mark one answer
a) switch off the fog lights
b) reduce your speed
c) switch off the demister
d) close any open windows
HC rules 201 211

Question: 6.9
You are driving in heavy traffic on a wet road. Spray makes it difficult to be seen. You should use your
Mark two answers
a) full beam headlights
b) rear fog lights if visibility is less than 100 metres (328 feet)
c) rear fog lights if visibility is more than 100 metres (328 feet)
d) dipped headlights
e) side lights only
HC rules 201 211

Question: 6.10
You are driving at dusk. You should switch your lights on
Mark two answers
a) even when street lights are not lit
b) so others can see you
c) only when others have done so
d) only when street lights are lit
HC rules 201 95

Question: 6.11
Why are vehicles fitted with rear fog lights?
Mark one answer
a) To be seen when driving at high speed
b) To use if broken down in a dangerous position
c) To make them more visible in thick fog
d) To warn drivers following closely to drop back
HC rules 201 211

Question: 6.12
You are driving through a tunnel and the traffic is flowing normally. What should you do?
Mark one answer
a) Use parking lights
b) Use front spot lights
c) Use dipped headlights
d) Use rear fog lights
HC rule 201

Question: 6.13
You are driving along this motorway. It is raining. When following this lorry you should

Mark two answers
a) allow at least a two-second gap
b) move left and drive on the hard shoulder
c) allow at least a four-second gap
d) be aware of spray reducing your vision
e) move right and stay in the right hand lane
HC rules 202 105

Question: 6.14
You are driving in heavy rain. Your steering suddenly becomes very light. You should
Mark one answer
a) steer towards the side of the road
b) apply gentle acceleration
c) brake firmly to reduce speed
d) ease off the accelerator
HC rule 202

Question: 6.15
You are travelling in very heavy rain. Your overall stopping distance is likely to be
Mark one answer
a) doubled
b) halved
c) up to ten times greater
d) no different
HC rule 202

Question: 6.16
You are following a large lorry on a wet road. Spray makes it difficult to see. You should

Mark one answer
a) drop back until you can see better
b) put your headlights on full beam
c) keep close to the lorry, away from the spray
d) speed up and overtake quickly
HC rule 202

Question: 6.17
You are driving along a wet road. How can you tell if your vehicle is aquaplaning?
Mark one answer
a) The engine will stall
b) The engine noise will increase
c) The steering will feel very heavy
d) The steering will feel very light
HC rule 202

Question: 6.18
You are driving along a wet road. How can you tell if your vehicle's tyres are losing their grip on the surface?
Mark one answer
a) The engine will stall
b) The steering will feel very heavy
c) The engine noise will increase
d) The steering will feel very light
HC rule 202

Question: 6.19
Your overall stopping distance will be much longer when driving
Mark one answer
a) in the rain
b) in fog
c) at night
d) in strong winds
HC rule 202

Question: 6.20
When snow is falling heavily you should
Mark one answer
a) only drive with your hazard lights on
b) not drive unless you have a mobile phone
c) only drive when your journey is short
d) not drive unless it is essential
HC rule 203

Question: 6.21
Before starting a journey in freezing weather you should clear ice and snow from your vehicle's
Mark four answers
a) aerial
b) windows
c) bumper
d) lights
e) mirrors
f) number plates
HC rule 204

Question: 6.22
You are driving on an icy road. What distance should you drive from the car in front?
Mark one answer
a) four times the normal distance
b) six times the normal distance
c) eight times the normal distance
d) ten times the normal distance
HC rule 205

Question: 6.23
Braking distances on ice can be
Mark one answer
a) twice the normal distance
b) five times the normal distance
c) seven times the normal distance
d) ten times the normal distance
HC rule 205

Question: 6.24
Freezing conditions will affect the distance it takes you to come to a stop. You should expect stopping distances to increase by up to
Mark one answer
a) two times
b) three times
c) five times
d) ten times
HC rule 205

Question: 6.25
How can you tell if you are driving on ice?
Mark two answers
a) The tyres make a rumbling noise
b) The tyres make hardly any noise
c) The steering becomes heavier
d) The steering becomes lighter
HC rule 206

Question: 6.26
You are trying to move off on snow. You should use
Mark one answer
a) the lowest gear you can
b) the highest gear you can
c) a high engine speed
d) the handbrake and footbrake together
HC rule 206

Question: 6.27
You are driving on an icy road. How can you avoid wheelspin?
Mark one answer
a) Drive at a slow speed in as high a gear as possible
b) Use the handbrake if the wheels start to slip
c) Brake gently and repeatedly
d) Drive in a low gear at all times
HC rule 206

Question: 6.28
How can you tell when you are driving over black ice?
Mark one answer
a) It is easier to brake
b) The noise from your tyres sounds louder
c) You will see tyre tracks on the road
d) Your steering feels light
HC rule 206

Question: 6.29
The roads are icy. You should drive slowly
Mark one answer
a) in the highest gear possible
b) in the lowest gear possible
c) with the handbrake partly on
d) with your left foot on the brake
HC rule 206

Question: 6.30
When driving in falling snow you should
Mark one answer
a) brake firmly and quickly
b) be ready to steer sharply
c) use sidelights only
d) brake gently in plenty of time
HC rule 206

Question: 6.31
You are driving in freezing conditions. What should you do when approaching a sharp bend?
Mark two answers
a) Slow down before you reach the bend
b) Gently apply your handbrake
c) Firmly use your footbrake
d) Coast into the bend
e) Avoid sudden steering movements
HC rule 206

Question: 6.32
Which of these is LEAST likely to be affected by crosswinds?
Mark one answer
a) Cyclists
b) Motorcyclists
c) High-sided vehicles
d) Cars
HC rule 207

Question: 6.33
Where are you most likely to be affected by a side wind?
Mark one answer
a) On a narrow country lane
b) On an open stretch of road
c) On a busy stretch of road
d) On a long, straight road
HC rule 207

Question: 6.34
What does this sign mean?

Mark one answer
a) Crosswinds
b) Road noise
c) Airport
d) Adverse camber
HC rule 207

Question: 6.35
You are driving on the motorway in windy conditions. When passing high-sided vehicles you should
Mark one answer
a) increase your speed
b) be wary of a sudden gust
c) drive alongside very closely
d) expect normal conditions
HC rule 207

Question: 6.36
In windy conditions you need to take extra care when
Mark one answer
a) using the brakes
b) making a hill start
c) turning into a narrow road
d) passing pedal cyclists
HC rule 207

Question: 6.37
It is a very windy day and you are about to overtake a cyclist. What should you do?
Mark one answer
a) Overtake very closely
b) Keep close as you pass
c) Sound your horn repeatedly
d) Allow extra room
HC rule 207

Question: 6.38
It is very windy. You are behind a motorcyclist who is overtaking a high-sided vehicle. What should you do?
Mark one answer
a) Overtake the motorcyclist immediately
b) Keep well back
c) Stay level with the motorcyclist
d) Keep close to the motorcyclist
HC rule 208

Question: 6.39
You are about to overtake a slow-moving motorcyclist. Which one of these signs would make you take special care?

Sign A   Sign B
Sign C   Sign D

Mark one answer
a) Sign A
b) Sign B
c) Sign C
d) Sign D
HC rule 208

Question: 6.40
You have to make a journey in foggy conditions. You should
Mark one answer
a) follow other vehicles' tail lights closely
b) avoid using dipped headlights
c) leave plenty of time for your journey
d) keep two seconds behind other vehicles
HC rule 209

Question: 6.41
You are driving in fog. Why should you keep well back from the vehicle in front?
Mark one answer
a) In case it changes direction suddenly
b) In case its fog lights dazzle you
c) In case it stops suddenly
d) In case its brake lights dazzle you
HC rules 209 210

Question: 6.42
Why should you always reduce your speed when travelling in fog?
Mark one answer
a) The brakes do not work as well
b) You will be dazzled by other headlights
c) The engine will take longer to warm up
d) It is more difficult to see events ahead
HC rules 209 210

Question: 6.43
You are following other vehicles in fog with your lights on. How else can you reduce the chances of being involved in an accident?
Mark one answer
a) Keep close to the vehicle in front
b) Use your main beam instead of dipped headlights
c) Keep together with the faster vehicles
d) Reduce your speed and increase the gap
HC rule 210

Question: 6.44
You have to make a journey in fog. What are the TWO most important things you should do before you set out?
Mark two answers
a) Top up the radiator with antifreeze
b) Make sure that you have a warning triangle in the vehicle
c) Check that your lights are working
d) Check the battery
e) Make sure that the windows are clean
HC rules 210 204

Question: 6.45
Why is it dangerous to leave rear fog lights on when they are not needed?
Mark two answers
a) Brake lights are less clear
b) Following drivers can be dazzled
c) Electrical systems could be overloaded
d) Direction indicators may not work properly
e) The battery could fail
HC rule 211

Question: 6.46
You are driving on a clear dry night with your rear fog lights switched on. This may
Mark two answers
a) reduce glare from the road surface
b) make other drivers think you are braking
c) give a better view of the road ahead
d) dazzle following drivers
e) help your indicators to be seen more clearly
HC rule 211

Question: 6.47
You forget to switch off your rear fog lights when the fog has cleared. This may
Mark three answers
a) dazzle other road users
b) reduce battery life
c) cause brake lights to be less clear
d) be breaking the law
e) seriously affect engine power
HC rule 211

Question: 6.48
You have been driving in thick fog which has now cleared. You must switch OFF your rear fog lights because
Mark one answer
a) they use a lot of power from the battery
b) they make your brake lights less clear
c) they will cause dazzle in your rear view mirrors
d) they may not be properly adjusted
HC rule 211

Question: 6.49
Using front fog lights in clear daylight will
Mark one answer
a) flatten the battery
b) dazzle other drivers
c) improve your visibility
d) increase your awareness
HC rule 211

Question: 6.50
While you are driving in fog, it becomes necessary to use front fog lights. You should
Mark one answer
a) only turn them on in heavy traffic conditions
b) remember not to use them on motorways
c) only use them on dual carriageways
d) remember to switch them off as visibility improves
HC rule 211

Question: 6.51
Front fog lights may be used ONLY if
Mark one answer
a) visibility is seriously reduced
b) they are fitted above the bumper
c) they are not as bright as the headlights
d) an audible warning device is used
HC rule 211

Question: 6.52
You have just driven out of fog. Visibility is now good. You MUST
Mark one answer
a) switch off all your fog lights
b) keep your rear fog lights on
c) keep your front fog lights on
d) leave fog lights on in case fog returns
HC rule 211

Question: 6.53
In very hot weather the road surface can become soft. Which TWO of the following will be most affected?
Mark two answers
a) The suspension
b) The grip of the tyres
c) The braking
d) The exhaust
HC rule 212

The Highway Code quiz programme

Question: 6.54
In very hot weather the road surface can get soft. Which TWO of the following will be affected most?
Mark two answers
a) The suspension
b) The steering
c) The braking
d) The exhaust
HC rule 212

Question: 6.55
You are leaving your vehicle parked on a road. When may you leave the engine running?
Mark one answer
a) If you will be parked for less than five minutes
b) If the battery is flat
c) When in a 20 mph zone
d) Never on any occasion
HC rule 214

Question: 6.56
On a clearway you must not stop
Mark one answer
a) at any time
b) when it is busy
c) in the rush hour
d) during daylight hours
HC rule 215

Question: 6.57
You are driving on an urban clearway. You may stop only to
Mark one answer
a) set down and pick up passengers
b) use a mobile telephone
c) ask for directions
d) load or unload goods
HC rule 215

Question: 6.58
When can you park on the left opposite these road markings?

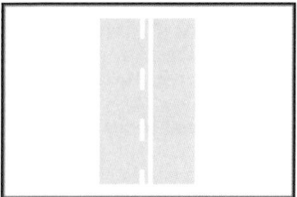

Mark one answer
a) If the line nearest to you is broken
b) When there are no yellow lines
c) To pick up or set down passengers
d) During daylight hours only
HC rule 215

Question: 6.59
What MUST you have to park in a disabled space?

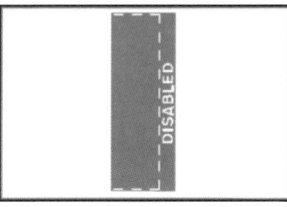

Mark one answer
a) An orange or blue badge
b) A wheelchair
c) An advanced driver certificate
d) A modified vehicle
HC rule 216

Question: 6.60
You are looking for somewhere to park your vehicle. The area is full EXCEPT for spaces marked 'disabled use'. You can

Mark one answer
a) use these spaces when elsewhere is full
b) park if you stay with your vehicle
c) use these spaces, disabled or not
d) not park there unless permitted
HC rule 216

Question: 6.61
In which THREE places would parking cause an obstruction to others?
Mark three answers
a) Near the brow of a hill
b) In a lay-by
c) Where the kerb is raised
d) Where the kerb has been lowered for wheelchairs
e) At or near a bus stop
HC rule 217

Question: 6.62
In which THREE places would parking your vehicle cause danger or obstruction to other road users?
Mark three answers
a) In front of a property entrance
b) At or near a bus stop
c) On your driveway
d) In a marked parking space
e) On the approach to a level crossing
HC rule 217

Question: 6.63
In which THREE places must you NOT park?
Mark three answers
a) Near the brow of a hill
b) At or near a bus stop
c) Where there is no pavement
d) Within 10 metres (32 feet) of a junction
e) On a 40 mph road
HC rule 217

Question: 6.64
What is the nearest you may park to a junction?
Mark one answer
a) 10 metres (32 feet)
b) 12 metres (39 feet)
c) 15 metres (49 feet)
d) 20 metres (66 feet)
HC rule 217

Question: 6.65
In which FOUR places must you NOT park or wait?
Mark four answers
a) On a dual carriageway
b) At a bus stop
c) On the slope of a hill
d) Opposite a traffic island
e) In front of someone else's drive
f) On the brow of a hill
HC rule 217

Question: 6.66
In which TWO places should you NOT park?
Mark two answers
a) Near a school entrance
b) Near a police station
c) In a side road
d) At a bus stop
e) In a one-way street
HC rule 217

Question: 6.67
You are parking on a two-way road at night. The speed limit is 40 mph. You should park on the
Mark one answer
a) left with parking lights on
b) left with no lights on
c) right with parking lights on
d) right with dipped headlights on
HC rules 222 223

Question: 6.68
You can park on the right-hand side of a road at night
Mark one answer
a) in a one-way street
b) with your sidelights on
c) more than 10 rnetres (32 feet) from a junction
d) under a lamp-post
HC rules 222 121

Question: 6.69
You are parked on the road at night. Where must you use parking lights?
Mark one answer
a) Where there are continuous white lines in the middle of the road
b) Where the speed limit exceeds 30 mph
c) Where you are facing oncoming traffic
d) Where you are near a bus stop
HC rules 223 222

Question: 6.70
Your vehicle is parked on the road at night. When must you use sidelights?
Mark one answer
a) Where there are continuous white lines in the middle of the road
b) Where the speed limit exceeds 30 mph
c) Where you are facing oncoming traffic
d) Where you are near a bus stop
HC rule 223

Question: 6.71
You park at night on a road with a 40 mph speed limit. You should park
Mark one answer
a) facing the traffic
b) with parking lights on
c) with dipped headlights on
d) near a street light
HC rule 223

Question: 6.72
On a foggy day you unavoidably have to park your car on the road. You should
Mark one answer
a) leave your headlights on
b) leave your fog lights on
c) leave your sidelights on
d) leave your hazard lights on
HC rule 225

Question: 6.73
You have to park on the road in fog. You should
Mark one answer
a) leave sidelights on
b) leave dipped headlights and fog lights on
c) leave dipped headlights on
d) leave main beam headlights on
HC rule 225

Question: 6.74
You wish to park facing DOWNHILL. Which TWO of the following should you do?
Mark two answers
a) Turn the steering wheel towards the kerb
b) Park close to the bumper of another car
c) Park with two wheels on the kerb
d) Put the handbrake on firmly
e) Turn the steering wheel away from the kerb
HC rule 226

7. Motorways
Before completing quiz 7 read Highway Code rules 227 - 247.

Question: 7.1
Which FOUR of these must NOT use motorways?
Mark four answers
a) Learner car drivers
b) Motorcycles over 50cc
c) Double deck buses
d) Farm tractors
e) Horse riders
f) Cyclists
HC rule 227

Question: 7.2
Which FOUR of these must NOT use motorways?
Mark four answers
a) Learner car drivers
b) Motorcycles over 50cc
c) Double-decker buses
d) Farm tractors
e) Learner motorcyclists
f) Cyclists
HC rule 227

Question: 7.3
As a provisional licence holder you should not drive a car
Mark one answer
a) over 30 mph
b) at night
c) on the motorway
d) with passengers in rear seats
HC rule 227

The Highway Code quiz programme

Question: 7.4
You are on a motorway. There are red flashing lights above every lane. You must

Mark one answer
a) pull onto the hard shoulder
b) slow down and watch for further signals
c) leave at the next exit
d) stop and wait
HC rule 232

Question: 7.5
You are driving on a road with several lanes. You see these signs above the lanes. What do they mean?

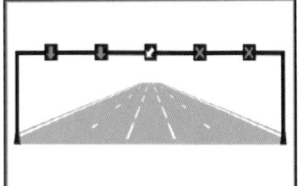

Mark one answer
a) The two right lanes are open
b) The two left lanes are open
c) Traffic in the left lanes should stop
d) Traffic in the right lanes should stop
HC rule 232

Question: 7.6
You are on a motorway. Red flashing lights appear above your lane only. What should you do?
Mark one answer
a) Continue in that lane and look for further information
b) Move into another lane in good time
c) Pull onto the hard shoulder
d) Stop and wait for an instruction to proceed
HC rule 232

Question: 7.7
Immediately after joining a motorway you should normally
Mark one answer
a) try to overtake
b) readjust your mirrors
c) position your vehicle in the centre lane
d) keep in the left lane
HC rule 233

Question: 7.8
When joining a motorway you must always
Mark one answer
a) use the hard shoulder
b) stop at the end of the acceleration lane
c) come to a stop before joining the motorway
d) give way to traffic already on the motorway
HC rule 233

Question: 7.9
You are joining a motorway. Why is it important to make full use of the slip road?
Mark one answer
a) Because there is space available to turn round if you need to
b) To allow you direct access to the overtaking lanes
c) To build up a speed similar to traffic on the motorway
d) Because you can continue on the hard shoulder
HC rule 233

Question: 7.10
What is the national speed limit on motorways for cars and motorcycles?
Mark one answer
a) 30 mph
b) 50 mph
c) 60 mph
d) 70 mph
HC rule 235

Question: 7.11
On a motorway what is used to reduce traffic bunching?
Mark one answer
a) Variable speed limits
b) Contraflow systems
c) National speed limits
d) Lane closures
HC rule 235

Question: 7.12
You are travelling on a motorway. Unless signs show a lower speed limit you must NOT exceed (NI exempt)
Mark one answer
a) 50 mph
b) 60 mph
c) 70 mph
d) 80 mph
HC rule 235

Question: 7.13
You are driving on a motorway. By mistake, you go past the exit that you wanted to take. You should
Mark one answer
a) carefully reverse on the hard shoulder
b) carry on to the next exit
c) carefully reverse in the left-hand lane
d) make a U-turn at the next gap in the central reservation
HC rule 237

Question: 7.14
On a three-lane motorway which lane should you normally use?
Mark one answer
a) Left
b) Right
c) Centre
d) Either the right or centre
HC rule 238

Question: 7.15
The left-hand lane on a three-lane motorway is for use by

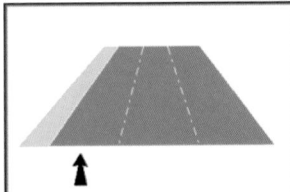

Mark one answer
a) any vehicle
b) large vehicles only
c) emergency vehicles only
d) slow vehicles only
HC rule 238

Question: 7.16
The left-hand lane of a motorway should be used for

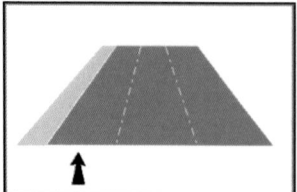

Mark one answer
a) breakdowns and emergencies only
b) overtaking slower traffic in the other lanes
c) slow vehicles only
d) normal driving
HC rule 238

Question: 7.17
What is the right-hand lane used for on a three-lane motorway?
Mark one answer
a) Emergency vehicles only
b) Overtaking
c) Vehicles towing trailers
d) Coaches only
HC rule 238

Question: 7.18
A basic rule when on motorways is
Mark one answer
a) use the lane that has least traffic
b) keep to the left lane unless overtaking
c) overtake on the side that is clearest
d) try to keep above 50 mph to prevent congestion
HC rule 238

Question: 7.19
For what reason may you use the right-hand lane of a motorway?

Mark one answer
a) For keeping out of the way of lorries
b) For driving at more than 70 mph
c) For turning right
d) For overtaking other vehicles
HC rule 238

Question: 7.20
The right-hand lane of a three-lane motorway is
Mark one answer
a) for lorries only
b) an overtaking lane
c) the right-turn lane
d) an acceleration lane
HC rule 238

Question: 7.21
You are driving at 70 mph on a three-lane motorway. There is no traffic ahead. Which lane should you use?
Mark one answer
a) Any lane
b) Middle lane
c) Right lane
d) Left lane
HC rule 238

Question: 7.22
Which of these IS NOT allowed to travel in the right-hand lane of a three-lane motorway?
Mark one answer
a) A small delivery van
b) A motorcycle
c) A vehicle towing a trailer
d) A motorcycle and side-car
HC rule 239

Question: 7.23
You are on a three-lane motorway towing a trailer. You may use the right-hand lane when
Mark one answer
a) there are lane closures
b) there is slow moving traffic
c) you can maintain a high speed
d) large vehicles are in the left and centre lanes
HC rule 239

Question: 7.24
On motorways you should never overtake on the left UNLESS
Mark one answer
a) you can see well ahead that the hard shoulder is clear
b) the traffic in the right-hand lane is signalling right
c) you warn drivers behind by signalling left
d) there is a queue of slow moving traffic to your right that is moving slower than you
HC rule 242

Question: 7.25
You are allowed to stop on a motorway when you
Mark one answer
a) need to walk and get fresh air
b) wish to pick up hitch hikers
c) are told to do so by flashing red lights
d) need to use a mobile telephone
HC rule 244

Question: 7.26
When should you stop on a motorway?
Mark three answers
a) If you have to read a map
b) When you are tired and need a rest
c) If red lights show above every lane
d) When told to by the police
e) If your mobile phone rings
f) When signalled by a Highways Agency Traffic Officer
HC rule 244

Question: 7.27

You are intending to leave the motorway at the next exit. Before you reach the exit you should normally position your vehicle

Mark one answer

a) in the middle lane
b) in the left-hand lane
c) on the hard shoulder
d) in any lane

HC rule 246

Question: 7.28

You should not normally travel on the hard shoulder of a motorway. When can you use it?

Mark one answer

a) When taking the next exit
b) When traffic is stopped
c) When signs direct you to
d) When traffic is slow moving

HC page 60 and rule 238

8. Breakdowns, accidents, road works, railway level crossings and tramways

Before completing quiz 8 read Highway Code rules 248 - 278.

Question: 8.1

You are on a motorway. When can you use hazard warning lights?

Mark two answers

a) When a vehicle is following too closely
b) When you slow down quickly because of danger ahead
c) When you are towing another vehicle
d) When driving on the hard shoulder
e) When you have broken down on the hard shoulder

HC rules 248 96

Question: 8.2

You have an accident while driving through a tunnel. You are not injured but your vehicle cannot be driven. What should you do first?

Mark one answer

a) Rely on other drivers phoning for the Police
b) Switch off the engine and switch on hazard lights
c) Take the names of witnesses and other drivers
d) Sweep up any debris that is in the road

HC rule 248

Question: 8.3

You are on a motorway at night. You MUST have your headlights switched on unless

Mark one answer

a) there are vehicles close in front of you
b) you are travelling below 50 mph
c) the motorway is lit
d) your vehicle is broken down on the hard shoulder

HC rules 248 249

Question: 8.4

You have broken down on a two-way road. You have a warning triangle. It should be displayed

Mark one answer

a) on the roof of your vehicle
b) at least 150 metres (492 feet) behind your vehicle
c) at least 45 metres (147 feet) behind your vehicle
d) just behind your vehicle

HC rule 248

Question: 8.5

You are in an accident on a two-way road. You have a warning triangle with you. At what distance before the obstruction should you place the warning triangle?

Mark one answer

a) 25 metres (82 feet)
b) 45 metres (147 feet)
c) 100 metres (328 feet)
d) 150 metres (492 feet)

HC rule 248

Question: 8.6

You have broken down on a two-way road. You have a warning triangle. You should place the warning triangle at least how far from your vehicle?

Mark one answer

a) 5 metres (16 feet)
b) 25 metres (82 feet)
c) 45 metres (147 feet)
d) 100 metres (328 feet)

HC rule 248

Question: 8.7
Which of these items should you carry in your vehicle for use in the event of an accident?
Mark three answers
a) Road map
b) Can of petrol
c) Jump leads
d) Fire extinguisher
e) First Aid kit
f) Warning triangle
HC rule 248

Question: 8.8
On the motorway, the hard shoulder should be used
Mark one answer
a) to answer a mobile phone
b) when an emergency arises
c) for a short rest when tired
d) to check a road atlas
HC rule 249

Question: 8.9
You have broken down on a motorway. To find the nearest emergency telephone you should always walk
Mark one answer
a) with the traffic flow
b) facing oncoming traffic
c) in the direction shown on the marker posts
d) in the direction of the nearest exit
HC rule 249

Question: 8.10
What should you use the hard shoulder of a motorway for?

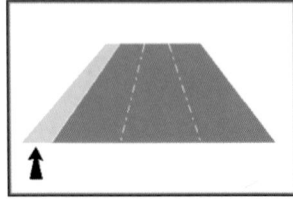

Mark one answer
a) Stopping in an emergency
b) Leaving the motorway
c) Stopping when you are tired
d) Joining the motorway
HC rule 249

Question: 8.11
You get a puncture on the motorway. You manage to get your vehicle onto the hard shoulder. You should
Mark one answer
a) change the wheel yourself immediately
b) use the emergency telephone and call for assistance
c) try to wave down another vehicle for help
d) only change the wheel if you have a passenger to help you
HC rule 249

Question: 8.12
Your vehicle has a puncture on a motorway. What should you do?
Mark one answer
a) Drive slowly to the next service area to get assistance
b) Pull up on the hard shoulder. Change the wheel as quickly as possible
c) Pull up on the hard shoulder. Use the emergency phone to get assistance
d) Switch on your hazard lights. Stop in your lane
HC rule 249

Question: 8.13
On a motorway you may ONLY stop on the hard shoulder

Mark one answer
a) in an emergency
b) if you feel tired and need to rest
c) if you accidentally go past the exit that you wanted to take
d) to pick up a hitchhiker
HC rule 249

Question: 8.14
After a breakdown you need to rejoin the main carriageway of a motorway from the hard shoulder. You should
Mark one answer
a) move out onto the carriageway then build up your speed
b) move out onto the carriageway using your hazard lights
c) gain speed on the hard shoulder before moving out onto the carriageway
d) wait on the hard shoulder until someone flashes their headlights at you
HC rule 250

Question: 8.15
Your vehicle has broken down on a motorway. You are not able to stop on the hard shoulder. What should you do?
Mark one answer
a) Switch on your hazard warning lights
b) Stop following traffic and ask for help
c) Attempt to repair your vehicle quickly
d) Stand behind your vehicle to warn others
HC rule 251

Question: 8.16
You are on a motorway. A large box falls onto the road from a lorry. The lorry does not stop. You should
Mark one answer
a) go to the next emergency telephone and inform the police
b) catch up with the lorry and try to get the driver's attention
c) stop close to the box until the police arrive
d) pull over to the hard shoulder, then remove the box
HC rule 254

The Highway Code quiz programme

Question: 8.17
You are on the motorway. Luggage falls from your vehicle. What should you do?
Mark one answer
a) Stop at the next emergency telephone and contact the police
b) Stop on the motorway and put on hazard lights whilst you pick it up
c) Walk back up the motorway to pick it up
d) Pull up on the hard shoulder and wave traffic down
HC rule 254

Question: 8.18
After an accident, someone is unconscious in their vehicle. When should you call the emergency services?
Mark one answer
a) Only as a last resort
b) As soon as possible
c) After you have woken them up
d) After checking for broken bones
HC rule 257

Question: 8.19
You are the first person to arrive at an accident where people are badly injured. Which THREE should you do?
Mark three answers
a) Switch on your own hazard warning lights
b) Make sure that someone telephones for an ambulance
c) Try and get people who are injured to drink something
d) Move the people who are injured clear of their vehicles
e) Get people who are not injured clear of the scene
HC rule 257

Question: 8.20
An accident has just happened. An injured person is lying in a busy road. What is the FIRST thing you should do to help?
Mark one answer
a) Treat the person for shock
b) Warn other traffic
c) Place them in the recovery position
d) Make sure the injured person is kept warm
HC rule 257

Question: 8.21
You have broken down on a motorway. When you use the emergency telephone you will be asked
Mark three answers
a) for the number on the telephone that you are using
b) for your driving licence details
c) for the name of your vehicle insurance company
d) for details of yourself and your vehicle
e) whether you belong to a motoring organisation
HC rule 257

Question: 8.22
At the scene of an accident you should
Mark one answer
a) not put yourself at risk
b) go to those casualties who are screaming
c) pull everybody out of their vehicles
d) leave vehicle engines switched on
HC rule 257

Question: 8.23
You break down on a motorway. You need to call for help. Why may it be better to use an emergency roadside telephone rather than a mobile phone?
Mark one answer
a) It connects you to a local garage
b) Using a mobile phone will distract other drivers
c) It allows easy location by the emergency services
d) Mobile phones do not work on motorways
HC rule 257

Question: 8.24
At an accident it is important to look after the casualty. When the area is safe, you should
Mark one answer
a) get them out of the vehicle
b) give them a drink
c) give them something to eat
d) keep them in the vehicle
HC rule 257

Question: 8.25
You have stopped at the scene of an accident to give help. Which THREE things should you do?
Mark three answers
a) Keep injured people warm and comfortable
b) Keep injured people calm by talking to them reassuringly
c) Keep injured people on the move by walking them around
d) Give injured people a warm drink
e) Make sure that injured people are not left alone
HC rule 257

Question: 8.26
You arrive at a serious motorcycle accident. The motorcyclist is unconscious and bleeding. Your main priorities should be to
Mark three answers
a) try to stop the bleeding
b) make a list of witnesses
c) check the casualty's breathing
d) take the numbers of the vehicles involved
e) sweep up any loose debris
f) check the casualty's airways
HC rule 257

Question: 8.27
An injured motorcyclist is lying unconscious in the road. You should
Mark one answer
a) remove the safety helmet
b) seek medical assistance
c) move the person off the road
d) remove the leather jacket
HC rule 257

Question: 8.28
You are the first to arrive at the scene of an accident. Which FOUR of these should you do?
Mark four answers
a) Leave as soon as another motorist arrives
b) Switch off the vehicle engine(s)
c) Move uninjured people away from the vehicle(s)
d) Call the emergency services
e) Warn other traffic
HC rule 257

Question: 8.29
Which of the following should you NOT do at the scene of an accident?
Mark one answer
a) Warn other traffic by switching on your hazard warning lights
b) Call the emergency services immediately
c) Offer someone a cigarette to calm them down
d) Ask drivers to switch off their engines
HC rule 257

Question: 8.30
Your vehicle breaks down on the hard shoulder of a motorway. You decide to use your mobile phone to call for help. You should
Mark one answer
a) stand at the rear of the vehicle while making the call
b) try to repair the vehicle yourself
c) get out of the vehicle by the right hand door
d) check your location from the marker posts on the left
HC rule 257

Question: 8.31
You arrive at the scene of a motorcycle accident. No other vehicle is involved. The rider is unconscious, lying in the middle of the road. The first thing you should do is
Mark one answer
a) move the rider out of the road
b) warn other traffic
c) clear the road of debris
d) give the rider reassurance
HC rule 257

Question: 8.32
You arrive at the scene of a motorcycle accident. The rider is injured. When should the helmet be removed?
Mark one answer
a) Only when it is essential
b) Always straight away
c) Only when the motorcyclist asks
d) Always, unless they are in shock
HC rule 257

Question: 8.33
You arrive at an accident. A motorcyclist is unconscious. Your FIRST priority is the casualty's
Mark one answer
a) breathing
b) bleeding
c) broken bones
d) bruising
HC rule 257

Question: 8.34
You have a collision whilst your car is moving. What is the first thing you must do?
Mark one answer
a) Stop only if there are injured people
b) Call the emergency services
c) Stop at the scene of the accident
d) Call your insurance company
HC rule 260

Question: 8.35
You lose control of your car and damage a garden wall. No one is around. What must you do?
Mark one answer
a) Report the accident to the police within 24 hours
b) Go back to tell the house owner the next day
c) Report the accident to your insurance company when you get home
d) Find someone in the area to tell them about it immediately
HC rule 260

Question: 8.36
You are involved in an accident with another vehicle. Someone is injured. Your vehicle is damaged. Which FOUR of the following should you find out?
Mark four answers
a) Whether the driver owns the other vehicle involved
b) The other driver's name, address and telephone number
c) The make and registration number of the other vehicle
d) The occupation of the other driver
e) The details of the other driver's vehicle insurance
f) Whether the other driver is licensed to drive
HC rules 260 261

Question: 8.37
The police may ask you to produce which three of these documents following an accident?
Mark three answers
a) Vehicle registration document
b) Driving licence
c) Theory test certificate
d) Insurance certificate
e) MOT test certificate
f) Road tax disc
HC rule 260

Question: 8.38
A police officer asks to see your documents. You do not have them with you. You may produce them at a police station within
Mark one answer
a) five days
b) seven days
c) 14 days
d) 21 days
HC rule 261

Question: 8.39
At roadworks which of the following can control traffic flow?
Mark three answers
a) A STOP-GO board
b) Flashing amber lights
c) A police officer
d) Flashing red lights
e) Temporary traffic lights
HC rule 262

Question: 8.40
You are entering an area of roadworks. There is a temporary speed limit displayed. You should
Mark one answer
a) not exceed the speed limit
b) obey the limit only during rush hour
c) ignore the displayed limit
d) obey the limit except at night
HC rule 262

Question: 8.41
You are approaching roadworks on a motorway. What should you do?
Mark one answer
a) Speed up to clear the works quickly
b) Always use the hard shoulder
c) Obey all speed limits
d) Stay very close to the vehicle in front
HC rules 262 263

Question: 8.42
You are driving on this dual carriageway. Why may you need to slow down?

Mark one answer
a) There is a broken white line in the centre
b) There are solid white lines either side
c) There are roadworks ahead of you
d) There are no footpaths
HC rules 262 263

Question: 8.43
To avoid an accident when entering a contraflow system, you should
Mark three answers
a) reduce speed in good time
b) switch lanes anytime to make progress
c) choose an appropriate lane early
d) keep the correct separation distance
e) increase speed to pass through quickly
f) follow other motorists closely to avoid long queues
HC rules 262 263 264

Question: 8.44
What does this sign mean?

Mark one answer
a) The right-hand lane ahead is narrow
b) Right-hand lane for buses only
c) Right-hand lane for turning right
d) The right-hand lane is closed
HC rule 263

Question: 8.45
You are in the right-hand lane of a dual carriageway. You see signs showing that the right-hand lane is closed 800 yards ahead. You should

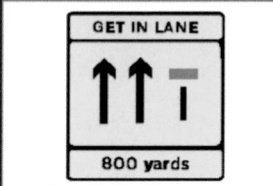

Mark one answer
a) keep in that lane until you reach the queue
b) move to the left immediately
c) wait and see which lane is moving faster
d) move to the left in good time
HC rule 263

Question: 8.46
When going through a contraflow system on a motorway you should

Mark one answer
a) ensure that you do not exceed 30 mph
b) keep a good distance from the vehicle ahead
c) switch lanes to keep the traffic flowing
d) stay close to the vehicle ahead to reduce queues
HC rule 264

Question: 8.47
You are on a motorway. There is a contraflow system ahead. What would you expect to find?
Mark one answer
a) Temporary traffic lights
b) Lower speed limits
c) Wider lanes than normal
d) Speed humps
HC rule 264

Question: 8.48
What does this sign mean?

Mark one answer
a) Change to the left lane
b) Leave at the next exit
c) Contraflow system
d) One-way street
HC rule 264

Question: 8.49
You are driving over a level crossing. The warning lights come on and a bell rings. What should you do?
Mark one answer
a) Get everyone out of the vehicle immediately
b) Stop and reverse back to clear the crossing
c) Keep going and clear the crossing
d) Stop immediately and use your hazard warning lights
HC rule 266

Question: 8.50
You are waiting at a level crossing. The red warning lights continue to flash after a train has passed by. What should you do?

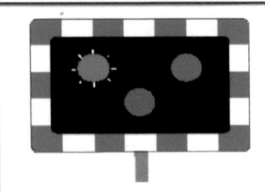

Mark one answer
a) Get out and investigate
b) Telephone the signal operator
c) Continue to wait
d) Drive across carefully
HC rule 266

Question: 8.51
You are waiting at a level crossing. A train has passed but the lights keep flashing. You must
Mark one answer
a) carry on waiting
b) phone the signal operator
c) edge over the stop line and look for trains
d) park and investigate
HC rule 266

Question: 8.52
The red lights are flashing. What should you do when approaching this level crossing?

Mark one answer
a) Go through quickly
b) Go through carefully
c) Stop before the barrier
d) Switch on hazard warning lights
HC rule 266

Question: 8.53
At a railway level crossing the red light signal continues to flash after a train has gone by. What should you do?
Mark one answer
a) Phone the signal operator
b) Alert drivers behind you
c) Wait
d) Proceed with caution
HC rule 266

Question: 8.54
You are driving towards this level crossing. What would be the first warning of an approaching train?

Mark one answer
a) Both half barriers down
b) A steady amber light
c) One half barrier down
d) Twin flashing red lights
HC rule 266

Question: 8.55
Your vehicle has broken down on an automatic railway level crossing. What should you do FIRST?
Mark one answer
a) Get everyone out of the vehicle and clear of the crossing
b) Phone the signal operator so that trains can be stopped
c) Walk along the track to give warning to any approaching trains
d) Try to push the vehicle clear of the crossing as soon as possible
HC rule 272

Question: 8.56
You break down on a level crossing. The lights have not yet begun to flash. Which THREE things should you do?
Mark three answers
a) Telephone the signal operator
b) Leave your vehicle and get everyone clear
c) Walk down the track and signal the next train
d) Move the vehicle if a signal operator tells you to
e) Tell drivers behind what has happened
HC rule 272

Question: 8.57
You have stalled in the middle of a level crossing and cannot restart the engine. The warning bell starts to ring. You should
Mark one answer
a) get out and clear of the crossing
b) run down the track to warn the signal operator
c) carry on trying to restart the engine
d) push the vehicle clear of the crossing
HC rule 272

Question: 8.58
Areas reserved for trams may have
Mark three answers
a) metal studs around them
b) white line markings
c) zig zag markings
d) a different coloured surface
e) yellow hatch markings
f) a different surface texture
HC rule 273

Question: 8.59

Diamond-shaped signs give instructions to

Mark one answer
a) tram drivers
b) bus drivers
c) lorry drivers
d) taxi drivers
HC rule 273

Question: 8.60

On a road where trams operate, which of these vehicles will be most at risk from the tram rails?

Mark one answer
a) Cars
b) Cycles
c) Buses
d) Lorries
HC rule 278

9. Signals and traffic signs part 1

Before completing quiz 9 read Highway Code pages 70 - 73.

Question: 9.1

What does this sign mean?

Mark one answer
a) End of motorway
b) End of restriction
c) Lane ends ahead
d) Free recovery ends
HC page 70

Question: 9.2

You see this amber traffic light ahead. Which light or lights, will come on next?

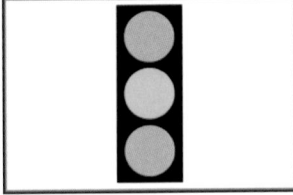

Mark one answer
a) Red alone
b) Red and amber together
c) Green and amber together
d) Green alone
HC page 70

Question: 9.3

You are approaching a red traffic light. The signal will change from red to

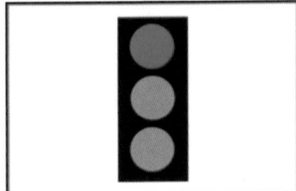

Mark one answer
a) red and amber, then green
b) green, then amber
c) amber, then green
d) green and amber, then green
HC page 70

Question: 9.4

These flashing red lights mean STOP. In which THREE of the following places could you find them?

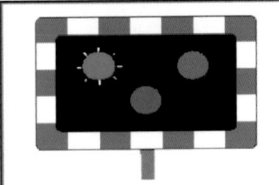

Mark three answers
a) Pelican crossings
b) Lifting bridges
c) Zebra crossings
d) Level crossings
e) Motorway exits
f) Fire stations
HC page 70

Question: 9.5
What does this motorway sign mean?

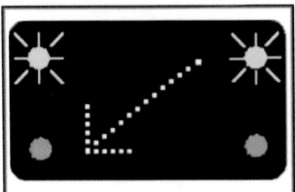

Mark one answer
a) Change to the lane on your left
b) Leave the motorway at the next exit
c) Change to the opposite carriageway
d) Pull up on the hard shoulder
HC page 70

Question: 9.6
What does this motorway sign mean?

Mark one answer
a) Temporary minimum speed 50 mph
b) No services for 50 miles
c) Obstruction 50 metres (164 feet) ahead
d) Temporary maximum speed 50 mph
HC page 70

Question: 9.7
What does this sign mean?

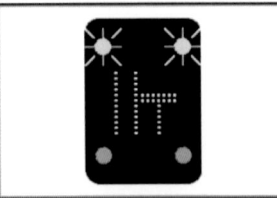

Mark one answer
a) Through traffic to use left lane
b) Right-hand lane T-junction only
c) Right-hand lane closed ahead
d) 11 tonne weight limit
HC page 70

Question: 9.8
On a motorway this sign means

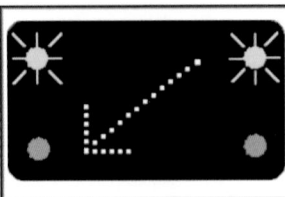

Mark one answer
a) move over onto the hard shoulder
b) overtaking on the left only
c) leave the motorway at the next exit
d) move to the lane on your left
HC page 70

Question: 9.9
You see this signal overhead on the motorway. What does it mean?

Mark one answer
a) Leave the motorway at the next exit
b) All vehicles use the hard shoulder
c) Sharp bend to the left ahead
d) Stop, all lanes ahead closed
HC page 70

Question: 9.10
At a junction you see this signal. It means

Mark one answer
a) cars must stop
b) trams must stop
c) both trams and cars must stop
d) both trams and cars can continue
HC page 70

Question: 9.11
You are in the right-hand lane on a motorway. You see these overhead signs. This means

Mark one answer
a) move to the left and reduce your speed to 50 mph
b) there are roadworks 50 metres (55 yards) ahead
c) use the hard shoulder until you have passed the hazard
d) leave the motorway at the next exit
HC page 70

Question: 9.12
You are travelling along a motorway. You see this sign. You should

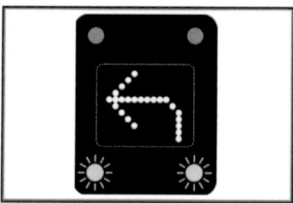

Mark one answer
a) leave the motorway at the next exit
b) turn left immediately
c) change lane
d) move onto the hard shoulder
HC page 70

Question: 9.13
You are approaching a zebra crossing where pedestrians are waiting. Which arm signal might you give?

Mark one answer
a) Sign A
b) Sign B
c) Sign C
d) Sign D
HC page 71

Question: 9.14
Which arm signal tells you that the car you are following is going to turn left?

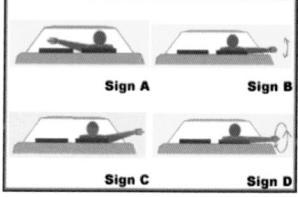

Mark one answer
a) Sign A
b) Sign B
c) Sign C
d) Sign D
HC page 71

Question: 9.15
The driver of this car is giving an arm signal. What are they about to do?

Mark one answer
a) Turn to the right
b) Turn to the left
c) Go straight ahead
d) Let pedestrians cross
HC page 71

Question: 9.16
The driver of the car in front is giving this arm signal. What does it mean?

Mark one answer
a) The driver is slowing down
b) The driver intends to turn right
c) The driver wishes to overtake
d) The driver intends to turn left
HC page 71

Question: 9.17
How should you give an arm signal to turn left?

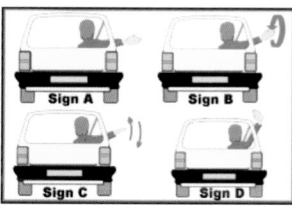

Mark one answer
a) Sign A
b) Sign B
c) Sign C
d) Sign D
HC page 71

Question: 9.18
You approach a junction. The traffic lights are not working. A police officer gives this signal. You should

Mark one answer
a) turn left only
b) turn right only
c) stop level with the officer's arm
d) stop at the stop line
HC page 72 87

Question: 9.19
What does this signal from a police officer mean to oncoming traffic?

Mark one answer
a) Go ahead
b) Stop
c) Turn left
d) Turn right
HC page 72 87

Question: 9.20
What is the meaning of this sign?

Mark one answer
a) Local speed limit applies
b) No waiting on the carriageway
c) National speed limit applies
d) No entry to vehicular traffic
HC page 73

Question: 9.21
What does this sign mean?

Mark one answer
a) Bend to the right
b) Road on the right closed
c) No traffic from the right
d) No right turn
HC page 73

Question: 9.22
What does this sign mean?

Mark one answer
a) No overtaking
b) No motor vehicles
c) Clearway (no stopping)
d) Cars and motorcycles only
HC page 73

Question: 9.23
Which of these signs means no motor vehicles?

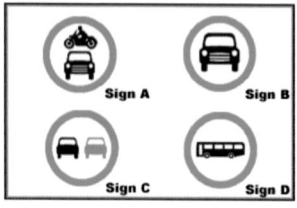

Mark one answer
a) Sign A
b) Sign B
c) Sign C
d) Sign D
HC page 73

Question: 9.24
What does this sign mean?

Mark one answer
a) No parking
b) No road markings
c) No through road
d) No entry
HC page 73

Question: 9.25
Which sign means no motor vehicles are allowed?

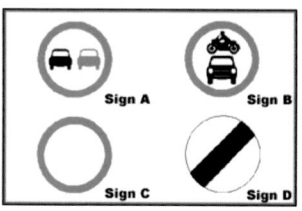

Mark one answer
a) Sign A
b) Sign B
c) Sign C
d) Sign D
HC page 73

Question: 9.26
Which type of sign tells you NOT to do something?

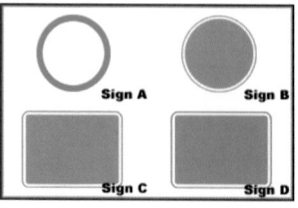

Mark one answer
a) Sign A
b) Sign B
c) Sign C
d) Sign D
HC page 73

Question: 9.27
Traffic signs giving orders are generally which shape?

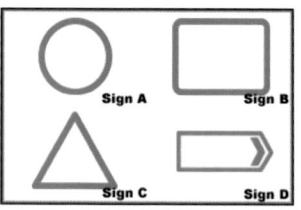

Mark one answer
a) Sign A
b) Sign B
c) Sign C
d) Sign D
HC page 73

Question: 9.28
What is the meaning of this sign?

Mark one answer
a) No entry
b) Waiting restrictions
c) National speed limit
d) School crossing patrol
HC page 73

Question: 9.29
Which sign means 'no entry'?

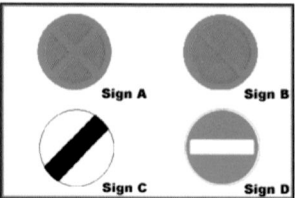

Mark one answer
a) Sign A
b) Sign B
c) Sign C
d) Sign D
HC page 73

The Highway Code quiz programme

Question: 9.30
What does this sign mean?

Mark one answer
a) Roundabout
b) Crossroads
c) No stopping
d) No entry
HC page 73

Question: 9.31
You MUST obey signs giving orders.
These signs are mostly in
Mark one answer
a) green rectangles
b) red triangles
c) blue rectangles
d) red circles
HC page 73

Question: 9.32
You see this sign ahead. It means

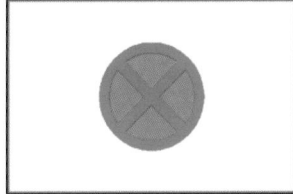

Mark one answer
a) national speed limit applies
b) waiting restrictions apply
c) no stopping
d) no entry
HC page 73

Question: 9.33
What does this sign mean?

Mark one answer
a) Motorcycles only
b) No cars
c) Cars only
d) No motorcycles
HC page 73

Question: 9.34
This traffic sign means there is

Mark one answer
a) a compulsory maximum speed limit
b) an advisory maximum speed limit
c) a compulsory minimum speed limit
d) an advised separation distance
HC page 73

Question: 9.35
At this junction there is a stop sign with a solid white line on the road surface. Why is there a stop sign here?

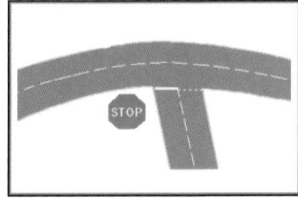

Mark one answer
a) Speed on the major road is de-restricted
b) It is a busy junction
c) Visibility along the major road is restricted
d) There are hazard warning lines in the centre of the road
HC page 73 147

Question: 9.36
Which of these signs means that the national speed limit applies?

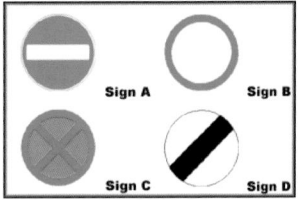

Mark one answer
a) Sign A
b) Sign B
c) Sign C
d) Sign D
HC page 73

Question: 9.37
Which shape is used for a 'give way' sign?

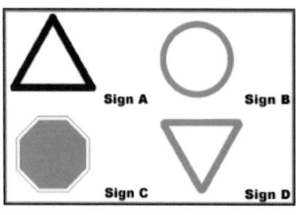

Sign A   Sign B

Sign C   Sign D

Mark one answer
a) Sign A
b) Sign B
c) Sign C
d) Sign D
HC page 73

Question: 9.38
At a junction you see this sign partly covered by snow. What does it mean?

Mark one answer
a) Cross roads
b) Give way
c) Stop
d) Turn right
HC page 73 147

Question: 9.39
What does this sign mean?

Mark one answer
a) You can park on the days and times shown
b) No parking on the days and times shown
c) No parking at all from Monday to Friday
d) End of the urban clearway restrictions
HC page 73

Question: 9.40
What does this traffic sign mean?

Mark one answer
a) No overtaking allowed
b) Give priority to oncoming traffic
c) Two way traffic
d) One-way traffic only
HC page 73

Question: 9.41
Which type of vehicle does this sign apply to?

Mark one answer
a) Wide vehicles
b) Long vehicles
c) High vehicles
d) Heavy vehicles
HC page 73

Question: 9.42
Which sign means 'no stopping'?

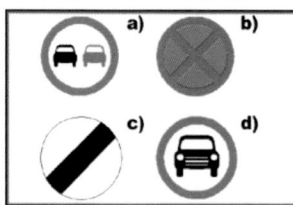

Mark one answer
a) Sign A
b) Sign B
c) Sign C
d) Sign D
HC page 73

Question: 9.43
What does this sign mean?

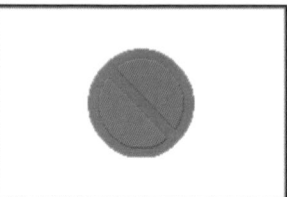

Mark one answer
a) Waiting restrictions apply
b) Waiting permitted
c) National speed limit applies
d) Clearway (no stopping)
HC page 73

Question: 9.44
Which sign means no overtaking?

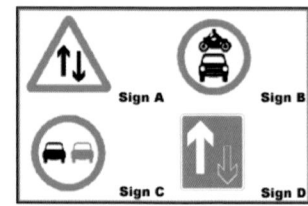

Sign A   Sign B

Sign C   Sign D

Mark one answer
a) Sign A
b) Sign B
c) Sign C
d) Sign D
HC page 73

Question: 9.45
What does this sign mean?

Mark one answer
a) Keep in one lane
b) Give way to oncoming traffic
c) Do not overtake
d) Form two lanes
HC page 73

Question: 9.46
What does this sign mean?

Mark one answer
a) You have priority
b) No motor vehicles
c) Two-way traffic
d) No overtaking
HC page 73

Question: 9.47
Which sign means NO motor vehicles allowed?

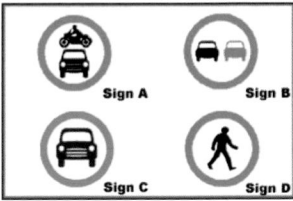

Mark one answer
a) Sign A
b) Sign B
c) Sign C
d) Sign D
HC page 73

Question: 9.48
What shape is a STOP sign at a junction?

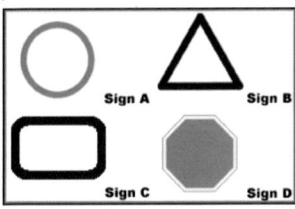

Mark one answer
a) Sign A
b) Sign B
c) Sign C
d) Sign D
HC page 73 147

10. Traffic signs part 2 and road/vehicle markings
Before completing quiz 10 read Highway Code pages 74 - 81.

Question: 10.1
What does this sign mean?

Mark one answer
a) Route for trams
b) Give way to trams
c) Route for buses
d) Give way to buses
HC page 74

Question: 10.2
What does this sign mean?

Mark one answer
a) Two-way traffic straight ahead
b) Two-way traffic crossing a one-way street
c) Two-way traffic over a bridge
d) Two-way traffic crosses a two-way road
HC page 74

Question: 10.3
What does this sign mean?

Mark one answer
a) Wait at the barriers
b) Wait at the crossroads
c) Give way to trams
d) Give way to farm vehicles
HC page 74

Question: 10.4
Which of these signs means there is a double bend ahead?

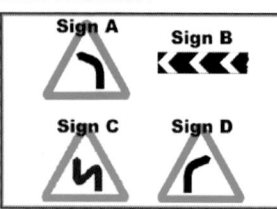

Mark one answer
a) Sign A
b) Sign B
c) Sign C
d) Sign D
HC page 74

Question: 10.5
Which FOUR of these would be indicated by a triangular road sign?

Mark four answers
a) Road narrows
b) Ahead only
c) Low bridge
d) Minimum speed
e) Children crossing
f) T-junction
HC page 74

Question: 10.6
What does this sign mean?

Mark one answer
a) Ring road
b) Mini-roundabout
c) No vehicles
d) Roundabout
HC page 74

Question: 10.7
What does this sign mean?

Mark one answer
a) Crossroads
b) Level crossing with gate
c) Level crossing without gate
d) Ahead only
HC page 74

Question: 10.8
What are triangular signs for?

Mark one answer
a) To give warnings
b) To give information
c) To give orders
d) To give directions
HC page 74

Question: 10.9
What does this sign mean?

Mark one answer
a) With-flow bus and cycle lane
b) Contraflow bus and cycle lane
c) No buses and cycles allowed
d) No waiting for buses and cycles
HC page 74

Question: 10.10
What does this sign mean?

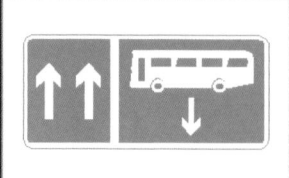

Mark one answer
a) Bus station on the right
b) Contraflow bus lane
c) With-flow bus lane
d) Give way to buses
HC page 74

Question: 10.11
Which sign means 'two-way traffic crosses a one-way road'?

Mark one answer
a) Sign A
b) Sign B
c) Sign C
d) Sign D
HC page 74

Question: 10.12
What does a circular traffic sign with a blue background do?

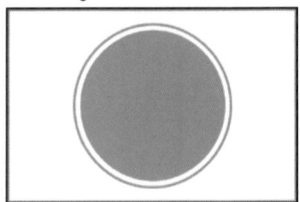

Mark one answer
a) Give warning of a motorway ahead
b) Give directions to a car park
c) Give motorway information
d) Give an instruction
HC page 74

Question: 10.13
What does this sign mean?

Mark one answer
a) Turn left ahead
b) T-junction
c) No through road
d) Give way
HC page 74

Question: 10.14
What does this sign mean?

Mark one answer
a) Give way to oncoming vehicles
b) Approaching traffic passes you on both sides
c) Turn off at the next available junction
d) Pass either side to get to the same destination
HC page 74

Question: 10.15
What does this sign mean?

Mark one answer
a) Buses turning
b) Ring road
c) Mini roundabout
d) Keep right
HC page 74

Question: 10.16
Which of these signs means turn left ahead?

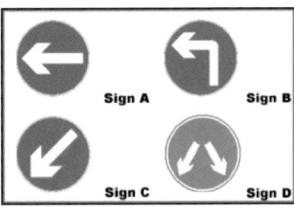

Mark one answer
a) Sign A
b) Sign B
c) Sign C
d) Sign D
HC page 74

Question: 10.17
What does this sign mean?

Mark one answer
a) Service area 30 miles ahead
b) Maximum speed 30 mph
c) Minimum speed 30 mph
d) Lay-by 30 miles ahead
HC page 74

Question: 10.18
What does this sign mean?

Mark one answer
a) Route for trams only
b) Route for buses only
c) Parking for buses only
d) Parking for trams only
HC page 74

Question: 10.19
What does this sign mean?

Mark one answer
a) Adverse camber
b) Steep hill downwards
c) Uneven road
d) Steep hill upwards
HC page 74

Question: 10.20
What does this sign mean?

Mark one answer
a) Minimum speed 30 mph
b) End of maximum speed
c) End of minimum speed
d) Maximum speed 30 mph
HC page 74

Question: 10.21
What does this sign mean?

Mark one answer
a) Contra-flow pedal cycle lane
b) With-flow pedal cycle lane
c) Pedal cycles and buses only
d) No pedal cycles or buses
HC page 74 119

Question: 10.22
What does this sign mean?

Mark one answer
a) No route for pedestrians and cyclists
b) A route for pedestrians only
c) A route for cyclists only
d) A route for pedestrians and cyclists
HC page 74 119

Question: 10.23
You see this sign ahead. You should expect the road to

Mark one answer
a) go steeply uphill
b) go steeply downhill
c) bend sharply to the left
d) bend sharply to the right
HC page 74

Question: 10.24
Which of these signs means that you are entering a one-way street?

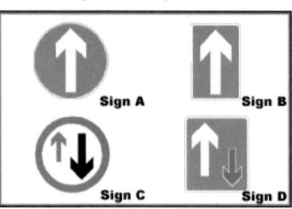

Mark one answer
a) Sign A
b) Sign B
c) Sign C
d) Sign D
HC page 74

Question: 10.25
What does this sign mean?

Mark one answer
a) End of dual carriageway
b) Tall bridge
c) Road narrows
d) End of narrow bridge
HC page 74

Question: 10.26
What does this sign mean?

Mark one answer
a) Two-way traffic ahead across a one-way street
b) Traffic approaching you has priority
c) Two-way traffic straight ahead
d) Motorway contraflow system ahead
HC page 74

Question: 10.27
What does this sign mean?

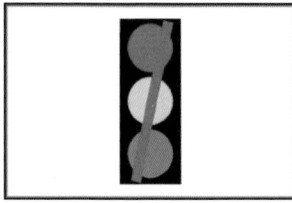

Mark one answer
a) Traffic lights out of order
b) Amber signal out of order
c) Temporary traffic lights ahead
d) New traffic lights ahead
HC page 74

Question: 10.28
Which of these signs means the end of a dual carriageway?

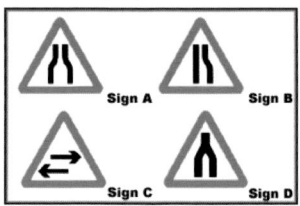

Mark one answer
a) Sign A
b) Sign B
c) Sign C
d) Sign D
HC page 74

Question: 10.29
You should reduce your speed when driving along this road because

Mark one answer
a) there is a staggered junction ahead
b) there is a low bridge ahead
c) there is a change in the road surface
d) the road ahead narrows
HC page 74

Question: 10.30
You see this sign at a crossroads. You should

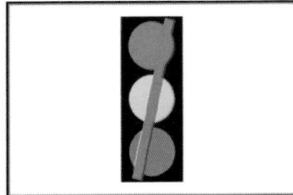

Mark one answer
a) maintain the same speed
b) carry on with great care
c) find another route
d) telephone the police
HC page 74

Question: 10.31
What does this sign mean?

Mark one answer
a) Cyclists must dismount
b) Cycles are not allowed
c) Cycle route ahead
d) Cycle in single file
HC page 75

Question: 10.32
What does this sign tell you?

Mark one answer
a) No cycling
b) Cycle route ahead
c) Cycles parking only
d) End of cycle route
HC page 75

Question: 10.33
Which sign tells you that pedestrians may be walking in the road as there is no pavement?

Mark one answer
a) Sign A
b) Sign B
c) Sign C
d) Sign D
HC page 75

Question: 10.34
What does this sign mean?

Mark one answer
a) Multi-exit roundabout
b) Risk of ice
c) Six roads converge
d) Place of historical interest
HC page 75

Question: 10.35
What does this sign mean?

Mark one answer
a) Humpback bridge
b) Traffic calming hump
c) Low bridge
d) Uneven road
HC page 75

Question: 10.36
What does this sign mean?

Mark one answer
a) Quayside or river bank
b) Steep hill downwards
c) Uneven road surface
d) Road liable to flooding
HC page 75

Question: 10.37
What does this sign mean?

Mark one answer
a) Level crossing with gate or barrier
b) Gated road ahead
c) Level crossing without gate or barrier
d) Cattle grid ahead
HC page 75

Question: 10.38
Which sign means that there may be people walking along the road?

Mark one answer
a) Sign A
b) Sign B
c) Sign C
d) Sign D
HC page 75

Question: 10.39
Which sign means that pedestrians may be walking along the road?

Mark one answer
a) Sign A
b) Sign B
c) Sign C
d) Sign D
HC page 75

Question: 10.40
Which of these signs warn you of a pedestrian crossing?

Mark one answer
a) Sign A
b) Sign B
c) Sign C
d) Sign D
HC page 75

Question: 10.41
What does this sign mean?

Mark one answer
a) No footpath ahead
b) Pedestrians only ahead
c) Pedestrian crossing ahead
d) School crossing ahead
HC page 75

Question: 10.42
What does this sign mean?

Mark one answer
a) School crossing patrol
b) No pedestrians allowed
c) Pedestrian zone – no vehicles
d) Pedestrian crossing ahead
HC page 75

Question: 10.43
You are about to overtake when you see this sign. You should

Mark one answer
a) overtake the other driver as quickly as possible
b) move to the right to get a better view
c) switch your headlights on before overtaking
d) hold back until you can see clearly ahead
HC page 75

Question: 10.44
What does this traffic sign mean?

Mark one answer
a) Slippery road ahead
b) Tyres liable to punctures ahead
c) Danger ahead
d) Service area ahead
HC page 75

Question: 10.45
What does this sign mean?

Mark one answer
a) Low bridge ahead
b) Tunnel ahead
c) Ancient monument ahead
d) Accident black spot ahead
HC page 75

Question: 10.46
What does this sign mean?

Mark one answer
a) No trams ahead
b) Oncoming trams
c) Trams crossing ahead
d) Trams only
HC page 75

Question: 10.47
What does '25' mean on this motorway sign?

Mark one answer
a) The distance to the nearest town
b) The route number of the road
c) The number of the next junction
d) The speed limit on the slip road
HC page 76

Question: 10.48
What does this sign mean?

Mark one answer
a) Distance to parking place ahead
b) Distance to public telephone ahead
c) Distance to public house ahead
d) Distance to passing place ahead
HC page 77

Question: 10.49
Which of the following signs informs you that you are coming to a 'no through road'?

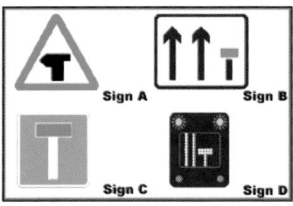

Mark one answer
a) Sign A
b) Sign B
c) Sign C
d) Sign D
HC page 77

Question: 10.50
What does this sign tell you?

Mark one answer
a) That it is a no-through road
b) End of traffic calming zone
c) Free parking zone ends
d) No waiting zone ends
HC page 77

Question: 10.51
What does this sign mean?

Mark one answer
a) Hilly road
b) Humps in road
c) Holiday route
d) Hospital route
HC page 77

Question: 10.52
What does this sign mean?

Mark one answer
a) Turn left for parking area
b) No through road on the left
c) No entry for traffic turning left
d) Turn left for ferry terminal
HC page 77

Question: 10.53
What does this sign mean?

Mark one answer
a) T-junction
b) No through road
c) Telephone box ahead
d) Toilet ahead
HC page 77

Question: 10.54
Which sign means 'no through road'?

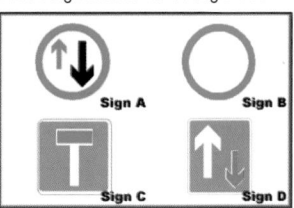

Mark one answer
a) Sign A
b) Sign B
c) Sign C
d) Sign D
HC page 77

Question: 10.55
What does this sign mean?

Mark one answer
a) No motor vehicles
b) End of motorway
c) No through road
d) End of bus lane
HC page 77

Question: 10.56
What does this sign mean?

Mark one answer
a) End of restricted speed area
b) End of restricted parking area
c) End of clearway
d) End of cycle route
HC page 77

Question: 10.57
What do these motorway signs show?

Mark one answer
a) They are countdown markers to a bridge
b) They are distance markers to the next telephone
c) They are countdown markers to the next exit
d) They warn of a police control ahead
HC page 77

Question: 10.58
What is the meaning of this traffic sign?

Mark one answer
a) End of two-way road
b) Give priority to vehicles coming towards you
c) You have priority over vehicles coming towards you
d) Bus lane ahead
HC page 77

Question: 10.59
Which sign means you have priority over oncoming vehicles?

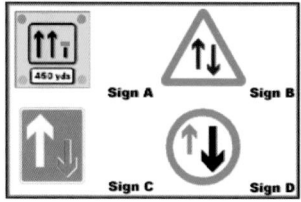

Mark one answer
a) Sign A
b) Sign B
c) Sign C
d) Sign D
HC page 77

Question: 10.60
This sign means

Mark one answer
a) tourist attraction
b) beware of trains
c) level crossing
d) beware of trams
HC page 77

Question: 10.61
What does a sign with a brown background show?

Mark one answer
a) Tourist directions
b) Primary roads
c) Motorway routes
d) Minor routes
HC page 77

Question: 10.62
What does this sign mean?

Mark one answer
a) No overtaking
b) You are entering a one-way street
c) Two-way traffic ahead
d) You have priority over vehicles from the opposite direction
HC page 77

Question: 10.63
You want to park and you see this sign. On the days and times shown you should

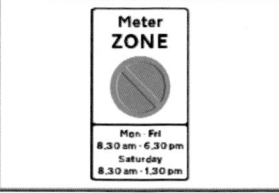

Mark one answer
a) park in a bay and not pay
b) park on yellow lines and pay
c) park on yellow lines and not pay
d) park in a bay and pay
HC page 77

Question: 10.64
This sign is advising you to

Mark one answer
a) follow the route diversion
b) follow the signs to the picnic area
c) give way to pedestrians
d) give way to cyclists
HC page 77

Question: 10.65
You see this sign on the rear of a slow-moving lorry that you want to pass. It is travelling in the middle lane of a three-lane motorway. You should

Mark one answer
a) cautiously approach the lorry then pass on either side
b) follow the lorry until you can leave the motorway
c) wait on the hard shoulder until the lorry has stopped
d) approach with care and keep to the left of the lorry
HC page 78

Question: 10.66
Why would this temporary speed limit sign be shown?

Mark one answer
a) To warn of the end of the motorway
b) To warn you of a low bridge
c) To warn you of a junction ahead
d) To warn of road works ahead
HC page 78

Question: 10.67
What might you expect to happen in this situation?

Mark one answer
a) Traffic will move into the right-hand lane
b) Traffic speed will increase
c) Traffic will move into the left-hand lane
d) Traffic will not need to change position
HC page 78 262

Question: 10.68
What does the solid white line at the side of the road indicate?

Mark one answer
a) Traffic lights ahead
b) Edge of the carriageway
c) Footpath on the left
d) Cycle path
HC page 78

Question: 10.69
The white line along the side of the road

Mark one answer
a) shows the edge of the carriageway
b) shows the approach to a hazard
c) means no parking
d) means no overtaking
HC page 78

Question: 10.70
You are on a motorway. You see this sign on a lorry that has stopped in the right-hand lane. You should

Mark one answer
a) move into the right-hand lane
b) stop behind the flashing lights
c) pass the lorry on the left
d) leave the motorway at the next exit
HC page 78

Question: 10.71
You see this line across the road at the entrance to a roundabout. What does it mean?

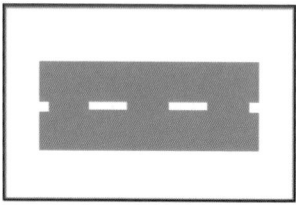

Mark one answer
a) Give way to traffic from the right
b) Traffic from the left has right of way
c) You have right of way
d) Stop at the line
HC page 78

Question: 10.72
You are driving on a motorway. There is a slow-moving vehicle ahead. On the back you see this sign. You should

Mark one answer
a) pass on the right
b) pass on the left
c) leave at the next exit
d) drive no further
HC page 78

Question: 10.73
'Red routes' in major cities have been introduced to
Mark one answer
a) raise the speed limits
b) help the traffic flow
c) provide better parking
d) allow lorries to load more freely
HC page 79

Question: 10.74
Yellow zigzag lines on the road outside schools mean

Mark one answer
a) sound your horn to alert other road users
b) stop to allow children to cross
c) you must not wait or park on these lines
d) you must not drive over these lines
HC page 80

Question: 10.75
You should NOT normally stop on these markings near schools

Mark one answer
a) except when picking up children
b) under any circumstances
c) unless there is nowhere else available
d) except to set down children
HC page 80

Question: 10.76
These road markings must be kept clear to allow

Mark one answer
a) school children to be dropped off
b) for teachers to park
c) school children to be picked up
d) a clear view of the crossing area
HC page 80

Question: 10.77
The road outside this school is marked with yellow zigzag lines. What do these lines mean?

Mark one answer
a) You may park on the lines when dropping off schoolchildren
b) You may park on the lines when picking schoolchildren up
c) You must not wait or park your vehicle here at all
d) You must stay with your vehicle if you park here
HC page 80

Question: 10.78
A tanker is involved in an accident. Which sign would show that the tanker is carrying dangerous goods?

Mark one answer
a) Sign A
b) Sign B
c) Sign C
d) Sign D
HC page 81

Question: 10.79
Where would you expect to see these markers?

Mark two answers
a) On a motorway sign
b) At the entrance to a narrow bridge
c) On a large goods vehicle
d) On a builder's skip placed on the road
HC page 81

11. Annexes
Before completing quiz 11 read Highway Code pages 82 - 93.

Question: 11.1
Motor cars must FIRST have an MOT test certificate when they are
Mark one answer
a) one year old
b) three years old
c) five years old
d) seven years old
HC page 84

Question: 11.2
When is it legal to drive a car over three years old without an MOT certificate?
Mark one answer
a) Up to seven days after the old certificate has run out
b) When driving to an MOT centre to arrange an appointment
c) Just after buying a secondhand car with no MOT
d) When driving to an appointment at an MOT centre
HC page 84

Question: 11.3
Your car needs an MOT certificate. If you drive without one this could invalidate your
Mark one answer
a) vehicle service record
b) insurance
c) road tax disc
d) vehicle registration document
HC page 84

Question: 11.4
An MOT certificate is normally valid for
Mark one answer
a) three years after the date it was issued
b) 10,000 miles
c) one year after the date it was issued
d) 30,000 miles
HC page 84

Question: 11.5
What is the legal minimum insurance cover you must have to drive on public roads?
Mark one answer
a) Third party, fire and theft
b) Fully comprehensive
c) Third party only
d) Personal injury cover
HC page 84

Question: 11.6
Vehicle excise duty is often called 'Road Tax' or 'The Tax Disc'. You must
Mark one answer
a) keep it with your registration document
b) display it clearly on your vehicle
c) keep it concealed safely in your vehicle
d) carry it on you at all times
HC page 85

Question: 11.7
Before driving anyone else's motor vehicle you should make sure that
Mark one answer
a) the vehicle owner has third party insurance cover
b) your own vehicle has insurance cover
c) the vehicle is insured for your use
d) the owner has left the insurance documents in the vehicle
HC page 84

Question: 11.8
Your vehicle needs a current MOT certificate. You do not have one. Until you do have one you will not be able to renew your
Mark one answer
a) driving licence
b) vehicle insurance
c) road tax disc
d) vehicle registration document
HC page 84

Question: 11.9

Which THREE of the following do you need before you can drive legally?

Mark three answers

a) A valid driving licence with signature
b) A valid tax disc displayed on your vehicle
c) A vehicle service record
d) Proper insurance cover
e) Breakdown cover
f) A vehicle handbook
HC page 84

Question: 11.10

Which THREE pieces of information are found on a vehicle registration document?

Mark three answers

a) Registered keeper
b) Make of the vehicle
c) Service history details
d) Date of the MOT
e) Type of insurance cover
f) Engine size
HC page 84

Question: 11.11

You have a duty to contact the licensing authority when

Mark three answers

a) you go abroad on holiday
b) you change your vehicle
c) you change your name
d) your job status is changed
e) your permanent address changes
f) your job involves travelling abroad
HC page 84

Question: 11.12

What is the legal minimum insurance cover you must have to drive on public roads?

Mark one answer

a) Fire and theft
b) Theft only
c) Third party
d) Fire only
HC page 84

Question: 11.13

For which TWO of these must you show your motor insurance certificate?

Mark two answers

a) When you are taking your driving test
b) When buying or selling a vehicle
c) When a police officer asks you for it
d) When you are taxing your vehicle
e) When having an MOT inspection
HC page 85

Question: 11.14

How old must you be to supervise a learner driver?

Mark one answer

a) 18 years old
b) 19 years old
c) 20 years old
d) 21 years old
HC page 85

Question: 11.15

As a provisional licence holder, you must not drive a motor car

Mark two answers

a) at more than 50 mph
b) on your own
c) on the motorway
d) under the age of 18 years of age at night
e) with passengers in the rear seats
HC page 85 227

Question: 11.16

To supervise a learner driver you must

Mark two answers

a) have held a full licence for at least 3 years
b) be at least 21
c) be an approved driving instructor
d) hold an advanced driving certificate
HC page 85

Question: 11.17

A friend wants to help you learn to drive. They must be

Mark one answer

a) be over 21 and have held a full licence for at least two years
b) be over 18 and hold an advanced driver's certificate
c) be over 18 and have fully comprehensive insurance
d) be over 21 and have held a full licence for at least three years
HC page 85

Question: 11.18

To drive on the road learners MUST

Mark one answer

a) have NO penalty points on their licence
b) have taken professional instruction
c) have a signed, valid provisional licence
d) apply for a driving test within 12 months
HC page 84

Question: 11.19

You have just passed your practical test. You do not hold a full licence in another category. Within two years you get six penalty points on your licence. What will you have to do?

Mark two answers

a) Retake only your theory test
b) Retake your theory and practical tests
c) Retake only your practical test
d) Reapply for your full licence immediately
e) Reapply for your provisional licence
HC page 89

Question: 11.20

You have been convicted of driving whilst unfit through drink or drugs. You will find this is likely to cause the cost of one of the following to rise considerably. Which one?

Mark one answer

a) Road fund licence
b) Insurance premiums
c) Vehicle test certificate
d) Driving licence
HC page 89

Question: 11.21
Which FOUR of these MUST be in good working order for your car to be roadworthy?
Mark four answers
a) Temperature gauge
b) Speedometer
c) Windscreen washers
d) Windscreen wiper
e) Oil warning light
f) Horn
HC page 89

Question: 11.22
Which THREE does the law require you to keep in good condition?
Mark three answers
a) Gears
b) Transmission
c) Headlights
d) Windscreen
e) Seat belts
HC page 89

Question: 11.23
While driving, a warning light on your vehicle's instrument panel comes on. You should
Mark one answer
a) continue if the engine sounds alright
b) hope that it is just a temporary electrical fault
c) deal with the problem when there is more time
d) check out the problem quickly and safely
HC page 90

Question: 11.24
Which TWO are badly affected if the tyres are under-inflated?
Mark two answers
a) Braking
b) Steering
c) Changing gear
d) Parking
HC page 90

Question: 11.25
It is illegal to drive with tyres that
Mark one answer
a) have been bought second-hand
b) have a large deep cut in the side wall
c) are of different makes
d) are of different tread patterns
HC page 90

Question: 11.26
The legal minimum depth of tread for car tyres over three quarters of the breadth is
Mark one answer
a) 1 mm
b) 1.6 mm
c) 2.5 mm
d) 4 mm
HC page 90

Question: 11.27
It is essential that tyre pressures are checked regularly. When should this be done?
Mark one answer
a) After any lengthy journey
b) After travelling at high speed
c) When tyres are hot
d) When tyres are cold
HC page 90

Question: 11.28
Excessive or uneven tyre wear can be caused by faults in which THREE of the following?
Mark three answers
a) The gearbox
b) The braking system
c) The accelerator
d) The exhaust system
e) Wheel alignment
f) The suspension
HC page 90

Question: 11.29
Your tyre bursts while you are driving. Which TWO things should you do?
Mark two answers
a) Pull on the handbrake
b) Brake as quickly as possible
c) Pull up slowly at the side of the road
d) Hold the steering wheel firmly to keep control
e) Continue on at a normal speed
HC page 90

Question: 11.30
Excessive or uneven tyre wear can be caused by faults in the
Mark two answers
a) gearbox
b) braking system
c) suspension
d) exhaust system
HC page 90

Question: 11.31
Which TWO things should you do when a front tyre bursts?
Mark two answers
a) Apply the handbrake to stop the vehicle
b) Brake firmly and quickly
c) Let the vehicle roll to a stop
d) Hold the steering wheel lightly
e) Grip the steering wheel firmly
HC page 90

Question: 11.32
You are checking your trailer tyres. What is the legal minimum tread depth over the central three quarters of its breadth?
Mark one answer
a) 1 mm
b) 1.6 mm
c) 2 mm
d) 2.6 mm
HC page 90

Question: 11.33
Which of these, if allowed to get low, could cause an accident?
Mark one answer
a) Antifreeze level
b) Brake fluid level
c) Battery water level
d) Radiator coolant level
HC page 91

Question: 11.34
Your vehicle pulls to one side when braking. You should
Mark one answer
a) change the tyres around
b) consult your garage as soon as possible
c) pump the pedal when braking
d) use your handbrake at the same time
HC page 91

Question: 11.35
You are testing your suspension. You notice that your vehicle keeps bouncing when you press down on the front wing. What does this mean?
Mark one answer
a) Worn tyres
b) Tyres under-inflated
c) Steering wheel not located centrally
d) Worn shock absorbers
HC page 91

129

Question: 11.36
Your engine catches fire. What should you do first?
Mark one answer
a) Lift the bonnet and disconnect the battery
b) Lift the bonnet and warn other traffic
c) Call the breakdown service
d) Call the fire brigade
HC page 91

Question: 11.37
What TWO safeguards could you take against fire risk to your vehicle?
Mark two answers
a) Keep water levels above maximum
b) Carry a fire extinguisher
c) Avoid driving with a full tank of petrol
d) Use unleaded petrol
e) Check out any strong smell of petrol
f) Use low octane fuel
HC page 91

Question: 11.38
When leaving your vehicle parked and unattended you should
Mark one answer
a) park near a busy junction
b) park in a housing estate
c) remove the key and lock it
d) leave the left indicator on
HC page 92

Question: 11.39
Which of the following should not be kept in your vehicle?
Mark one answer
a) A first aid kit
b) A road atlas
c) The tax disc
d) The vehicle documents
HC page 92

Question: 11.40
Which of these is most likely to deter the theft of your vehicle?
Mark one answer
a) An immobiliser
b) Tinted windows
c) Locking wheel nuts
d) A sun screen
HC page 92

Question: 11.41
When leaving your car unattended for a few minutes you should
Mark one answer
a) leave the engine running
b) switch the engine off but leave the key in
c) lock it and remove the key
d) park near a traffic warden
HC page 92

Question: 11.42
You are parking your car. You have some valuables which you are unable to take with you. What should you do?
Mark one answer
a) Park near a police station
b) Put them under the drivers seat
c) Lock them out of sight
d) Park in an unlit side road
HC page 92

Question: 11.43
What should you do when leaving your vehicle?
Mark one answer
a) Put valuable documents under the seats
b) Remove all valuables
c) Cover valuables with a blanket
d) Leave the interior light on
HC page 92

Question: 11.44
Which of the following may help to deter a thief from stealing your car?
Mark one answer
a) Always keeping the headlights on
b) Fitting reflective glass windows
c) Always keeping the interior light on
d) Etching the car number on the windows
HC page 92

Question: 11.45
How could you deter theft from your car when leaving it unattended?
Mark one answer
a) Leave valuables in a carrier bag
b) Lock valuables out of sight
c) Put valuables on the seats
d) Leave valuables on the floor
HC page 92

Question: 11.46
You have to leave valuables in your car. It would be safer to
Mark one answer
a) put them in a carrier bag
b) park near a school entrance
c) lock them out of sight
d) park near a bus stop
HC page 92

Question: 11.47
How can you reduce the chances of your car being broken into when leaving it unattended?
Mark one answer
a) Take all contents with you
b) Park near a taxi rank
c) Place any valuables on the floor
d) Park near a fire station
HC page 92

Question: 11.48
When leaving your car to help keep it secure you should
Mark one answer
a) leave the hazard warning lights on
b) lock it and remove the key
c) park on a one way street
d) park in a residential area
HC page 92

Question: 11.49
When parking and leaving your car for a few minutes you should
Mark one answer
a) leave it unlocked
b) lock it and remove the key
c) leave the hazard warning lights on
d) leave the interior light on
HC page 92

Question: 11.50
When parking and leaving your car you should
Mark one answer
a) park under a shady tree
b) remove the tax disc
c) park in a quiet road
d) engage the steering lock
HC page 92

The Highway Code quiz programme

Question: 11.51
You arrive at the scene of an accident. A pedestrian has a severe bleeding wound on their leg, although it is not broken. What should you do?
Mark two answers
a) Dab the wound to stop bleeding
b) Keep both legs flat on the ground
c) Apply firm pressure to the wound
d) Raise the leg to lessen bleeding
e) Fetch them a warm drink
HC page 93

Question: 11.52
At an accident someone is unconscious. Your main priorities should be to
Mark three answers
a) sweep up the broken glass
b) take the names of witnesses
c) count the number of vehicles involved
d) check the airway is clear
e) make sure they are breathing
f) stop any heavy bleeding
HC page 93

Question: 11.53
You arrive at the scene of an accident. It has just happened and someone is injured. Which THREE of the following should be given urgent priority?
Mark three answers
a) Stop any severe bleeding
b) Get them a warm drink
c) Check that their breathing is OK
d) Take numbers of vehicles involved
e) Look for witnesses
f) Clear their airway and keep it open
HC page 93

Question: 11.54
At an accident a casualty has stopped breathing. You should
Mark two answers
a) remove anything that is blocking the mouth
b) keep the head tilted forwards as far as possible
c) raise the legs to help with circulation
d) try to give the casualty something to drink
e) keep the head tilted back as far as possible
HC page 93

Question: 11.55
At an accident a casualty is unconscious but still breathing. You should only move them if
Mark one answer
a) an ambulance is on its way
b) bystanders advise you to
c) there is further danger
d) bystanders will help you to
HC page 92

Question: 11.56
An accident casualty has an injured arm. They can move it freely, but it is bleeding. Why should you get them to keep it in a raised position?
Mark one answer
a) Because it will ease the pain
b) It will help them to be seen more easily
c) To stop them touching other people
d) It will help to reduce the bleeding
HC page 92

Question: 11.57
At an accident a casualty is unconscious. Which THREE of the following should you check urgently?
Mark three answers
a) Circulation
b) Airway
c) Shock
d) Breathing
e) Broken bones
HC page 93

Question: 11.58
You arrive at the scene of an accident. It has just happened and someone is unconscious. Which of the following should be given urgent priority to help them?
Mark three answers
a) Clear the airway and keep it open
b) Try to get them to drink water
c) Check that they are breathing
d) Look for any witnesses
e) Stop any heavy bleeding
f) Take the numbers of vehicles involved
HC page 93

Question: 11.59
You are at the scene of an accident. Someone is suffering from shock. You should
Mark four answers
a) reassure them constantly
b) offer them a cigarette
c) keep them warm
d) avoid moving them if possible
e) loosen any tight clothing
f) give them a warm drink
HC page 92

Question: 11.60
There has been an accident. The driver is suffering from shock. You should
Mark two answers
a) give them a drink
b) reassure them
c) not leave them alone
d) offer them a cigarette
e) ask who caused the accident
HC page 92

Question: 11.61
You are at the scene of an accident. Someone is suffering from shock. You should
Mark three answers
a) offer them a cigarette
b) offer them a warm drink
c) keep them warm
d) loosen any tight clothing
e) reassure them constantly
HC page 92

Question: 11.62
You have to treat someone for shock at the scene of an accident. You should
Mark one answer
a) reassure them constantly
b) walk them around to calm them down
c) give them something cold to drink
d) cool them down as soon as possible
HC page 92

Question: 11.63
When you are giving mouth to mouth you should only stop when
Mark one answer
a) you think the casualty is dead
b) the casualty can breathe without help
c) the casualty has turned blue
d) you think the ambulance is coming
HC page 93

Question: 11.64
You arrive at the scene of an accident. A passenger is bleeding badly from an arm wound. What should you do?
Mark one answer
a) Apply pressure over the wound and keep the arm down
b) Dab the wound
c) Get them a drink
d) Apply pressure over the wound and raise the arm
HC page 93

Question: 11.65
You arrive at the scene of an accident. A pedestrian is bleeding heavily from a leg wound but the leg is not broken. What should you do?
Mark one answer
a) Dab the wound to stop the bleeding
b) Keep both legs flat on the ground
c) Apply firm pressure to the wound
d) Fetch them a warm drink
HC page 93

Question: 11.66
There has been an accident. A motorcyclist is lying injured and unconscious. Unless it's essential, why should you usually not attempt to remove their helmet?
Mark one answer
a) Because they may not want you to
b) This could result in more serious injury
c) They will get too cold if you do this
d) Because you could scratch the helmet
HC page 92

Question: 11.67
To start mouth to mouth on a casualty you should
Mark three answers
a) tilt their head forward
b) clear the airway
c) turn them on their side
d) tilt their head back
e) pinch the nostrils together
f) put their arms across their chest
HC page 93

Question: 11.68
What is the maximum specified fine for driving without insurance?
Mark one answer
a) £50
b) £500
c) £1000
d) £5000
HC page 88

12. Supplementary notes
Before completing quiz 12 read the Highway Code supplementary notes in this book.

Question: 12.1
The Pass Plus scheme has been created for new drivers. What is its main purpose?
Mark one answer
a) To allow you to drive faster
b) To allow you to carry passengers
c) To improve your basic skills
d) To let you drive on motorways
Supplementary note 1

Question: 12.2
You have third party insurance. What does this cover?
Mark three answers
a) Damage to your own vehicle
b) Damage to your vehicle by fire
c) Injury to another person
d) Damage to someone's property
e) Damage to other vehicles
f) Injury to yourself
Supplementary note 1

Question: 12.3
A newly qualified driver must
Mark one answer
a) display green 'L' plates
b) not exceed 40 mph for 12 months
c) be accompanied on a motorway
d) have valid motor insurance
Supplementary note 1

Question: 12.4
The cost of your insurance may reduce if you
Mark one answer
a) are under 25 years old
b) do not wear glasses
c) pass the driving test first time
d) take the Pass Plus scheme
Supplementary note 1

Question: 12.5
The cost of your insurance may be reduced if
Mark one answer
a) your car is large and powerful
b) you are using the car for work purposes
c) you have penalty points on your licence
d) you are over 25 years old
Supplementary note 1

Question: 12.6
Your vehicle is insured third party only. This covers
Mark two answers
a) damage to your vehicle
b) damage to other vehicles
c) injury to yourself
d) injury to others
e) all damage and injury
Supplementary note 1

Question: 12.7
Your motor insurance policy has an excess of £100. What does this mean?
Mark one answer
a) The insurance company will pay the first £100 of any claim
b) You will be paid £100 if you do not have an accident
c) Your vehicle is insured for a value of £100 if it is stolen
d) You will have to pay the first £100 of any claim
Supplementary note 1

Question: 12.8
When you apply to renew your vehicle excise licence (tax disc) you must produce
Mark one answer
a) a valid insurance certificate
b) the old tax disc
c) the vehicle handbook
d) a valid driving licence
Supplementary note 1

Question: 12.9
Which age group of drivers is most likely to be involved in a road accident?
Mark one answer
a) 36 to 45-year-olds
b) 55-year-olds and over
c) 46 to 55-year-olds
d) 17 to 25-year-olds
Supplementary note 1

Question: 12.10
You have just passed your test. How can you decrease your risk of accidents on the motorway?
Mark one answer
a) By keeping up with the car in front
b) By never going over 40 mph
c) By staying only in the left hand lane
d) By taking further training
Supplementary note 1

Question: 12.11
A cover note is a document issued before you receive your
Mark one answer
a) driving licence
b) insurance certificate
c) registration document
d) MOT certificate
Supplementary note 1

Question: 12.12
Which of the following may reduce the cost of your insurance?
Mark one answer
a) Having a valid MOT certificate
b) Taking a Pass Plus course
c) Driving a powerful car
d) Having penalty points on your licence
Supplementary note 1

Question: 12.13
How long will a Statutory Off Road Notification (SORN) last for?
Mark one answer
a) 12 months
b) 24 months
c) 3 years
d) 10 years
Supplementary note 1

Question: 12.14
What is a Statutory Off Road Notification (SORN) declaration?
Mark one answer
a) A notification to tell VOSA that a vehicle does not have a current MOT
b) Information kept by the police about the owner of the vehicle
c) A notification to tell DVLA that a vehicle is not being used on the road
d) Information held by insurance companies to check the vehicle is insured
Supplementary note 1

Question: 12.15
A Statutory Off Road Notification (SORN) declaration is
Mark one answer
a to tell DVLA that your vehicle is being used on the road but the MOT has expired
b) to tell DVLA that you no longer own the vehicle
c) to tell DVLA that your vehicle is not being used on the road
d) to tell DVLA that you are buying a personal number plate
Supplementary note 1

Question: 12.16
A Statutory Off Road Notification (SORN) is valid
Mark one answer
a) for as long as the vehicle has an MOT
b) for 12 months only
c) only if the vehicle is more than 3 years old
d) provided the vehicle is insured
Supplementary note 1

Question: 12.17
A Statutory Off Road Notification (SORN) will last
Mark one answer
a) for the life of the vehicle
b) for as long as you own the vehicle
c) for 12 months only
d) until the vehicle warranty expires
Supplementary note 1

Question: 12.18
You claim on your insurance to have your car repaired. Your policy has an excess of £100.
What does this mean?
Mark one answer
a) The insurance company will pay the first £100 of any claim
b) You will be paid £100 if you do not claim within one year
c) Your vehicle is insured for a value of £100 if it is stolen
d) You will have to pay the first £100 of the cost of repair to your car
Supplementary note 1

Question: 12.19
The Pass Plus scheme is designed to (NI exempt)
Mark one answer
a) give you a discount on your MOT
b) improve your basic driving skills
c) increase your mechanical knowledge
d) allow you to drive anyone else's vehicle
Supplementary note 1

Question: 12.20
By taking part in the Pass Plus scheme you will (NI exempt)
Mark one answer
a) never get any points on your licence
b) be able to service your own car
c) allow you to drive anyone else's vehicle
d) improve your basic driving skills
Supplementary note 1

Question: 12.21
Supertrams or Light Rapid Transit (LRT) systems are environmentally friendly because
Mark one answer
a) they use diesel power
b) they use quieter roads
c) they use electric power
d) they do not operate during rush hour
Supplementary note 2

Question: 12.22
How can you, as a driver, help the environment?
Mark three answers
a) By reducing your speed
b) By gentle acceleration
c) By using leaded fuel
d) By driving faster
e) By harsh acceleration
f) By servicing your vehicle properly
Supplementary note 2

Question: 12.23
Motor vehicles can harm the environment. This has resulted in
Mark three answers
a) air pollution
b) damage to buildings
c) reduced health risks
d) improved public transport
e) less use of electrical vehicles
f) using up natural resources
Supplementary note 2

Question: 12.24
To help the environment, you can avoid wasting fuel by
Mark three answers
a) having your vehicle properly serviced
b) making sure your tyres are correctly inflated
c) not over-revving in the lower gears
d) driving at higher speeds where possible
e) keeping an empty roof rack properly fitted
f) servicing your vehicle less regularly
Supplementary note 2

Question: 12.25
Which THREE of the following are most likely to waste fuel?
Mark three answers
a) Reducing your speed
b) Carrying unnecessary weight
c) Using the wrong grade of fuel
d) Under-inflated tyres
e) Using different brands of fuel
f) A fitted, empty roof rack
Supplementary note 2

Question: 12.26
You service your own vehicle. How should you get rid of the old engine oil?
Mark one answer
a) Take it to a local authority site
b) Pour it down a drain
c) Tip it into a hole in the ground
d) Put it into your dustbin
Supplementary note 2

Question: 12.27
On a vehicle, where would you find a catalytic converter?
Mark one answer
a) In the fuel tank
b) In the air filter
c) On the cooling system
d) On the exhaust system
Supplementary note 2

Question: 12.28
New petrol-engined cars must be fitted with catalytic converters. The reason for this is to
Mark one answer
a) control exhaust noise levels
b) prolong the life of the exhaust system
c) allow the exhaust system to be recycled
d) reduce harmful exhaust emissions
Supplementary note 2

Question: 12.29
Why do MOT tests include a strict exhaust emission test?
Mark one answer
a) To recover the cost of expensive garage equipment
b) To help protect the environment against pollution
c) To discover which fuel supplier is used the most
d) To make sure diesel and petrol engines emit the same fumes
Supplementary note 2

Question: 12.30
To reduce the damage your vehicle causes to the environment you should
Mark three answers
a) use narrow side streets
b) avoid harsh acceleration
c) brake in good time
d) anticipate well ahead
e) use busy routes
Supplementary note 2

Question: 12.31

When a roof rack is not in use it should be removed. Why is this?

Mark one answer

a) It will affect the suspension
b) It is illegal
c) It will affect your braking
d) It will waste fuel

Supplementary note 2

Question: 12.32

How should you dispose of a used battery?

Mark two answers

a) Take it to a local authority site
b) Put it in the dustbin
c) Break it up into pieces
d) Leave it on waste land
e) Take it to a garage
f) Burn it on a fire

Supplementary note 2

Question: 12.33

The pictured vehicle is 'environmentally friendly' because it

Mark three answers

a) reduces noise pollution
b) uses diesel fuel
c) uses electricity
d) uses unleaded fuel
e) reduces parking spaces
f) reduces town traffic

Supplementary note 2

Question: 12.34

Driving at 70 mph uses more fuel than driving at 50 mph by up to

Mark one answer

a) 10%
b) 30%
c) 75%
d) 100%

Supplementary note 2

Question: 12.35

The purpose of a catalytic converter is to reduce

Mark one answer

a) fuel consumption
b) the risk of fire
c) toxic exhaust gases
d) engine wear

Supplementary note 2

Question: 12.36

What is most likely to cause high fuel consumption?

Mark one answer

a) Poor steering control
b) Accelerating around bends
c) Staying in high gears
d) Harsh braking and accelerating

Supplementary note 2

Question: 12.37

A properly serviced vehicle will give

Mark two answers

a) lower insurance premiums
b) you a refund on your road tax
c) better fuel economy
d) cleaner exhaust emissions

Supplementary note 2

Question: 12.38

Catalytic converters are fitted to make the

Mark one answer

a) engine produce more power
b) exhaust system easier to replace
c) engine run quietly
d) exhaust fumes cleaner

Supplementary note 2

Question: 12.39

To reduce the volume of traffic on the roads you could

Mark three answers

a) use public transport more often
b) share a car when possible
c) walk or cycle on short journeys
d) travel by car at all times
e) use a car with a smaller engine
f) drive in a bus lane

Supplementary note 2

Question: 12.40

Which TWO of the following will improve fuel consumption?

Mark two answers

a) Reducing your road speed
b) Planning well ahead
c) Late and harsh braking
d) Driving in lower gears
e) Short journeys with a cold engine
f) Rapid acceleration

Supplementary note 2

Question: 12.41

Which THREE things can you, as a road user, do to help the environment?

Mark three answers

a) Cycle when possible
b) Drive on under-inflated tyres
c) Use the choke for as long as possible on a cold engine
d) Have your vehicle properly tuned and serviced
e) Watch the traffic and plan ahead
f) Brake as late as possible without skidding

Supplementary note 2

Question: 12.42

As a driver, you can help reduce pollution levels in town centres by

Mark one answer

a) driving more quickly
b) using leaded fuel
c) walking or cycling
d) driving short journeys

Supplementary note 2

Question: 12.43

A roof rack fitted to your car will

Mark one answer

a) reduce fuel consumption
b) improve the road handling
c) make your car go faster
d) increase fuel consumption

Supplementary note 2

Question: 12.44
As a driver you can cause MORE damage to the environment by
Mark three answers
a) choosing a fuel efficient vehicle
b) making a lot of short journeys
c) driving in as high a gear as possible
d) accelerating as quickly as possible
e) having your vehicle regularly serviced
f) using leaded fuel
Supplementary note 2

Question: 12.45
To help protect the environment you should NOT
Mark one answer
a) remove your roof rack when unloaded
b) use your car for very short journeys
c) walk, cycle, or use public transport
d) empty the boot of unnecessary weight
Supplementary note 2

Question: 12.46
Your vehicle has a catalytic converter. Its purpose is to reduce
Mark one answer
a) exhaust noise
b) fuel consumption
c) exhaust emissions
d) engine noise
Supplementary note 2

Question: 12.47
Why can it be an advantage for traffic speed to stay constant over a longer distance?
Mark one answer
a) You will do more stop-start driving
b) You will use far more fuel
c) You will be able to use more direct routes
d) Your overall journey time will normally improve
Supplementary note 2

Question: 12.48
On which TWO occasions might you inflate your tyres to more than the recommended normal pressure?
Mark two answers
a) When the roads are slippery
b) When driving fast for a long distance
c) When the tyre tread is worn below 2mm
d) When carrying a heavy load
e) When the weather is cold
f) When the vehicle is fitted with anti-lock brakes
Supplementary note 3

Question: 12.49
What can cause heavy steering?
Mark one answer
a) Driving on ice
b) Badly worn brakes
c) Over-inflated tyres
d) Under-inflated tyres
Supplementary note 3

Question: 12.50
Unbalanced wheels on a car may cause
Mark one answer
a) the steering to pull to one side
b) the steering to vibrate
c) the brakes to fail
d) the tyres to deflate
Supplementary note 3

Question: 12.51
You will use more fuel if your tyres are
Mark one answer
a) under-inflated
b) of different makes
c) over-inflated
d) new and hardly used
Supplementary note 3

Question: 12.52
Driving with under-inflated tyres can affect
Mark two answers
a) engine temperature
b) fuel consumption
c) braking
d) oil pressure
Supplementary note 3

Question: 12.53
Turning the steering wheel while your car is stationary can cause damage to the
Mark two answers
a) gearbox
b) engine
c) brakes
d) steering
e) tyres
Supplementary note 5

Question: 12.54
When should you especially check the engine oil level?
Mark one answer
a) Before a long journey
b) When the engine is hot
c) Early in the morning
d) Every 6000 miles
Supplementary note 6

Question: 12.55
You need top up your battery. What level should you fill to?
Mark one answer
a) The top of the battery
b) Half-way up the battery
c) Just below the cell plates
d) Just above the cell plates
Supplementary note 6

Question: 12.56
You have too much oil in your engine. What could this cause?
Mark one answer
a) Low oil pressure
b) Engine overheating
c) Chain wear
d) Oil leaks
Supplementary note 6

Question: 12.57
The fluid level in your battery is low. What should you top it up with?
Mark one answer
a) Battery acid
b) Distilled water
c) Engine oil
d) Engine oil
Supplementary note 6

Question: 12.58
You are driving down a long steep hill. You suddenly notice your brakes are not working as well as normal. What is the usual cause of this?
Mark one answer
a) The brakes overheating
b) Air in the brake fluid
c) Oil on the brakes
d) Badly adjusted brakes
Supplementary note 7

Question: 12.59
The main cause of brake fade is
Mark one answer
a) the brakes overheating
b) air in the brake fluid
c) oil on the brakes
d) the brakes out of adjustment
Supplementary note 7

Question: 12.60
You have been involved in an argument before starting your journey. This has made you feel angry. You should
Mark one answer
a) start to drive, but open a window
b) drive slower than normal and turn your radio on
c) have an alcoholic drink to help you relax before driving
d) calm down before you start to drive
Supplementary note 9

Question: 12.61
Objects hanging from your interior mirror may
Mark two answers
a) restrict your view
b) improve your driving
c) distract your attention
d) help your concentration
Supplementary note 9

Question: 12.62
You are driving on a motorway and want to use your mobile phone. What should you do?
Mark one answer
a) Try to find a safe place on the hard shoulder
b) Leave the motorway and stop in a safe place
c) Use the next exit and pull up on the slip road
d) Move to the left lane and reduce your speed
Supplementary note 9

Question: 12.63
Using a mobile phone when driving is illegal. The chance of you having an accident while using one is
Mark one answer
a) two times higher
b) four times higher
c) six times higher
d) ten times higher
Supplementary note 9

Question: 12.64
Using a mobile phone when driving is illegal. Your chances of having an accident increase by
Mark one answer
a) two times
b) four times
c) eight times
d) twelve times
Supplementary note 9

Question: 12.65
Using a mobile phone when driving is illegal. If you do so your chances of having an accident increase by how many times?
Mark one answer
a) two
b) four
c) ten
d) twenty
Supplementary note 9

Question: 12.66
Why are mirrors often slightly curved (convex)?
Mark one answer
a) They give a wider field of vision
b) They totally cover blind spots
c) They make it easier to judge the speed of following traffic
d) They make following traffic look bigger
Supplementary note 10

Question: 12.67
You are dazzled at night by a vehicle behind you. You should
Mark one answer
a) set your mirror to anti dazzle
b) set your mirror to dazzle the other driver
c) brake sharply to a stop
d) switch your rear lights on and off
Supplementary note 10

Question: 12.68
When you see a hazard ahead you should use the mirrors. Why is this?
Mark one answer
a) Because you will need to accelerate out of danger
b) To assess how your actions will affect following traffic
c) Because you will need to brake sharply to a stop
d) To check what is happening on the road ahead
Supplementary note 10

Question: 12.69
While driving, this warning light on your dashboard comes on. It means

Mark one answer
a) a fault in the braking system
b) the engine oil is low
c) a rear light has failed
d) your seat belt is not fastened
Supplementary note 11

Question: 12.70

Which instrument panel warning light would show that headlights are on full beam ?

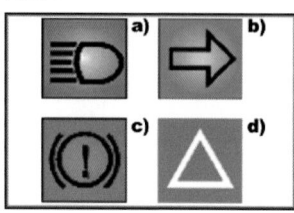

Mark one answer
a) Sign A
b) Sign B
c) Sign C
d) Sign D
Supplementary note 11

Question: 12.71

What does this instrument panel light mean when lit ?

Mark one answer
a) Gear lever in park
b) Gear lever in neutral
c) Handbrake on
d) Handbrake off
Supplementary note 11

Question: 12.72

Anti-lock brakes may not work as effectively if the road surface is
Mark two answers
a) dry
b) loose
c) wet
d) good
e) firm
Supplementary note 12

Question: 12.73

You are driving on a wet road. You have to stop your vehicle in an emergency. You should
Mark one answer
a) apply the handbrake and footbrake together
b) keep both hands on the wheel
c) select reverse gear
d) give an arm signal
Supplementary note 12

Question: 12.74

You arrive at an accident where someone is suffering from severe burns. You should
Mark one answer
a) apply lotions to the injury
b) burst any blisters
c) remove anything stuck to the burns
d) douse the burns with cool liquid
Supplementary note 13

Question: 12.75

You arrive at the scene of an accident. There has been an engine fire and someone's hands and arms have been burnt. You should NOT
Mark one answer
a) douse the burn thoroughly with cool liquid
b) lay the casualty down
c) remove anything sticking to the burn
d) reassure them constantly
Supplementary note 13

Question: 12.76

At an accident you suspect a casualty has back injuries. The area is safe. You should
Mark one answer
a) offer them a drink
b) not move them
c) raise their legs
d) offer them a cigarette
Supplementary note 13

Question: 12.77

At an accident a small child is not breathing. When giving mouth to mouth you should breathe
Mark one answer
a) sharply
b) gently
c) heavily
d) rapidly
Supplementary note 13

Question: 12.78

How can you use the engine of your vehicle to control your speed?
Mark one answer
a) By changing to a lower gear
b) By selecting reverse gear
c) By changing to a higher gear
d) By selecting neutral
Supplementary note 14

Question: 12.79

You will feel the effects of engine braking when you
Mark one answer
a) only use the handbrake
b) only use neutral
c) change to a lower gear
d) change to a higher gear
Supplementary note 14

Question: 12.80

Hills can affect the performance of your vehicle. Which TWO apply when driving up steep hills?
Mark two answers
a) Higher gears will pull better
b) You will slow down sooner
c) Overtaking will be easier
d) The engine will work harder
e) The steering will feel heavier
Supplementary note 14

Question: 12.81

If your vehicle uses diesel fuel, take extra care when refuelling, Diesel fuel when spilt is
Mark one answer
a) sticky
b) odourless
c) clear
d) slippery
Supplementary note 15

Question: 12.82

To avoid spillage after refuelling, you should make sure that
Mark one answer
a) your tank is only 3/4 full
b) you have used a locking filler cap
c) you check your fuel gauge is working
d) your filler cap is securely fastened
Supplementary note 15

Question: 12.83
You have a loose filler cap on your diesel fuel tank. This will
Mark two answers
a) waste fuel and money
b) make roads slippery for other road users
c) improve your vehicles fuel consumption
d) increase the level of exhaust emissions
Supplementary note 15

Question: 12.84
You may remove your seat belt when carrying out a manoeuvre that involves
Mark one answer
a) reversing
b) a hill start
c) an emergency stop
d) driving slowly
Supplementary note 16

Question: 12.85
When you are NOT sure that it is safe to reverse your vehicle you should
Mark one answer
a) use your horn
b) rev your engine
c) get out and check
d) reverse slowly
Supplementary note 16

Question: 12.86
You are reversing your vehicle into a side road. When would the greatest hazard to passing traffic occur?
Mark one answer
a) After you've completed the manoeuvre
b) Just before you actually begin to manoeuvre
c) After you've entered the side road
d) When the front of your vehicle swings out
Supplementary note 16

Question: 12.87
A heavy load on your roof rack will
Mark one answer
a) improve the road holding
b) reduce the stopping distance
c) make the steering lighter
d) reduce stability
Supplementary note 17

Question: 12.88
What does this sign mean?

Mark one answer
a) Vehicles may not park on the verge or footway
b) Vehicles may park on the left-hand side of the road only
c) Vehicles may park fully on the verge or footway
d) Vehicles may park on the right-hand side of the road only
Supplementary note 18

Question: 12.89
What does this sign mean?

Mark one answer
a) Direction to park and ride car park
b) No parking for buses or coaches
c) Directions to bus and coach park
d) Parking area for cars and coaches
Supplementary note 18

Question: 12.90
You are in a tunnel and you see this sign. What does it mean?

Mark one answer
a) Direction to emergency pedestrian exit
b) Beware of pedestrians, no footpath ahead
c) No access for pedestrians
d) Beware of pedestrians crossing ahead
Supplementary note 18

Question: 12.91
Which is the sign for a ring road?

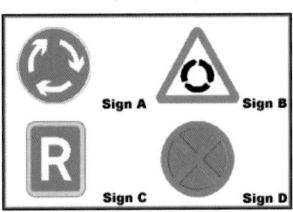

Mark one answer
a) Sign A
b) Sign B
c) Sign C
d) Sign D
Supplementary note 18

Question: 12.92
What does this sign mean?

Mark one answer
a) Route for lorries
b) Ring road
c) Rest area
d) Roundabout
Supplementary note 18

Question: 12.93
What do these road markings outside a school mean?

Mark one answer
a) You may park here if you are a teacher
b) Sound your horn before parking
c) When parking use your hazard warning lights
d) You must not wait or park your vehicle here
Supplementary note 18

Question: 12.94
What is the reason for the area marked in red and white along the centre of this road?

Mark one answer
a) It is to separate traffic flowing in opposite directions
b) It marks an area to be used by overtaking motorcyclists
c) It is a temporary marking to warn of the roadworks
d) It is separating the two sides of the dual carriageway
Supplementary note 18

Question: 12.95
Why are these yellow lines painted across the road?

Mark one answer
a) To help you choose the correct lane
b) To help you keep the correct separation distance
c) To make you aware of your speed
d) To tell you the distance to the roundabout
Supplementary note 18

Question: 12.96
When driving through a tunnel you should
Mark one answer
a) Look out for variable message signs
b) Use your air conditioning system
c) Switch on your rear fog lights
d) Always use your windscreen wipers
Supplementary note 18

Question: 12.97
You are going through a tunnel. What systems are provided to warn of any accidents or congestion?
Mark one answer
a) Double white centre lines
b) Variable message signs
c) Chevron 'distance markers'
d) Rumble strips
Supplementary note 18

Question: 12.98
You must not stop on these road markings because you may obstruct

Mark one answer
a) childrens view of the crossing area
b) teachers access to the school
c) delivery vehicles access to the school
d) emergency vehicles access to the school
Supplementary note 18

Question: 12.99
You will see these red and white markers when approaching

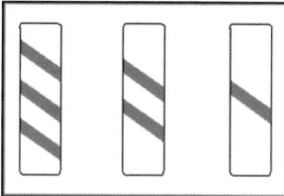

Mark one answer
a) the end of a motorway
b) a concealed level crossing
c) a concealed speed limit sign
d) the end of a dual carriageway
Supplementary note 18

Question: 12.100
A rumble device is designed to

Mark two answers
a) give directions
b) prevent cattle escaping
c) alert you to low tyre pressure
d) alert you to a hazard
e) encourage you to reduce speed
Supplementary note 18

The Highway Code quiz programme

Question: 12.101
You are going through a tunnel. What should you look out for that warns of accidents or congestion?
Mark one answer
a) Hazard warning lines
b) Other drivers flashing their lights
c) Variable message signs
d) Areas marked with hatch markings
Supplementary note 18

Question: 12.102
You see these markings on the road. Why are they there?

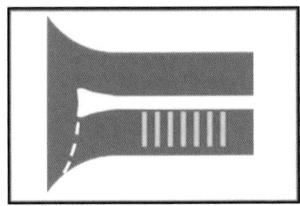

Mark one answer
a) To show a safe distance between vehicles
b) To keep the area clear of traffic
c) To make you aware of your speed
d) To warn you to change direction
Supplementary note 18

Question: 12.103
You are approaching a busy junction. There are several lanes with road markings. At the last moment you realise that you are in the wrong lane. You should
Mark one answer
a) continue in that lane
b) force your way across
c) stop until the area has cleared
d) use clear arm signals to cut across
Supplementary note 19

Question: 12.104
You take the wrong route and find you are on a one-way street. You should

Mark one answer
a) reverse out of the road
b) turn round in a side road
c) continue to the end of the road
d) reverse into a driveway
Supplementary note 19

Question: 12.105
You are towing a caravan. Which is the safest type of rear-view mirror to use?
Mark one answer
a) Interior wide-angle-view mirror
b) Extended-arm side mirrors
c) Ordinary door mirrors
d) Ordinary interior mirror
Supplementary note 20

Question: 12.106
Are passengers allowed to ride in a caravan that is being towed?
Mark one answer
a) Yes if they are over fourteen
b) No not at any time
c) Only if all the seats in the towing vehicle are full
d) Only if a stabilizer is fitted
Supplementary note 20

Question: 12.107
A trailer must stay securely hitched up to the towing vehicle. What additional safety device can be fitted to the trailer braking system?
Mark one answer
a) Stabiliser
b) Jockey wheel
c) Corner steadies
d) Breakaway cable
Supplementary note 20

Question: 12.108
You are planning to tow a caravan. Which of these will mostly help to aid the vehicle handling?
Mark one answer
a) A jockey-wheel fitted to the towbar
b) Power steering fitted to the towing vehicle
c) Anti-lock brakes fitted to the towing vehicle
d) A stabiliser fitted to the towbar
Supplementary note 20

Question: 12.109
Why would you fit a stabiliser before towing a caravan?
Mark one answer
a) It will help with stability when driving in crosswinds
b) It will allow heavy items to be loaded behind the axle
c) It will help you to raise and lower the jockey wheel
d) It will allow you to tow without the breakaway cable
Supplementary note 20

Question: 12.110
You wish to tow a trailer. Where would you find the maximum noseweight of your vehicle's tow ball?
Mark one answer
a) In the vehicle handbook
b) In The Highway Code
c) In your vehicle registration certificate
d) In your licence documents
Supplementary note 20

Question: 12.111
When driving a car fitted with automatic transmission what would you use 'kick down' for?
Mark one answer
a) Cruise control
b) Quick acceleration
c) Slow braking
d) Fuel economy
Supplementary note 21

Question: 12.112

The MAIN benefit of having four-wheel drive is to improve

Mark one answer

a) road holding
b) fuel consumption
c) stopping distances
d) passenger comfort

Supplementary note 22

Question: 12.113

What type of emergency vehicle is fitted with a green flashing beacon?

Mark one answer

a) Fire engine
b) Road gritter
c) Ambulance
d) Doctor's car

Supplementary note 23

Question: 12.114

A vehicle has a flashing green beacon. What does this mean?

Mark one answer

a) A doctor is answering an emergency call
b) The vehicle is slow-moving
c) It is a motorway police patrol vehicle
d) A vehicle is carrying hazardous chemicals

Supplementary note 23

Question: 12.115

Which of the following vehicles will use blue flashing beacons?

Mark three answers

a) Motorway maintenance
b) Bomb disposal
c) Blood transfusion
d) Police patrol
e) Breakdown recovery

Supplementary note 23

Question: 12.116

A flashing green beacon on a vehicle means

Mark one answer

a) police on non-urgent duties
b) doctor on an emergency call
c) road safety patrol operating
d) gritting in progress

Supplementary note 23

Question: 12.117

Which THREE of these emergency services might have blue flashing beacons?

Mark three answers

a) Coastguard
b) Bomb disposal
c) Gritting lorries
d) Animal ambulances
e) Mountain rescue
f) Doctors' cars

Supplementary note 23

Question: 12.118

Windscreen pillars can obstruct your view. You should take particular care when

Mark one answer

a) driving on a motorway
b) driving on a dual carriageway
c) approaching a one-way street
d) approaching bends and junctions

Supplementary note 24

Question: 12.119

You want to turn right from a junction but your view is restricted by parked vehicles. What should you do?

Mark one answer

a) Move out quickly, but be prepared to stop
b) Sound your horn and pull out if there is no reply
c) Stop, then move slowly forward until you have a clear view
d) Stop, get out and look along the main road to check

Supplementary note 24

Question: 12.120

You want to turn left at this junction. The view of the main road is restricted. What should you do?

Mark one answer

a) Stay well back and wait to see if something comes
b) Build up your speed so that you can emerge quickly
c) Stop and apply the handbrake even if the road is clear
d) Approach slowly and edge out until you can see more clearly

Supplementary note 24

Question: 12.121

You are waiting to emerge from a junction. The windscreen pillar is restricting your view. What should you be particularly aware of?

Mark one answer

a) Lorries
b) Buses
c) Motorcyclists
d) Coaches

Supplementary note 24

Question: 12.122
Why must you take extra care when turning right at this junction?

Mark one answer
a) Road surface is poor
b) Footpaths are narrow
c) Road markings are faint
d) There is reduced visibility
Supplementary note 24

Question: 12.123
You are driving in busy traffic. You want to pull up on the left just after a junction on the left. When should you signal?
Mark one answer
a) As you are passing or just after the junction
b) Just before you reach the junction
c) Well before you reach the junction
d) It would be better not to signal at all
Supplementary note 24

Question: 12.124
You are approaching unmarked crossroads. How should you deal with this type of junction?
Mark one answer
a) Accelerate and keep to the middle
b) Slow down and keep to the right
c) Accelerate looking to the left
d) Slow down and look both ways
Supplementary note 24

Question: 12.125
You are waiting to emerge left from a minor road. A large vehicle is approaching from the right. You have time to turn, but you should wait. Why?
Mark one answer
a) The large vehicle can easily hide an overtaking vehicle
b) The large vehicle can turn suddenly
c) The large vehicle is difficult to steer in a straight line
d) The large vehicle can easily hide vehicles from the left
Supplementary note 24

Question: 12.126
You are approaching crossroads. The traffic lights have failed. What should you do?
Mark one answer
a) Brake and stop only for large vehicles
b) Brake sharply to a stop before looking
c) Be prepared to brake sharply to a stop
d) Be prepared to stop for any traffic.
Supplementary note 24

Question: 12.127
When emerging from junctions, which is most likely to obstruct your view?
Mark one answer
a) Windscreen pillars
b) Steering wheel
c) Interior mirror
d) Windscreen wipers
Supplementary note 24

Question: 12.128
At a busy unmarked crossroads, which of the following has priority?
Mark one answer
a) Vehicles going straight ahead
b) Vehicles turning right
c) None of the vehicles
d) The vehicles that arrived first
Supplementary note 24

Question: 12.129
You are waiting to turn right at the end of a road. Your view is obstructed by parked vehicles. What should you do?
Mark one answer
a) Stop and then move forward slowly and carefully for a proper view
b) Move quickly to where you can see so you only block traffic from one direction
c) Wait for a pedestrian to let you know when it is safe for you to emerge
d) Turn your vehicle around immediately and find another junction to use
Supplementary note 24

Question: 12.130
You are waiting to emerge at a junction. Your view is restricted by parked vehicles. What can help you to see traffic on the road you are joining?
Mark one answer
a) Looking for traffic behind you
b) Reflections of traffic in shop windows
c) Making eye contact with other road users
d) Checking for traffic in your interior mirror
Supplementary note 24

Question: 12.131
You are driving in slow-moving queues of traffic. Just before changing lane you should
Mark one answer
a) sound the horn
b) look for motorcyclists filtering through the traffic
c) give a 'slowing down' arm signal
d) change down to first gear
Supplementary note 25

Question: 12.132
You are in a line of traffic. The driver behind you is following very closely. What action should you take?
Mark one answer
a) Ignore the following driver and continue to drive within the speed limit
b) Slow down, gradually increasing the gap between you and the vehicle in front
c) Signal left and wave the following driver past
d) Move over to a position just left of the centre line of the road
Supplementary note 26

Question: 12.133
'Tailgating' means
Mark one answer
a) using the rear door of a hatchback car
b) reversing into a parking space
c) following another vehicle too closely
d) driving with rear fog lights on
Supplementary note 26

Question: 12.134
You are on a road which has speed humps. A driver in front is travelling slower than you. You should
Mark one answer
a) sound your horn
b) overtake as soon as you can
c) flash your headlights
d) slow down and stay behind
Supplementary note 26

Question: 12.135
In heavy motorway traffic you are being followed closely by the vehicle behind. How can you lower the risk of an accident?

Mark one answer
a) Increase your distance from the vehicle in front
b) Tap your foot on the brake pedal sharply
c) Switch on your hazard lights
d) Move onto the hard shoulder and stop
Supplementary note 26

Question: 12.136
When following a large vehicle you should keep well back because this
Mark one answer
a) allows you to corner more quickly
b) helps the large vehicle to stop more easily
c) allows the driver to see you in the mirrors
d) helps you to keep out of the wind
Supplementary note 26

Question: 12.137
In which of these situations should you avoid overtaking?
Mark one answer
a) Just after a bend
b) In a one-way street
c) On a 30 mph road
d) Approaching a dip in the road
Supplementary note 27

Question: 12.138
As you approach this bridge you should

Mark three answers
a) move into the middle of the road to get a better view
b) slow down
c) get over the bridge as quickly as possible
d) consider using your horn
e) find another route
f) beware of pedestrians
Supplementary note 28

Question: 12.139
You are driving downhill. There is a car parked on the other side of the road. Large, slow lorries are coming towards you. You should
Mark one answer
a) keep going because you have the right of way
b) slow down and give way
c) speed up and get past quickly
d) pull over on the right behind the parked car
Supplementary note 29

Question: 12.140
When driving in fog, which of the following are correct?
Mark three answers
a) Use dipped headlights
b) Use headlights on full beam
c) Allow more time for your journey
d) Keep close to the car in front
e) Slow down
f) Use side lights only
Supplementary note 30

Question: 12.141
Using rear fog lights in clear daylight will
Mark one answer
a) be useful when towing a trailer
b) give extra protection
c) dazzle other drivers
d) make following drivers keep back
Supplementary note 30

Question: 12.142
Chains can be fitted to your wheels to help prevent
Mark one answer
a) damage to the road surface
b) wear to the tyres
c) skidding in deep snow
d) the brakes locking
Supplementary note 30

Question: 12.143
Who is legally responsible for ensuring that a Vehicle Registration Certificate (V5C) is updated?
Mark one answer
a) The registered vehicle keeper
b) The vehicle manufacturer
c) Your insurance company
d) The licensing authority
Supplementary note 30

Question: 12.144
When should you update your Vehicle Registration Certificate (V5C)?
Mark one answer
a) When you pass your driving test
b) When you move house
c) When your vehicle needs an MOT
d) When you have an accident
Supplementary note 30

Question: 12.145
Where is the safest place to park your vehicle at night?
Mark one answer
a) In a garage
b) On a busy road
c) In a quiet car park
d) Near a red route
Supplementary note 31

Question: 12.146
Wherever possible, which one of the following should you do when parking at night?
Mark one answer
a) Park in a quiet car park
b) Park in a well lit area
c) Park facing against the flow of traffic
d) Park next to a busy junction
Supplementary note 31

Question: 12.147
How can you help to prevent your car radio being stolen?
Mark one answer
a) Park in an unlit area
b) Hide the radio with a blanket
c) Park near a busy junction
d) Install a security coded radio
Supplementary note 31

Question: 12.148
You are away from home and have to park your vehicle overnight. Where should you leave it?
Mark one answer
a) Opposite another parked vehicle
b) In a quiet road
c) Opposite a traffic island
d) In a secure car park
Supplementary note 31

Question: 12.149
To help keep your car secure you could join a
Mark one answer
a) vehicle breakdown organisation
b) vehicle watch scheme
c) advanced drivers scheme
d) car maintenance class
Supplementary note 31

Question: 12.150
To help keep your vehicle secure at night, where should you park?
Mark one answer
a) Near a police station
b) In a quiet road
c) On a red route
d) In a well lit area
Supplementary note 31

Question: 12.151
When leaving your vehicle where should you park if possible?
Mark one answer
a) Opposite a traffic island
b) In a secure car park
c) On a bend
d) At or near a taxi rank
Supplementary note 31

Question: 12.152
How can you lessen the risk of your vehicle being broken into at night?
Mark one answer
a) Leave it in a well lit area
b) Park in a quiet side road
c) Don't engage the steering lock
d) Park in a poorly lit area
Supplementary note 31

Question: 12.153
Which of the following types of crossing can detect when people are on them?
Mark one answer
a) Pelican
b) Toucan
c) Zebra
d) Puffin
Supplementary note 32

Question: 12.154
You are approaching a red light at a puffin crossing. Pedestrians are on the crossing. The red light will stay on until
Mark one answer
a) you start to edge forward on to the crossing
b) the pedestrians have reached a safe position
c) the pedestrians are clear of the front of your vehicle
d) a driver from the opposite direction reaches the crossing
Supplementary note 32

Question: 12.155
You are approaching traffic lights that have been on green for some time. You should
Mark one answer
a) accelerate hard
b) maintain your speed
c) be ready to stop
d) brake hard
Supplementary note 32

Question: 12.156
You see a pedestrian with a dog. The dog has a yellow or burgundy coat. This especially warns you that the pedestrian is
Mark one answer
a) elderly
b) dog training
c) colour blind
d) deaf
Supplementary note 32

Question: 12.157
Which TWO of the following are correct? When overtaking at night you should
Mark two answers
a) WAIT until a bend so that you can see the oncoming headlights
b) sound your horn twice before moving out
c) be careful because you can see less
d) beware of bends in the road ahead
e) put headlights on full beam
Supplementary note 33

Question: 12.158
You are waiting in a traffic queue at night. To avoid dazzling following drivers you should
Mark one answer
a) apply the handbrake only
b) apply the footbrake only
c) switch off your headlights
d) use both the handbrake and footbrake
Supplementary note 33

Question: 12.159
You are driving at night with full beam headlights on. A vehicle is overtaking you. You should dip your lights
Mark one answer
a) some time after the vehicle has passed you
b) before the vehicle starts to pass you
c) only if the other driver dips their headlights
d) as soon as the vehicle passes you
Supplementary note 33

Question: 12.160
You are travelling along the left-hand lane of a three-lane motorway. Traffic is joining from a slip road. You should
Mark one answer
a) race the other vehicles
b) move to another lane
c) maintain a steady speed
d) switch on your hazard flashers
Supplementary note 34

Question: 12.161
Why is it particularly important to carry out a check on your vehicle before making a long motorway journey?
Mark one answer
a) You will have to do more harsh braking on motorways
b) Motorway service stations do not deal with breakdowns
c) The road surface will wear down the tyres faster
d) Continuous high speeds may increase the risk of your vehicle breaking down
Supplementary note 34

Question: 12.162
Where would you see these road markings?

Mark one answer
a) At a level crossing
b) On a motorway slip road
c) At a pedestrian crossing
d) On a single-track road
Supplementary note 34

Question: 12.163
You see a car on the hard shoulder of a motorway with a HELP pennant displayed. This means the driver is most likely to be
Mark one answer
a) a disabled person
b) first aid trained
c) a foreign visitor
d) a rescue patrol person
Supplementary note 34

Question: 12.164
How should you use the emergency telephone on a motorway?
Mark one answer
a) Stay close to the carriageway
b) Face the oncoming traffic
c) Keep your back to the traffic
d) Stand on the hard shoulder
Supplementary note 34

Question: 12.165
The emergency telephones on a motorway are connected to the
Mark one answer
a) ambulance service
b) police control
c) fire brigade
d) breakdown service
Supplementary note 34

Question: 12.166
Motorway emergency telephones are usually linked to the police. In some areas they are now linked to
Mark one answer
a) the Highways Agency Control Centre
b) the Driver Vehicle Licensing Agency
c) the Driving Standards Agency
d) the local Vehicle Registration Office
Supplementary note 34

Question: 12.167
When may you stop on a motorway?
Mark one answer
a) If you have to read a map
b) When you are tired and need a rest
c) If your mobile phone rings
d) In an emergency or breakdown
Supplementary note 34

Question: 12.168
An Emergency Refuge Area is an area
Mark one answer
a) on a motorway for use in cases of emergency or breakdown
b) for use if you think you will be involved in a road rage incident
c) on a motorway for a police patrol to park and watch traffic
d) for construction and road workers to store emergency equipment
Supplementary note 35

Question: 12.169

What is an Emergency Refuge Area on a motorway for?

Mark one answer

a) An area to park in when you want to use a mobile phone
b) To use in cases of emergency or breakdown
c) For an emergency recovery vehicle to park in a contra-flow system
d) To drive in when there is queuing traffic ahead

Supplementary note 35

Question: 12.170

Highways Agency Traffic Officers

Mark one answer

a) will not be able to assist at a breakdown or emergency
b) are not able to stop and direct anyone on a motorway
c) will tow a broken down vehicle and it's passengers home
d) are able to stop and direct anyone on a motorway

Supplementary note 35

Question: 12.171

You are on a motorway. A red cross is displayed above the hard shoulder. What does this mean?

Mark one answer

a) Pull up in this lane to answer your mobile phone
b) Use this lane as a running lane
c) This lane can be used if you need a rest
d) You should not travel in this lane

Supplementary note 35

Question: 12.172

You are on a motorway in an Active Traffic Management (ATM) area. A mandatory speed limit is displayed above the hard shoulder. What does this mean?

Mark one answer

a) You should not travel in this lane
b) The hard shoulder can be used as a running lane
c) You can park on the hard shoulder if you feel tired
d) You can pull up in this lane to answer a mobile phone

Supplementary note 35

Question: 12.173

The aim of an Active Traffic Management scheme on a motorway is to

Mark one answer

a) prevent overtaking
b) reduce rest stops
c) prevent tailgating
d) reduce congestion

Supplementary note 35

Question: 12.174

You are in an Active Traffic Management area on a motorway. When the Actively Managed mode is operating

Mark one answer

a) speed limits are only advisory
b) the national speed limit will apply
c) the speed limit is always 30 mph
d) all speed limit signals are set

Supplementary note 35

Question: 12.175

You are travelling on a motorway. A red cross is shown above the hard shoulder and mandatory speed limits above all other lanes. This means

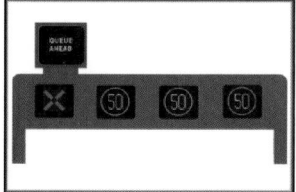

Mark one answer

a) the hard shoulder can be used as a rest area if you feel tired
b) the hard shoulder is for emergency or breakdown use only
c) the hard shoulder can be used as a normal running lane
d) the hard shoulder has a speed limit of 50 mph

Supplementary note 35

Question: 12.176

You are travelling on a motorway. A red cross is shown above the hard shoulder. What does this mean?

Mark one answer

a) Use this lane as a rest area
b) Use this as a normal running lane
c) Do not use this lane to travel in
d) National speed limit applies in this lane

Supplementary note 35

Question: 12.177
You see this sign on a motorway. It means you can use

Mark one answer
a) any lane except the hard shoulder
b) the hard shoulder only
c) the three right hand lanes only
d) all the lanes including the hard shoulder

Supplementary note 35

Question: 12.178
You are travelling on a motorway. You MUST stop when signalled to do so by which of these?
Mark one answer
a) Flashing amber lights above your lane
b) A Highways Agency Traffic Officer
c) Pedestrians on the hard shoulder
d) A driver who has broken down

Supplementary note 35

Question: 12.179
Before starting a journey it is wise to plan your route. How can you do this?
Mark one answer
a) Look at a map
b) Contact your local garage
c) Look in your vehicle handbook
d) Check your vehicle registration document

Supplementary note 36

Question: 12.180
It can help to plan your route before starting a journey. You can do this by contacting
Mark one answer
a) your local filling station
b) a motoring organisation
c) the Driver Vehicle Licensing Agency
d) your vehicle manufacturer

Supplementary note 36

Question: 12.181
How can you plan your route before starting a long journey?
Mark one answer
a) Check your vehicle's workshop manual
b) Ask your local garage
c) Use a route planner on the internet
d) Consult your travel agents

Supplementary note 36

Question: 12.182
Planning your route before setting out can be helpful. How can you do this?
Mark one answer
a) Look in a motoring magazine
b) Only visit places you know
c) Try to travel at busy times
d) Print or write down the route

Supplementary note 36

Question: 12.183
Why is it a good idea to plan your journey to avoid busy times?
Mark one answer
a) You will have an easier journey
b) You will have a more stressful journey
c) Your journey time will be longer
d) It will cause more traffic congestion

Supplementary note 36

Question: 12.184
Planning your journey to avoid busy times has a number of advantages. One of these is
Mark one answer
a) your journey will take longer
b) you will have a more pleasant journey
c) you will cause more pollution
d) your stress level will be greater

Supplementary note 36

Question: 12.185
It is a good idea to plan your journey to avoid busy times. This is because
Mark one answer
a) your vehicle will use more fuel
b) you will see less road works
c) it will help to ease congestion
d) you will travel a much shorter distance

Supplementary note 36

Question: 12.186
By avoiding busy times when travelling
Mark one answer
a) you are more likely to be held up
b) your journey time will be longer
c) you will travel a much shorter distance
d) you are less likely to be delayed

Supplementary note 36

Question: 12.187
It can help to plan your route before starting a journey. Why should you also plan an alternative route?
Mark one answer
a) Your original route may be blocked
b) Your maps may have different scales
c) You may find you have to pay a congestion charge
d) Because you may get held up by a tractor

Supplementary note 36

Question: 12.188
As well as planning your route before starting a journey, you should also plan an alternative route. Why is this?
Mark one answer
a) To let another driver overtake
b) Your first route may be blocked
c) To avoid a railway level crossing
d) In case you have to avoid emergency vehicles

Supplementary note 36

Question: 12.189
Who of these will not have to pay Congestion Charges in London?
Mark one answer
a) A van driver making deliveries
b) A rider of a two-wheeled vehicle
c) A car driver whose vehicle is more than 1000 cc
d) A driver who just wants to park in the area

Supplementary note 37

Question: 12.190
You are making an appointment and will have to travel a long distance. You should
Mark one answer
a) allow plenty of time for your journey
b) plan to go at busy times
c) avoid all national speed limit roads
d) prevent other drivers from overtaking
Supplementary note 37

Question: 12.191
Congestion Charges apply in the London area. Who of these will NOT have to pay?
Mark one answer
a) A person who lives in the area
b) A driver making deliveries
c) A person who is just driving through the area
d) A driver with no other passengers in the vehicle
Supplementary note 37

Question: 12.192
Fuel consumption is at its highest when you are
Mark one answer
a) braking
b) coasting
c) accelerating
d) steering
Supplementary note 38

Question: 12.193
Missing out some gears saves fuel by reducing the amount of time you spend
Mark one answer
a) braking
b) coasting
c) steering
d) accelerating
Supplementary note 38

Question: 12.194
Rapid acceleration and heavy braking can lead to
Mark one answer
a) reduced pollution
b) increased fuel consumption
c) reduced exhaust emissions
d) increased road safety
Supplementary note 38

Question: 12.195
What style of driving causes increased risk to everyone?
Mark one answer
a) Considerate
b) Defensive
c) Competitive
d) Responsible
Supplementary note 38

Question: 12.196
What percentage of all emissions does road transport account for?
Mark one answer
a) 10%
b) 20%
c) 30%
d) 40%
Supplementary note 38

Question: 12.197
How can driving in an Eco-safe manner help protect the environment?
Mark one answer
a) Through the legal enforcement of speed regulations
b) By increasing the number of cars on the road
c) Through increased fuel bills
d) By reducing exhaust emissions
Supplementary note 38

Question: 12.198
How can missing out some gear changes save fuel?
Mark one answer
a) By reducing the amount of time you are accelerating
b) Because there is less need to use the footbrake
c) By controlling the amount of steering
D) Because coasting is kept to a minimum
Supplementary note 38

Question: 12.199
You will find that driving smoothly can
Mark one answer
a) reduce journey times by about 15%
b) increase fuel consumption by about 15%
c) reduce fuel consumption by about 15%
d) increase journey times by about 15%
Supplementary note 38

Question: 12.200
You can save fuel when conditions allow by
Mark one answer
a) using lower gears as often as possible
b) accelerating sharply in each gear
c) using each gear in turn
d) missing out some gears
Supplementary note 38

Question: 12.201
What does Eco-safe driving achieve?
Mark one answer
a) Increased fuel consumption
b) Improved road safety
c) Damage to the environment
d) Increased exhaust emissions
Supplementary note 38

Question: 12.202
You are driving through a tunnel. Your vehicle catches fire. What should you do?
Mark one answer
a) Continue through the tunnel if you can
b) Turn your vehicle around immediately
c) Reverse out of the tunnel
d) Carry out an emergency stop
Supplementary note 39

Question: 12.203
You are driving through a tunnel. There has been an accident and the car in front is on fire and blocking the road. What should you do?
Mark one answer
a) Overtake and continue as quickly as you can
b) Lock all the doors and windows
c) Switch on hazard warning lights
d) Stop, then reverse out of the tunnel
Supplementary note 39

Question: 12.204

You are in a tunnel. Your vehicle is on fire and you CANNOT drive it. What should you do?

Mark two answers

a) Stay in the vehicle and close the windows
b) Switch on hazard warning lights
c) Leave the engine running
d) Try and put out the fire
e) Switch off all of your lights
f) Wait for other people to phone for help

Supplementary note 39

Question: 12.205

Your vehicle catches fire while driving through a tunnel. It is still driveable. What should you do?

Mark one answer

a) Leave it where it is with the engine running
b) Pull up, then walk to an emergency telephone point
c) Park it away from the carriageway
d) Drive it out of the tunnel if you can do so

Supplementary note 39

Quiz Answers

Answers Section: 1

Book No		DSA Cat
1.1	b	6
1.2	ad	6
1.3	a	6
1.4	d	10
1.5	d	6
1.6	a	2
1.7	bd	10
1.8	a	6
1.9	d	6
1.10	b	3
1.11	b	3
1.12	d	3
1.13	a	14
1.14	a	14
1.15	a	14
1.16	a	14
1.17	bc	14
1.18	d	14
1.19	c	14
1.20	d	3
1.21	b	3
1.22	c	3
1.23	a	14
1.24	a	3
1.25	d	5
1.26	abe	12
1.27	cd	5
1.28	a	5
1.29	b	5
1.30	ac	5
1.31	abe	5
1.32	d	5
1.33	cd	5
1.34	abc	5
1.35	a	5
1.36	b	5
1.37	b	5
1.38	a	5
1.39	ad	1
1.40	ab	5
1.41	be	9
1.42	b	5
1.43	d	5
1.44	d	13
1.45	b	13
1.46	d	5
1.47	c	5
1.48	abd	5
1.49	ace	5
1.50	abc	5
1.51	c	5
1.52	b	5
1.53	d	5
1.54	c	5
1.55	d	5
1.56	c	5
1.57	c	5
1.58	a	5
1.59	ab	5

Answers Section: 2

Book No		DSA Cat
2.1	a	10
2.2	b	4
2.3	b	11
2.4	b	11
2.5	d	5
2.6	b	11
2.7	ace	10
2.8	abc	10
2.9	b	11
2.10	a	11
2.11	c	11
2.12	d	2
2.13	d	2
2.14	c	3
2.15	c	11
2.16	a	3
2.17	a	11
2.18	a	2
2.19	c	5
2.20	c	2
2.21	d	8
2.22	b	8
2.23	c	8
2.24	b	8
2.25	d	10
2.26	a	8
2.27	b	2
2.28	c	8
2.29	b	8
2.30	a	9
2.31	a	13
2.32	a	5
2.33	d	5
2.34	a	5
2.35	ab	13
2.36	b	11
2.37	c	9
2.38	a	13
2.39	a	5
2.40	d	5
2.41	a	13
2.42	c	4
2.43	b	4
2.44	b	4
2.45	c	8
2.46	b	4
2.47	b	4
2.48	bc	4
2.49	d	4
2.50	c	4
2.51	b	4
2.52	d	3
2.53	b	4
2.54	c	4
2.55	b	4
2.56	b	4
2.57	c	4
2.58	c	4
2.59	b	4
2.60	c	4
2.61	d	4
2.62	d	4
2.63	b	4
2.64	d	11
2.65	abdf	8
2.66	b	8
2.67	b	8
2.68	d	8
2.69	bd	8
2.70	c	4
2.71	b	8
2.72	c	8
2.73	c	8
2.74	c	10
2.75	d	10
2.76	b	10
2.77	d	9
2.78	d	10
2.79	b	10
2.80	a	10
2.81	c	9
2.82	c	9
2.83	ad	14
2.84	b	11
2.85	b	10
2.86	b	5
2.87	ae	5
2.88	d	4
2.89	d	2
2.90	a	4
2.91	d	2
2.92	a	4
2.93	b	2
2.94	ae	5
2.95	c	4
2.96	b	4
2.97	b	2
2.98	abd	8
2.99	b	4

Answers Section: 3

Book No		DSA Cat
3.1	c	11
3.2	b	11
3.3	c	11
3.4	a	11
3.5	c	11
3.6	c	11
3.7	c	8
3.8	c	9
3.9	c	9
3.10	c	9
3.11	c	11
3.12	b	9
3.13	d	9
3.14	c	5
3.15	a	7
3.16	a	11
3.17	ae	10
3.18	b	10
3.19	a	9
3.20	b	11
3.21	d	10
3.22	d	10
3.23	bef	10
3.24	ab	10
3.25	a	10
3.26	c	2
3.27	d	10
3.28	a	2
3.29	d	11
3.30	c	1
3.31	d	10
3.32	b	5
3.33	b	10
3.34	a	10
3.35	a	5
3.36	c	2
3.37	a	5
3.38	a	5
3.39	abe	5
3.40	ab	1
3.41	abcd	1
3.42	abcd	1
3.43	b	1
3.44	b	1
3.45	b	1
3.46	c	1
3.47	d	1
3.48	b	1
3.49	b	1
3.50	c	1
3.51	c	1
3.52	d	1
3.53	d	1
3.54	c	13
3.55	a	5
3.56	ace	5
3.57	cde	10
3.58	a	3
3.59	bf	5
3.60	d	6
3.61	a	8
3.62	a	8
3.63	a	3
3.64	a	11
3.65	d	11
3.66	b	11
3.67	b	11
3.68	a	5
3.69	c	4
3.70	d	3
3.71	c	6
3.72	d	5
3.73	b	2
3.74	d	2
3.75	c	2
3.76	c	8
3.77	d	10

Answers Section: 4

Book No		DSA Cat
4.1	c	1
4.2	abe	1
4.3	d	1
4.4	b	4
4.5	a	4
4.6	a	4
4.7	c	1
4.8	b	1
4.9	ac	6
4.10	c	6
4.11	a	6
4.12	b	7
4.13	ace	8
4.14	c	1
4.15	b	10
4.16	b	6
4.17	a	7
4.18	d	7
4.19	d	7
4.20	c	11
4.21	c	1
4.22	d	10
4.23	ace	4
4.24	a	8
4.25	b	5
4.26	d	7
4.27	d	7
4.28	c	2
4.29	c	8
4.30	b	2
4.31	c	5
4.32	c	2
4.33	b	7
4.34	b	6
4.35	b	6
4.36	b	6
4.37	b	6
4.38	c	6
4.39	b	6
4.40	b	11
4.41	a	5
4.42	b	11
4.43	b	10
4.44	c	1
4.45	a	10
4.46	a	10
4.47	a	10
4.48	c	11
4.49	b	11
4.50	d	8
4.51	a	11
4.52	c	11
4.53	d	11
4.54	c	11
4.55	c	11
4.56	b	11
4.57	a	11
4.58	a	5
4.59	c	2

Book No		Cat	Book No		Cat	Book No		Cat	Book No		Cat	Book No		Cat
4.60	d	6	5.12	c	5	6.9	bd	7	6.70	b	10	8.25	abe	13
4.61	c	6	5.13	a	6	6.10	ab	1	6.71	b	10	8.26	acf	13
4.62	b	6	5.14	b	5	6.11	c	8	6.72	c	8	8.27	b	6
4.63	d	6	5.15	c	6	6.12	c	13	6.73	a	8	8.28	bcde	13
4.64	a	10	5.16	d	6	6.13	cd	5	6.74	ad	4	8.29	c	13
4.65	d	5	5.17	c	6	6.14	d	4				8.30	d	9
4.66	c	6	5.18	c	5	6.15	a	8	**Answers Section: 7**			8.31	b	13
4.67	d	6	5.19	c	6	6.16	a	7	Book No		DSA Cat	8.32	a	13
4.68	d	10	5.20	c	6	6.17	d	4	7.1	adef	9	8.33	a	13
4.69	d	10	5.21	ace	6	6.18	d	4	7.2	adef	9	8.34	c	6
4.70	a	10	5.22	b	5	6.19	a	4	7.3	c	9	8.35	a	13
4.71	adf	10	5.23	c	5	6.20	d	8	7.4	d	9	8.36	abce	13
4.72	d	10	5.24	c	6	6.21	bdef	4	7.5	b	5	8.37	bde	13
4.73	a	6	5.25	d	6	6.22	d	8	7.6	b	11	8.38	b	12
4.74	a	6	5.26	b	5	6.23	d	4	7.7	d	9	8.39	ace	11
4.75	d	6	5.27	b	7	6.24	d	4	7.8	d	9	8.40	a	10
4.76	c	6	5.28	c	6	6.25	bd	4	7.9	c	9	8.41	c	9
4.77	ac	6	5.29	b	2	6.26	b	4	7.10	d	9	8.42	c	5
4.78	d	6	5.30	abd	6	6.27	d	4	7.11	a	9	8.43	acd	11
4.79	b	11	5.31	d	2	6.28	d	4	7.12	c	9	8.44	d	11
4.80	a	11	5.32	b	6	6.29	a	4	7.13	b	9	8.45	d	10
4.81	a	5	5.33	de	2	6.30	d	4	7.14	a	9	8.46	b	9
4.82	a	3	5.34	d	6	6.31	ae	4	7.15	a	9	8.47	b	9
4.83	a	2	5.35	c	5	6.32	d	7	7.16	d	9	8.48	c	11
4.84	a	6	5.36	c	6	6.33	b	4	7.17	b	9	8.49	c	10
4.85	a	2	5.37	a	6	6.34	a	11	7.18	a	9	8.50	c	10
4.86	c	10	5.38	b	6	6.35	b	8	7.19	a	9	8.51	a	10
4.87	d	5	5.39	a	2	6.36	d	4	7.20	b	11	8.52	c	5
4.88	b	2	5.40	d	5	6.37	d	7	7.21	d	9	8.53	c	13
4.89	d	6	5.41	d	6	6.38	b	7	7.22	c	9	8.54	b	5
4.90	a	2	5.42	a	7	6.39	a	7	7.23	a	9	8.55	a	13
4.91	b	10	5.43	a	7	6.40	c	8	7.24	d	9	8.56	abd	13
4.92	a	2	5.44	c	7	6.41	c	8	7.25	c	9	8.57	a	13
4.93	c	6	5.45	b	7	6.42	c	8	7.26	cdf	9	8.58	bdf	8
4.94	a	10	5.46	b	5	6.43	d	8	7.27	b	9	8.59	a	2
4.95	d	6	5.47	a	5	6.44	ce	8	7.28	c	9	8.60	b	2
4.96	ae	6	5.48	c	5	6.45	ab	8						
4.97	a	2	5.49	b	7	6.46	bd	8	**Answers Section: 8**			**Answers Section: 9**		
4.98	c	2	5.50	a	2	6.47	acd	8	Book No		DSA Cat	Book No		DSA Cat
4.99	a	10	5.51	d	7	6.48	b	8	8.1	be	13	9.1	b	11
4.100	d	10	5.52	a	7	6.49	b	8	8.2	b	13	9.2	a	11
4.101	b	10	5.53	b	7	6.50	d	8	8.3	d	8	9.3	a	11
4.102	b	6	5.54	a	2	6.51	a	8	8.4	c	13	9.4	bdf	11
4.103	d	1	5.55	cd	7	6.52	a	8	8.5	b	13	9.5	a	11
4.104	d	6	5.56	ac	7	6.53	bc	4	8.6	c	13	9.6	d	11
4.105	a	10	5.57	b	2	6.54	bc	4	8.7	def	13	9.7	c	11
			5.58	c	5	6.55	d	3	8.8	b	13	9.8	d	11
Answers Section: 5			5.59	b	7	6.56	a	10	8.9	c	9	9.9	a	11
Book No		DSA Cat	5.60	bc	7	6.57	a	10	8.10	a	9	9.10	b	7
5.1	abc	6	5.61	d	7	6.58	c	10	8.11	b	9	9.11	a	9
5.2	c	6	5.62	a	6	6.59	a	10	8.12	c	13	9.12	a	11
5.3	d	6				6.60	d	10	8.13	a	9	9.13	a	11
5.4	c	6	**Answers Section: 6**			6.61	ade	3	8.14	c	9	9.14	b	11
5.5	b	6	Book No		DSA Cat	6.62	abe	3	8.15	a	9	9.15	b	11
5.6	c	6	6.1	b	7	6.63	abd	10	8.16	a	13	9.16	d	11
5.7	d	6	6.2	d	8	6.64	a	10	8.17	a	13	9.17	b	11
5.8	b	5	6.3	a	8	6.65	bdef	10	8.18	b	13	9.18	d	11
5.9	d	6	6.4	a	8	6.66	ad	10	8.19	abe	13	9.19	b	5
5.10	d	6	6.5	b	8	6.67	a	3	8.20	b	13	9.20	c	10
5.11	d	6	6.6	a	8	6.68	a	10	8.21	ade	13	9.21	d	11
						6.69	b	3	8.22	a	13			

Q	Ans	Cat
9.22	b	11
9.23	a	11
9.24	d	11
9.25	b	11
9.26	a	11
9.27	a	11
9.28	b	10
9.29	d	11
9.30	c	11
9.31	d	11
9.32	c	11
9.33	d	11
9.34	a	11
9.35	c	11
9.36	d	11
9.37	d	11
9.38	c	11
9.39	b	11
9.40	b	11
9.41	c	11
9.42	b	11
9.43	a	11
9.44	c	11
9.45	c	11
9.46	d	11
9.47	a	11
9.48	d	11

Answers Section: 10

Book No	DSA Cat	
10.1	a	11
10.2	b	11
10.3	c	11
10.4	c	11
10.5	acef	11
10.6	d	11
10.7	a	11
10.8	a	11
10.9	a	11
10.10	b	11
10.11	b	11
10.12	d	11
10.13	b	11
10.14	d	11
10.15	c	11
10.16	b	11
10.17	c	11
10.18	a	11
10.19	b	11
10.20	c	10
10.21	b	6
10.22	d	6
10.23	c	5
10.24	b	11
10.25	a	11
10.26	c	11
10.27	a	11
10.28	d	11
10.29	a	5
10.30	b	11
10.31	c	11
10.32	b	6
10.33	a	6
10.34	b	11
10.35	a	11
10.36	a	11
10.37	a	11
10.38	d	6
10.39	a	11
10.40	a	11
10.41	c	11
10.42	d	11
10.43	d	11
10.44	c	11
10.45	b	11
10.46	c	11
10.47	c	11
10.48	a	11
10.49	c	11
10.50	d	10
10.51	c	11
10.52	b	11
10.53	b	11
10.54	c	11
10.55	b	11
10.56	b	11
10.57	c	9
10.58	c	11
10.59	c	11
10.60	a	11
10.61	a	11
10.62	d	11
10.63	d	10
10.64	a	11
10.65	d	5
10.66	d	11
10.67	c	5
10.68	b	5
10.69	a	11
10.70	c	11
10.71	a	11
10.72	b	3
10.73	b	6
10.74	c	6
10.75	b	11
10.76	d	6
10.77	c	6
10.78	c	13
10.79	cd	5

Answers Section: 11

Book No	DSA Cat	
11.1	b	12
11.2	d	12
11.3	b	12
11.4	c	12
11.5	c	12
11.6	b	12
11.7	c	12
11.8	c	12
11.9	abd	12
11.10	abf	12
11.11	bce	12
11.12	c	12
11.13	cd	12
11.14	d	12
11.15	bc	5
11.16	ab	12
11.17	d	6
11.18	c	12
11.19	be	12
11.20	b	5
11.21	bcdf	3
11.22	cde	3
11.23	d	13
11.24	ab	3
11.25	b	3
11.26	b	3
11.27	d	3
11.28	bef	3
11.29	cd	13
11.30	bc	3
11.31	ce	13
11.32	b	3
11.33	b	3
11.34	b	3
11.35	d	3
11.36	d	13
11.37	be	13
11.38	c	3
11.39	d	3
11.40	a	3
11.41	c	3
11.42	c	3
11.43	b	3
11.44	d	3
11.45	b	3
11.46	c	3
11.47	a	3
11.48	b	3
11.49	b	3
11.50	d	3
11.51	cd	13
11.52	def	13
11.53	acf	13
11.54	ae	13
11.55	c	13
11.56	d	13
11.57	abd	13
11.58	ace	13
11.59	acde	13
11.60	bc	13
11.61	cde	13
11.62	a	13
11.63	b	13
11.64	d	13
11.65	c	13
11.66	b	13
11.67	bde	13
11.68	d	12

Answers Section: 12

Book No	DSA Cat	
12.1	c	12
12.2	cde	12
12.3	d	12
12.4	d	12
12.5	d	12
12.6	bd	12
12.7	d	12
12.8	a	12
12.9	d	6
12.10	d	6
12.11	b	12
12.12	b	12
12.13	a	12
12.14	c	12
12.15	c	12
12.16	b	12
12.17	c	12
12.18	d	12
13.19	b	12
13.20	b	12
12.21	c	3
12.22	abf	3
12.23	abf	3
12.24	abc	3
12.25	bdf	3
12.26	a	3
12.27	d	3
12.28	d	3
12.29	b	3
12.30	bcd	3
12.31	d	3
12.32	ae	3
12.33	acf	3
12.34	b	3
12.35	c	3
12.36	d	3
12.37	cd	3
12.38	d	3
12.39	abc	3
12.40	ab	3
12.41	ade	3
12.42	c	3
12.43	d	3
12.44	bdf	3
12.45	b	3
12.46	c	3
12.47	d	9
12.48	bd	14
12.49	d	3
12.50	b	3
12.51	a	3
12.52	bc	3
12.53	de	3
12.54	a	3
12.55	d	3
12.56	d	3
12.57	b	3
12.58	a	8
12.59	a	3
12.60	d	5
12.61	ac	1
13.62	b	1
13.63	b	1
13.64	b	1
13.65	b	1
12.66	a	5
12.67	a	6
13.68	b	1
12.69	a	3
12.70	a	2
12.71	c	3
12.72	bc	4
12.73	b	1
12.74	d	13
12.75	c	13
12.76	b	13
12.77	b	13
12.78	a	8
12.79	c	8
12.80	bd	8
12.81	d	3
12.82	d	3
12.83	ab	3
12.84	a	10
12.85	c	10
12.86	d	10
12.87	d	14
12.88	c	11
12.89	a	11
12.90	a	11
12.91	c	11
12.92	b	11
12.93	d	6
12.94	a	11
12.95	c	1
12.96	a	13
12.97	b	13
12.98	a	6
12.99	b	10
12.100	de	8
12.101	c	13
12.102	c	8
12.103	a	10
12.104	c	5
12.105	b	7
12.106	b	14
12.107	d	14
12.108	d	14
13.109	a	14
13.110	a	8
12.111	b	5
12.112	a	4
12.113	d	2
12.114	a	2
12.115	bcd	2
12.116	b	2
12.117	abe	2
12.118	d	1

12.119	c	6	12.178	b	10
12.120	d	5	12.179	a	3
12.121	c	1	12.180	b	3
12.122	d	5	12.181	c	3
12.123	a	11	12.182	d	3
12.124	d	2	12.183	a	3
12.125	a	7	12.184	b	3
12.126	d	5	12.185	c	3
12.127	a	1	12.186	d	3
12.128	c	10	12.187	a	3
12.129	a	1	12.188	b	3
12.130	b	5	12.189	b	3
12.131	b	6	12.190	a	3
12.132	b	2	12.191	a	3
12.133	c	2	12.192	c	3
12.134	d	8	12.193	d	3
12.135	a	5	12.194	b	3
12.136	c	1	12.195	c	2
12.137	d	1	12.196	b	3
12.138	bdf	1	12.197	d	3
12.139	b	7	12.198	a	3
12.140	ace	4	12.199	c	3
12.141	c	8	12.200	d	3
12.142	c	8	12.201	b	3
12.143	a	12	12.202	a	13
12.144	b	12	12.203	c	13
12.145	a	10	12.204	bd	13
12.146	b	3	12.205	d	13
12.147	d	3			
12.148	d	3			
12.149	b	3			
12.150	d	10			
12.151	b	3			
12.152	a	3			
12.153	d	6			
12.154	b	2			
12.155	c	1			
12.156	d	6			
12.157	cd	8			
12.158	a	2			
12.159	d	10			
12.160	b	9			
12.161	d	9			
12.162	b	11			
12.163	a	13			
12.164	b	9			
12.165	b	9			
12.166	a	9			
12.167	d	9			
12.168	a	9			
12.169	b	9			
12.170	d	9			
12.171	d	9			
12.172	b	9			
12.173	d	9			
12.174	d	9			
12.175	b	9			
12.176	c	9			
12.177	d	9			

Theory Test Centres

Aberdeen, Migvie House (Ground flr east wing), 23 North Silver Street, Aberdeen, Aberdeenshire, AB10 1RJ
Aberystwyth, 33 North Parade, Ground floor unit, Aberystwyth, Ceredigion, SY23 2JH
Aldershot, 1 London House (Ground flr), Pickford Street, Aldershot, Hampshire, GU11 1TY
Ayr, 7A Boswell Park (1st flr), Ayr, South Ayrshire, KA7 1NP
Ballymena, Tower Centre (Unit 19), Lower Mill Street, Ballymena, Antrim, BT43 6AH
Bangor, Bangor Railway Station, Station Road, Bangor, Gwynedd, LL57 ILZ
Barnstaple, Riverside Court, Castle Street, Barnstaple, Devon, EX31 1DR
Barrow, 111 Duke Street, Barrow in Furness, Barrow, Cumbria, LA14 1XA
Basildon, Southgate House Suite 1A (1st flr), Town Square, Basildon, Essex, SS14 1BN
Basingstoke, The Square (part Ground Floor), Basing View, Basingstoke, Hampshire, RG21 4EB
Bath, 1st floor East Suite, Charter House The Square Lower Bristol Road, Bath, Somerset, BA2 3BH
Belfast, Chambers of Commerce House (5th flr), 22 Great Victoria Street, Belfast, Nothern Ireland, BT2 7LX
Berwick, Shop Unit 3 Border Court, Woolmarket Berwick upon Tweed, Berwick, Berwick, TD15 1DP
Birkenhead, 2 Europa Boulevard (2nd flr), Conway Park, Birkenhead, Cheshire, CH41 4PE
Birmingham, St Chads Queensway, 1 Snowhill Plaza, Birmingham, West Midlands, B4 6JG
Blackpool, Darwin Court (Unit 9A Ground flr), Blackpool Technology Exchange, Blackpool, Lancashire, FY2 OJN
Bolton, 34 Queensbrook, Bolton Technology Exchange, Bolton, Lancashire, BL1 4AY
Boston, 3 Bridge Street, Boston, Lincolnshire, PE21 8QF
Bournemouth, Roddis House (3rd flr), Old Christchurch Road, Bournemouth, Dorset, BH1 1LG
Bradford, Caspian House (1st flr), 61 East Parade, Bradford, Yorkshire, BD1 5EP
Brighton, Fourth Floor, Victoria House, 125 Queens Road, Brighton, East Sussex, BN1 3WB
Bristol, Tower House (3rd flr), Fairfax Street, Bristol, Gloucestershire, BS1 3BN
Builth Wells, Spar Buildings (rear end), The Strand Grove Street, Builth Wells, Brecknockshire, LD2 3DN
Bury St Edmunds, St Edmunds House (2nd flr North Ent), Lower Baxter Street, Bury St Edmunds, Suffolk, IP33 1ET
Cambridge, St Andrews House (2nd flr), St Andrews Street, Cambridge, Cambridgeshire, CB2 3BZ
Canterbury, St.James House (1st flr), Castle Street, Canterbury, Kent, CT1 2QZ
Cardiff, Limerick House (3rd flr), 23 Churchill Way, Cardiff, South Glamorgan, CF10 2HE
Carlisle, 10 A Lowther Street, Carlisle, Cumbria, CA3 8DA
Chatham, 14-16 High Street, Chatham, London, Kent, ME4 4EP
Chelmsford, Grosvenor House (1st flr), 51 New London Road, Chelmsford, Essex, CM2 OND
Cheltenham, Unit D Pate Court North Place, St. Margarets Road, Cheltenham, Gloucestershire, GL50 4DY
Chester, 1 Corbridge House, The Square, Chester, Cheshire, CH1 3AN
Chesterfield, 6-8 Corporation street, Suite 1B (1st flr), Chesterfield, Derbyshire, S41 7TP
Clydebank, (1st Flr Suite F2 Unit 4), Blair Court Clydebank Business Park, Clydebank, Strathclyde, G81 2LA
Colchester, Century House South, Riverside Office Centre North Station Road, Colchester, Essex, CO1 1RD
Coventry, Warwick Gate (1st flr), 21/22 Warwick Row, Coventry, Warwickshire, CV1 1ET
Crawley, Belgrave House (1st flr), Station Road , Crawley, West Sussex, RH10 1HU
Croydon, Central House (2nd flr), 27 Park Street, Croydon, London, Surrey, CRO 1YD
Derby, Part Ground Floor East Wing, 100 Mansfield Road, Derby, Derbyshire, DE1 3TT
Doncaster, Office 6 Silver House, Silver Street, Doncaster, Yorkshire, DN1 1HL
Dudley, Trafalgar House (Lower Ground flr), 47-49 Kings Street, Dudley, West Midlands, DY2 8PS

Dumfries, 77/79 Whitesands, Unit 3, Dumfries, Dumfries & Galloway, DG1 2RX
Dundee, 14/22 Exchange Street, Unit 2, Dundee, Tayside, DD1 3DE
Dunfermline, Unit 3 Evans Business Centre, 15 Pitreavie Court Pitreavie Business Park, Dunfermline, Fife, KY11 8UU
Durham, Suite 1 Abbeywoods Business Park, Abbey Road, Durham, DH1 5TH
Eastbourne, Senlac House (Ground flr), 55 Seaside, Eastbourne, East Sussex, BN22 7NE
Edinburgh, Cairncross House (suite 2 2nd floor), 25 union Street, Edinburgh, Lothian, EH1 3LR
Exeter, Renslade House (Suite 2), Bonhay Road, Exeter, Devon, EX4 3AY
Fareham, Persimmon House Ground flr The Parkway, 100 Wickham Road, Fareham, Hampshire, PO16 7HT
Fort William, St. Marys House, Gordon Square, Fort William, Highland, OH33 6DY
Gairloch, Gairloch Community Centre, Achtercairn, Gairloch, Highland, IV21 2BP
Galashiels, 45 High Street, Galashiels, Scottish Borders, TD1 1RY
Glasgow, Newton House (3rd flr), 457 Sauchiehall Street, Glasgow, Strathclyde, G2 3LG
Gloucester, Eastgate House, 121-131 Eastgate Street, Gloucester, Gloucester, GL1 1PX
Grantham, Unit 39, The George Shopping Centre, Guildhall Street, Grantham, NG31 6NJ.
Greenock, Victory Court (ground flr north), Cartsburn Martime Arthur Street, Greenock, Inverclyde, PA15 4RT
Grimsby, Acorn Business Park (Ground Flr Unit 8&9), Moss Road, Grimsby, Lincolnshire, DN32 0LW
Guildford, The Old Magistrates Court, 71 North Street, Guildford, Surrey, GU1 4AW
Harlow, Terminus House (11th flr), Terminus Street, Harlow, Essex, CM20 1XA
Harrogate, Strayside House, 27 West Park, Harrogate, North Yorkshire, HG1 1BJ
Hastings, Phillips House, Drury Lane , Ponswood Industrial Estate, St Leonards, Hastings, East Sussex, TN38 9BA
Haverfordwest, 34 High St, 1st floor offices, Haverfordwest, Dyfed, SA61 2DA
Helmsdale, Helmsdale Community Centre, Dunrobin Street, Helmsdale, Sutherland, KW8 6JX
Hereford, Penn House (Ground flr rear), 9/10 Broad Street, Hereford, Herefordshire, HR4 9AP
Huddersfield, Ramsden House (5th flr), New Street, Huddersfield, Yorkshire, HD1 2TW
Hull, Kingston House South Unit 14/15, Bond Street, Hull, Yorkshire, HU1 3EN
Huntly, Market Muir Car Park, Huntly, Aberdeenshire, AB54 8ET
Ilford, Valentine House (4th flr), 51-69 Ilford Hill, Ilford, London, Essex, IG1 2DG
Inverness, Ballantyne House Suites 1&2 1st floor, 84 Academy Street, Inverness, Highland, IV1 1LU
Ipswich, Crown House, Crown Street, Ipswich, Suffolk, IP1 3HS
Isle of Arran, Auchrannie Country House & Hotel, Brodick, Isle of Arran, KA27 8BZ
Isle of Barra, Castlebay community High School, Castlebay, Isle of Barra, HS9 5XD
Isle of Benbecula, Unit 1, Benbecula College, Liniclate, Isle of Benbecula, HS7 5PJ
Isle of Islay, Islay & Jura CVS, High Street, Bowmore, Isle of Islay, PA43 7JE
Isle of Mull, Craignure Village Hall, Craignure, Isle of Mull, PA56 6AY
Isle of Tiree, Tiree High School, Tiree, Isle of Tiree, PA77 6XT
Isle of Wight, 48 Lugley Street, Newport, Isle of Wight, Isle of Wight, PO30 5HD
Isles of Scilly, The Scillonian Club, The Parade, St Marys, Isles of Scilly, TR21 0LP
Kings Lynn, The Mission Hall, Ship Lane St Anns Street, Kings Lynn, Norfolk, PE30 1LT
Kingston upon Thames, Drapers Court (4th floor), Kingston Hall Road, Kingston upon Thames, London, KT1 2BQ
Kirkwall, 7/13 Laing Street (Ground flr), Kirkwall, Orkney Islands, KW15 1NW
Kyle of Lochalsh, Harbour Car Park Railway Pier, Kyle of Lochalsh, Rosshire, IV40 8AQ

155

Leeds, Gallery House (1st flr), The Headrow, Leeds, Leeds, LS1 5RD

Leicester, Rutland centre (Office suite 3A 3rd flr), 56 Halford Street, Leicester, Leicestershire, LE1 1TQ

Lerwick, Toll Clock Shopping Centre (Unit 6V), 26 North Road, Lerwick, Shetland, ZE1 OPE

Lincoln, Queensgate House (1st flr), Silver Street, Lincoln, Lincolnshire, LN2 1EW

Liverpool, Orleans House (3rd flr), Edmund Street, Liverpool, Merseyside, L3 9NG

Londonderry, City Factory (part ground flr), 19 Queen Street, Londonderry, Derry, BT48 7EF

Lowestoft, Waveney Chambers (2nd flr), Waveney Road, Lowestoft, Suffolk, NR32 1BN

Luton, 70/78 Collingdon Street, Luton, Bedfordshire, LU1 1RX

Manchester, 111 Piccadilly (5th flr), Manchester, Greater Manchester, M1 2HY

Mansfield, Ground Floor Offices, 32-34 Rosemary Street, Mansfield, Nottinghamshire, NG18 1QL

Merthyr Tydfill, Castle House (1st flr), Glebeland Street, Merthyr Tydfill, Mid Glamorgan, CF47 8AT

Middlesbrough, Cleveland Business Centre (Unit 6), 1 Watson Street, Middlesbrough, Cleveland, TS1 2RQ

Milton Keynes, Tempus House (Ground flr), 249 Midsummer boulevard, Milton Keynes, Buckinghamshire, MK9 1YA

Motherwell, Unit 1B, Orbiston Business Park, 347 Orbiston Street, Motherwell, North Lanarkshire, ML1 1QW

Newcastle upon Tyne, Collingwood House (1st Flr), 3 Collingwood Street, Newcastle upon Tyne, Newcastle upon Tyne, NE1 1JW

Newport, Clarence House (6th floor), Clarence Place, Newport, Gwent, NP19 7AA

Newry, 12 John Mitchel Place (2nd flr), Newry, Co Down, BT34 2BP

Northampton, Sol House (Suite 201), St.Katherines Street, Northampton, Northampton, NN1 2QZ

Norwich, St.Cuthberts House (1st flr), 7 Upper King Street, Norwich, Norfolk, NR3 1RB

Nottingham, Rodney House (Suite G2 ground flr), Castle Gate, Nottingham, Nottinghamshire, NG1 7AW

Oban, The Corran Halls, No. 54 The Esplanade, Oban, Oban, Argyll, PA34 5RT

Oldham, 5a/6a Whitney Court, Southlink Business Park, Oldham, Gter Manchester, OL4 1DE

Omagh, Anderson House (2nd flr), 33 Market Street, Omagh, County Tyrone, BT78 1EE

Oxford, 58 St Aldates (3rd flr), Oxford, Oxfordshire, OX1 1ST

Southgate, Crown House 2nd floor, 47 Chase Side Southgate, London, London, N14 5BP

Penzance, Market House (Upper 1st flr), Market Place Market Jew Street, Penzance, Cornwall, TR18 2JE

Peterborough, 41 Broadway (1st Flr), Peterborough, Cambridgeshire, PE1 1SJ

Pitlochry, 2 BurnsideRoad, Pitlochry, Perthshire, P16 5AL

Plymouth, Princess Court (1st flr), Princess Street, Plymouth, Devon, PL1 2EX

Portadown, Lismore House, 23 Church Street, Portadown, County Armagh, BT62 3LN

Portsmouth, Venture Tower (4th flr), Fratton Road, Portsmouth, Hampshire, PO1 5DL

Preston, Norwest Court (ground flr), Guildhall Street, Preston, Lancashire, PR1 3NU

Reading, Hanover House (3rd flr), 202 Kings Road, Reading, Berkshire, RG1 4NN

Redditch, Grosvenor House (2nd flr), Prospect Hill, Redditch, Worcestershire, B97 4DL

Rhyl, 3 Bodfor Street, Rhyl, North Wales, LL18 1AS

Runcorn, 1A Whitworth Court (Ground Flr), Manor Farm Road, Runcorn, Cheshire, WA7 1WA

Salford, The Lighthouse, 14 The Quays, Salford Quays, Salford, Greater Manchester, M50 3XT

Salisbury, 39 Brown Street, Salisbury, Wiltshire, SP1 2AS

Scarborough, 29-30 St Nicholas Street, Suite 2, Scarborough, Yorkshire, YO11 2HF

Scunthorpe, Haldenby House (Unit 2), Berkeley Business Park Doncaster Road, Scunthorpe, South Humberside, DN15 7DQ

Sheffield, Orchard House (3rd flr), Leopold Street, Sheffield, Yorkshire, S1 2GY

Shrewsbury, Canon Court West (Suite 2), Abbey Lawn Abbey Foregate, Shrewsbury, Shropshire, SY2 5DE

Sidcup, Kingswood House (1st florr), High Street, Sidcup Hill, Sidcup, Kent, DA14 6HQ

Slough, Brooklands House, Petersfield Avenue, Slough, SL2 5DY

Solihull, Corner Oaks (part 1st floor), 1 Homer Road, Solihull, West Midlands, B91 3QG

Southampton, Capital house (6th floor), Houndwell Place, Southampton, Hampshire, SO14 1HU

Southend-On-Sea, Baryta House (4th flr), West Wing 29 Victoria Avenue, Southend-On-Sea, Essex, SS2 6AZ

Southgate, Crown House (1st flr), 47 Chase Side, Southgate, N14 5BP

Southport, Gordon House (Suite 6), Leicester Street, Southport, Lancashire, PR9 OER

Southwark, 9 Holyrood Street (1st flr), Southwark, London, London, SE1 2EL

St Helens, Century House (2nd flr), Hardshaw Street, St Helens, Merseyside, WA10 1QU

Staines, Church House (ground flr), Church Street Staines, Staines, London, TW18 4EP

Stevenage, Southgate House (6th flr), St Georges Way, Stevenage, Hertsfordshire, SG1 1HG

Stirling, Hillside House (suite 1A), Laurelhill Business Park, Stirling, Stirlingshire, FK7 9JQ

Stockport, Kingsgate (Ground floor), Wellington, Stockport, Gter Manchester, SK4 1EX

Stoke on Trent, Whittle Court (Unit 8A), Town Road, Stoke on Trent, Staffordshire, ST1 2QE

Stornoway, Cromwell Street Quay (Unit 3), Harbour View, Stornoway, Isle of Lewis, HS1 2DF

Stranraer, 56 George Street, Stranraer, Dumfries & Galloway, DG9 7RH

Stratford Upon Avon, Packwood House (2nd flr), Guild Street, Stratford Upon Avon, Warwickshire, CV37 6RP

Sunderland, Havelock Buildings (2nd flr), 6 Fawcett Street, Sunderland, Tyne and Wear, SR1 1SJ

Sutton Coldfield, Four Oaks House (Ground flr), Lichfield Road, Sutton Coldfield, West Midlands, B74 2TZ

Swansea, Grove House (2nd flr), 3 Grove Place, Swansea, Glamorgan, SA1 5DF

Swindon, South Suite (Ground Flr), 30-33 Milton Road, Swindon, Wiltshire, SN1 5JA

Tarbert , The Surgery, School Street, Tarbert, Argyll & Bute, PA29 6UL

Taunton, Victoria House (2nd flr), Victoria Street, Taunton, Somerset, TA1 3JA

Tongue, St Andrews Glebe Industial Estate, Tongue, Highland, IV27 4XB

Torquay, Rooms 37, 38 and 39, Castle Circus House, 136 Union Street, Torquay, TQ2 5QB.

Truro, Palace Buildings Public rooms, Quay Street, Truro, Cornwall, TR1 2HE

Uxbridge, Wellington House (Ground flr), 4/10 Cowley Road, Uxbridge, Middlesex, UB8 2XW

Watford, Cassiobury House 1st floor, 11-19 Station Road, Watford, Hertfordshire, WD17 1AN

Weymouth, Phoenix House, St. Nicholas Street, Weymouth, Dorset, DT4 8AA

Wick, Unit 5D Airport House, Airport Industrail Estate, Wick, KW1 4QS

Wigan, Ground and Basement, 38/40 Market Street, Wigan, Gter Manchester, WN1 1JG

Wolverhampton, Derwent House (2nd flr), 42-46 Waterloo Road, Wolverhampton, West Midlands, WV1 4XB

Worcester, Haswell House (3rd floor), Block B1 St Nicolas Street, Worcester, West Midlands, WR1 1UN

Workington, Solway House, Oxford Street, Workington, Cumbria, CA14 2AL

Worthing, Chatsworth House (first floor), 31 Chatsworth Road, Worthing, West Sussex, BN11 1LY

Yeovil, The Coach House (Ground Flr), St Nicholas Close Penn Hill, Yeovil, Somerset, BA20 1SF

York, Stirling House, Station Business Park, Holgate Park Drive, York, North Yorkshire, YO26 4GB

Driving Test Centres

Aberdeen (Altens), Unit, 10 Burnbank Business Centre, Aberdeen, Aberdeenshire, AB12 3LF

Aberdeen (Balgownie Road), Balgownie Road, Bridge of Don, Aberdeen, AB22 8GT

Aberfeldy, Town Hall, Crieff Road, Aberfeldy, Perth and Kinross, PH15 2BJ

Abergavenny, Station Road, Abergavenny, Gwent, NP7 5HT

Aberystwyth (Park Avenue), Yr Hen Ysgol, Alexandra Road, Aberystwyth, SY23 1LE

Airdrie, 7 Aitchison Street, Sword Street, Airdrie, ML6 0DA

Aldershot, The Portacabin, North Lane, Aldershot, GU12 4SU

Alness, Unit 22 Fyrish Way, Alness, Scotland, IV17 0PJ

Alnwick, Roxburgh House, Green Batt, Alnwick, NE66 1LA

Arbroath, 1 Lochlands Drive, Arbroath, Scotland, DD11 3AT

Ashford (Kent), Crown Buildings, Wellesley Road, Ashford, TN24 8EN

Ashford (Middlesex), 18/19 Fir Tree Place, Church Road, Ashford, TW15 2PH

Aylesbury, Morgan House, Walton Grove, Aylesbury, HP21 7SL

Ayr, 161 Whitletts Road, Ayr, South Ayrshire, KA8 9JQ

Bala, Unit 4, Penllyn Workshops, Bala, LL23

Ballachulish, Mountain Rescue Centre, Glencoe, Balachulish, PA49 4HP

Ballater, The Lecture Room, Ballater Fire Station Anderson Road, Ballater, AB35 5QW

Banbury, 3 West Bar Street, Banbury, Oxfordshire, OX16 9SD

Banff, C/O Dept. of Employment, 23/25 Castle Street, Banff, AB45 1DJ

Bangor, Bryn Llwyd, Coed Mawr, Bangor, LL57 4SW

Barking, 84 Tanner Street, Barking, Essex, IG11 8QF

Barnet, Raydean House 15/17 Western Parade, Barnet, Middlesex, EN5 1AD

Barnsley, West Road, Barnsley, South Yorkshire, S75 2DH

Barnstaple, Portmarsh, Victoria, Barnstaple, EX32 9HT

Barra Island, The Pier, Castlebay, Isle of Barra, HS9 5XD

Barrow In Furness, Trinity Enterprise Centre, Unit 11 Ironworks Road, Barrow-In-Furness, LA14 2PN

Barry, 41 Dock View Road, Barry, Vale of Glamorgan, CF63 4JP

Basingstoke, Brighton Hill Centre, Basingstoke, Hampshire, RG22 4LR

Bathgate, 74 Glasgow Road, Bathgate, Edinburgh, EH48 2AG

Bedford, Portman House, 59/63 Goldington Road, Bedford, MK40 3LT

Belvedere, 33 Woolwich Road, Belvedere, Kent, DA17 5EE

Benbecula Island, Balivanich Airport, Benbecula Island, Scotland, HS7 5LA

Berwick upon Tweed, Tweedmouth Ind. Estate, Northumberland Street, Berwick upon Tweed, TD15 2UY

Bettyhill, C/O Bettyhill Post Office, Bettyhill, Thurso, KW14 7SP

Beverley LGV, Old Beck Road, off Groveshill Road, Beverley, HU17 0JG

Bexleyheath, 38 Avenue Road, Bexleyheath, Kent, DA7 4EG

Birmingham (Kings Heath), 955 Alcester Road South, Birmingham, West Midlands, B14 5JA

Birmingham (Kingstanding), 205 Birdbrook Road, Kingstanding, Birmingham, B44 9UL

Birmingham (Quinton), Crown Buildings 74 Ridgacre Lane, Quinton, Birmingham, B32 1EN

Birmingham (Shirley), 401 Stratford Road, Shirley, Solihull, B90 4AA

Birmingham (South Yardley), Clay Lane, South Yardley, West Midlands, B26 1EA

Birmingham (Sutton Coldfield), 110/116 Boldmere Road, Sutton Coldfield, West Midlands, B73 5UB

Birmingham (Washwood Heath), 68/70 Coleshill Road, Hodgehill, Birmingham, B36 8AB

Bishop Auckland, Bob Hardisty Drive, Bishop Auckland, County Durham, DL14 7TL

Bishops Stortford, South Road, Bishops Stortford, Hertfordshire, CM23 3LD

Blackburn, 50 Preston New Road, Blackburn, Lancashire, BB02 6AH

Blackpool, Government Buildings, Warbreck Hill Road, Blackpool, FY02 0XE

Blairgowrie, Retained Fire Station, West George Street, Blairgowrie, PH10 6DZ

Bletchley, Block 4 Government Buildings, Wilton Hostel Wilton Avenue, Bletchley, MK3 6DH

Blyth, Unit 3 Sextant House, Freehold Street, Blyth, NE24 3EX

Bodmin, Bell Lane, Dennison Road, Bodmin, PL31 2JL

Bolton, Weston Street, Bolton, Lancashire, BL03 2AW

Borehamwood, Unit 1-3, Elstree Gate, Elstree Way, Borehamwood, Hertfordshire, WD6 1JD

Boston, Unit 2 Plot 3, Redstone Industrial Estate, Spalding Road, Boston, PE21 8AL

Bournemouth, 21/23 Gillam Road, Northbourne, Bournemouth, BH10 6BW

Bradford (Eccleshill), Victoria House, Victoria Road, Eccleshill, Bradford, BD02 2DD

Bradford (Heaton), 15 Farfield Street, Heaton, Bradford, BD09 5AS

Brecon, Camden Road, Brecon, Powys, LD3 7RY

Brentwood, 89 Warley Hill, Brentwood, Essex, CM14 5JN

Bridgend, Crown Buildings, Angel Street, Bridgend, CF31 4AD

Bridlington, Crown Buildings, Quay Road, Bridlington, YO16 4LY

Brighton, The Octagon, Village Square Complex, Brighton Marina Village, Brighton, BN2 1NB

Bristol (Brislington), Government Buildings, Flowers Hill, Bath Road, Bristol, BS4 5JX

Bristol (Southmead), 2 Concord Drive, Southmead, Bristol, BS10 6PZ

Bristol (St George), 226 Kingsway, St George, Bristol, BS5 8NF

Broadstairs (Thanet), The Cottage, Pierremont Hall, Broadstairs, CT10 1JH

Brodick (Isle of Arran), Royal Mail Delivery Office, Mayish Road, Brodick, KA27 8AU

Buckie, The Fire Station, East Cathcart Street, Buckie, AB56 1QJ

Burton-On-Trent, The Gatehouse, Victoria Crescent, Burton-On-Trent, DE14 2QD

Bury (Lancs), Smith Street, Bury, Lancashire, BL09 6HH

Bury St Edmunds, Tritron House, St Andrews Street North, Bury St Edmunds, IP33 1TJ

Buxton, The Dairy, 7 Green Lane, Buxton, SK17 9DS

Callander, Burgh Chambers, South Church Street, Callander, FK17 8BN

Camborne L + LGV, Wilson Way, Redruth, Cornwall, TR15 3RP

Cambridge (Chesterton Road), 73/79 Chesterton Road, Cambridge, CB4 3AP

Cambridge (Cowley Road), Cowley Road, Cambridge, Cambridgeshire, CB4 0DT

Campbeltown, Crown Buildings, Hall Street, Campbeltown, PA28 6BD

Cannock, Suite 3 ground floor, Commerce House, Ridings Park (off Phoenix Road), Hawks Green Lane, Cannock, Staffordshire, WS11 7FJ

Canterbury, 25 New Dover Road, Canterbury, Kent, CT1 3AS

Cardiff (Fairwater), 30 Norbury Road, Fairwater, Cardiff, CF5 5HU

Cardigan, Crown Building, Napier Street, Cardigan, SA43 1ED

Carlisle, Hill Crest Avenue, Carlisle, Cumbria, CA1 2QJ

Carmarthen, Ty Myrddin, Crown Building, Old Station Road, Carmarthen, SA31 1GS

Castle Douglas, 33-37 Cotton Street, Castle Douglas, DG7 1AJ

Cheetham Hill – Manchester, Alderglen Road, Cheetham, Manchester, M8 0TD

Chelmsford, Synergy Centre, 4 Hoffmanns Way, Chelmsford, CM1 1GU

Cheltenham, Bishopsgate House, 94 All Saints Road, Cheltenham, GL52 2HQ

Chertsey, Unit 4, The Forum, Hanworth Industrial Estate, Hanworth Lane, Chertsey, KT16 9JX

Chester, 95 Bond Parade, Dicksons Drive, Newton, CH02 2ND

Chesterfield, Bus Garage Approach Road, Stonegravels, Chesterfield, S41 7LF

Chichester, Wyman House , Shopwhyke Road, Chichester, PO20 6AA

Chingford, Doric House, 128 Station Road, Chingford, E4 6AD

Chippenham, Unit 11 Cavalier Court, Bumpers Farm, Chippenham, SN14 6LH

Chorley, Rossall Road, Chorley, Lancashire, PR06 0BT

Clacton-On-Sea, 103/105 Carnarvon Road, Clacton on Sea, Essex, CO15 6PR

Cleethorpes, 62 Sydney Street, Cleethorpes, South Humberside, DN35 7NQ

Colchester, Grange Way, Colchester, Essex, CO2 8HF

Colwyn Bay, Government Buildings, Dinerth Road, Rhos on Sea, LL28 4UL

Congleton, 27 West Street, Congleton, Cheshire, CW12 3JU
Coventry (Bayton Road), 42 Bayton Road, Coventry, West Midlands, CV7 9EJ
Crawley, Unit 2 The Pavillions, Brighton Road Pease Pottage, Crawley, RH11 9BJ
Crewe, 6 Nile Street, Crewe, Cheshire, CW2 7LL
Crieff, Crieff Fire Station, Broich Road, Crief, PH7 3SB
Croydon, 111 Canterbury Road, Croydon, Surrey, CR0 3HH
Cumnock, The Town Hall, Hall Terrace, Cumnock, KA18 1BY
Cupar, 29 East Burnside, Cupar, KY15 4HJ
Cwmbran, Unit 116, Springvale Industrial Estate, Cwmbran, NP44 5BG
Darlington, C/O CICT, Banks Road, Darlington, DL1 1YA
Derby (Sinfin Lane), Ordnance Cottage, Sinfin Lane, Derby, DE24 9GL
Doncaster, Shaftesbury Avenue, Intake, Doncaster, DN02 6DT
Dorchester, Government Buildings, Prince of Wales Road, Dorchester, DT1 1PU
Dumbarton, C/O The Benefits Agency, 15 Meadowbank street, Dumbarton, G82 1SJ
Dumfries, 161 Brooms Road, Dumfries, Dumfries & Galloway, DG1 2SH
Dundee, Unit 1 Faraday Court, Dryburgh Industrial Estate, Dundee, DD2 3UD
Dunfermline, Estantia House, Pitreavie Drive, Dunfermline, KY11 8UH
Dunoon, C/O The Job Centre, George Street, Dunoon, PA23 8BB
Duns, Scottish Borders Council, 8 Newton Street, Duns, TD11 3AU
Durham, Elvet House, Hallgarth Street, Durham, DH01 3AT
Eastbourne, 1 Coastguard Cottages, 84 Wartling Road, Sussex, BN22 7PT
Edinburgh (Currie), 13-15 Bryce Road, Currie, Edinburgh, EH14 5LT
Edinburgh (Joppa), Joppa Terrace, Edinburgh, Lothian, EH15 2HY
Elgin, Crown Buildings, 21 Trinity Road, Elgin, IV30 1UE
Ellesmere Port, 22 Chester Road, Whitby, Ellesmere Port, LO65 6RU
Elswick, Unit 2, Sirius House, Elswick, Newcastle-upon-Tyne, NE4 7YL
Enfield L + LGV, 33 Brancroft Way, Brimsdown, Enfield, Middlesex, EN3 7NJ
Exeter, Melrose House, Rydon Lane Pynes Hill, Exeter, EX2 5AZ
Failsworth, 2 Partington Street, Failsworth, Manchester, MO35 0RD
Falkirk, 11 Maggiewoods Loan, Falkirk, FK1 5HR
Folkestone, Palting House Trinity Road, Folkestone, Kent, CT20 2RH
Forfar, 38 Prior Road, Forfar, DD8 3DT
Fort Augustus, Memorial Hall, Fort Augustus, PH32 4DJ
Fort William, St Marys Manse, Belford Road, Fort William, PH33 6BT
Fraserburgh, World's End Basement Office Suite, 11 Dalrymple Street, Fraserburgh, AB43 9BH
Gainsborough, Turpin Close, Eastern Avenue, Gainsborough, DN21 1QF
Gairloch, Mihol Road, Gairloch, IV21 2BX
Galashiels, 1 Croft Street, Galashiels, Scottish Borders, TD1 3BH
Garston, 69 Woolton Road, Garston, Liverpool, L19 5ND
Gateshead, Seventh Avenue, Team Valley Trading Estate, Gateshead, NE11 0NG
Gillingham L + LGV, Unit 4 The Courtyard, Campus Way, Off Bailey Drive, Gillingham Business Park, Gillingham , Kent, ME8 0NZ
Girvan, 3 Beach Pavillion, Girvan, Ayrshire, KA26 9PH
Glasgow (Anniesland), 351 Anniesland Road, Glasgow, Strathclyde, G13 1XS
Glasgow (Baillieston), 341 Springhill Parkway, Glasgow Business Park, Glasgow, G69 6GA
Glasgow (MossPark), 111-115 Airth Drive, Mosspark, Glasgow, G52 1JU
Glasgow (Springburn Park), Springburn Park, 14A Balornock Road, Glasgow, G21 3UH
Gloucester, 95 Eastern Avenue, Barnwood, Gloucester, GL4 7TG
Golspie, Golspie Fire Station, Back Road, Golspie, KW10 6SP
Goodmayes, 98 Goodmayes Road, Ilford, Essex, IG3 9UZ
Gosport, South Street, Gosport, Hampshire, PO12 1EL

Grantham, Cecil Street, Grantham, Lincolnshire, NG31 9AQ
Grantown on Spey, Grantown on Spey Fire Station, Woodside Avenue, Grantown on Spey, PH26 3JR
Gravesend, 25 Pelham Road, Gravesend, Kent, DA11 0HU
Greenford (Horsenden Lane), 96 Horsenden Lane North, Greenford, Middlesex, UB6 7QH
Greenford (Ruislip Road), 112 Ruislip Road, Greenford, Middlesex, UB6 9QH
Greenock, 19A Union Street, Greenock, PA16 8DD
Guildford L + LGV, Slyfield Industrial Estate off Moorfield Road, Guildford, Surrey, GU1 1SA
Haddington, Herdmanflatt, Haddington, EH41 4NG
Halifax, 11 Cross Street West, Pellon, Halifax, HX02 0HA
Hamilton, 30 Selkirk Street, Hamilton, South Lanarkshire, ML3 6RQ
Harris Island, C/O Community Centre, Tarbert, Harris, HS3 3DL
Harrogate, Walcot, Alexandra Road, Harrogate, HG01 5JS
Hartlepool, Unit 20, Newburn Bridge Industrial Estate, Mainsforth Terrace, Hartlepool, County Durham, TS25 1TZ
Hastings, Heron House, 149/159 London Road, St Leonards on Sea, TN37 6LB
Haverfordwest L + LGV, Terminal Buildings, Withybush Airfield, Tangiers, Haverfordwest, SA62 4BY
Hawick, Government Buildings, North Bridge Street, Hawick, TD9 9BD
Hayes (Middlesex), Fourways House Rigby Lane Swallowfield Way, Hayes, Middlesex, UB3 1ET
Heckmondwike, Tower Buildings, High Street, Heckmondwike, WF16 0AS
Helmsdale, Masonic Hall, Sutherland Street, Helmsdale, KW8 6JE
Hendon, Petrel House Aerodrome Road, Hendon, London, NW9 5LW
Hereford, 1 Faraday Road, Westfield Trading Estate, Hereford, HR4 9NS
Herne Bay, 8b Sea Street, Herne Bay, Kent, CT6 8SP
Hessle, 28 The Weir, Hessle, East Yorkshire, HU13 0RU
Hexham, St Andrews House, Haugh Lane, Hexham, NE46 3EW
Heysham, 1A Sugham Lane, Heysham, Lancashire, LA03 2AH
High Wycombe, 19 Desborough Avenue, High Wycombe, Buckinghamshire, HP11 2RX
Hinckley, 33 Brookside, Hinckley, Leicestershire, LE10 2TG
Hither Green, Ennersdale Road, Hither Green, London, SE13 6JD
Holyhead (Kingsland Road), Unit 11, Kingsland Road, Holyhead, Wales, LL65 2HY
Hornchurch, 75 Station Lane, Hornchurch, Essex, RM12 6JX
Horsforth, Room 013 Woodside House, 261 Low Lane, Horsforth, Leeds, LS18 5NY
Hove, 9 Burwash Road, Hove, East Sussex, BN3 8GP
Huddersfield, Waverley House, Waverley Road, Huddersfield, HD01 5NA
Hull, Chamberlain Road, Hull, East Yorkshire, HU08 8HL
Huntly, Huntly Fire Station, Depot Road, Huntly, AB54 8JX
Hyde, 23 Perrin Street, Hyde, Cheshire, SK14 1JE
Inveraray (Argyll), The Pier, Inverary, PA32 8
Inverness, Ground Floor Suite B1, Elm House, Cradlehall Business Park, Off Caulfield Road North, Inverness, IV2 5NQ
Inverurie (Grampian), Garioch Indoor Bowling Centre, Harlaw Industrial Estate, Inverurie, AB51 4FR
Ipswich, 243 Woodbridge Road, Ipswich, Suffolk, IP4 2QX
Isle of Islay (Port Ellen), Glen Eckdale Airfield, Port Ellen, PA42 7
Isle of Mull (Salen), Post Office, Salen, Isle of Mull, PA72 6JD
Isle of Skye (Broadford), Broadford Fire Station, Old School House, Broadford, IV49 9AQ
Isle of Skye (Portree), Springfield Guest House, Home Farm Road, Portree, IV51 9LX
Isle of Tiree, The Airport, Isle of Tiree, PA77 6UW
Isles of Scilly, Town Hall, St Marys, Isles of Scilly, TR21 0LW
Isleworth, Worton Hall Worton Road, Isleworth, Middlesex, TW7 6ER
Keighley, Spencer Street rear of, 54 Devonshire Street, Keighley, BD21 2BL
Kelso, Croall Bryson Garage, Roxburgh Works, Pinnaclehill Industrial Estate, Kelso, TD5 8DW
Kendal, Eskdale House, Shap Road, Kendal, LA09 6NQ
Kettering, Northampton House, Station Road, Kettering, NN15 7HH
Kidderminster, Castle Road, Kidderminster, Worcestershire, DY11 6TT

Kilmarnock, 71 Whatriggs Road, Kilmarnock, East Ayrshire, KA1 3RB

Kings Lynn, Bergen Way, North Lynn Industrial Est, Kings Lynn, PE30 2JG

Kingussie, Kingussie Shinty Club, The Market Stance, Ruthven Road, Kingussie, PH21 1EN

Kirkcaldy, Park Road, Galatown, Kirkcaldy, KY1 3EL

Kyle of Lochalsh, Kyle of Lochalsh Fire Station, Stoney Road, Kyle of Lochalsh, IV40 8BP

Lairg, Lairg Fire Station, Main Street, Lairg, IV27 4DB

Lampeter, Government Buildings, Pontfaen Road, Lampeter, SA48 7BL

Lanark, Ross of Lanark, 171 St Leonards Street, Lanark, ML11 7DZ

Launceston, St Johns, Weston Road, Launceston, Cornwall, PL15 7AY

Leeds (Harehills), Hillcrest House, 386 Harehills Lane, Leeds, LS9 6NF

Leicester (Gipsy Lane), Opposite Oliver Road, Leicester, LE4 9DF

Leicester (Welford Road), Keble House, Welford Road, Leicester, LE2 6AS

Leicester (Wigston), Tigers Road off Saffron Road, South Wigston, Leicester, LE18 4WS

Leighton Buzzard, Van Dyke Road, Leighton Buzzard, Bedfordshire, LU7 3HA

Lerwick (Shetland), Isleburgh House, King Harald Street, Lerwick, ZE1 0DJ

Letchworth, Jackmans Place, Letchworth, Hertfordshire, SG6 1RF

Lichfield, Lower Sanford Street, Lichfield, West Midlands, WS13 6RB

Lincoln, Procter Road, off Outer Circle Road, Lincoln, LN2 4LA

Llandrindod Wells, Government Buildings, Spa Road East, Llandrindod Wells, LD1 5HA

Llanelli, Toft Place, Llanerch, Llanelli, SA15 3SB

Lochgilphead, County Offices, Manse Brae, Lochgilphead, PA31 8QU

Longbenton, Government Buildings, Whitley Road, Longbenton, NE12 9SE

Loughborough, Pinfold Gate Car Park, Pinfold Gate Road, Loughborough, LE11 1BG

Loughton, Crown Buildings, 284 High Road, Loughton, Essex, IG10 1RB

Louth, Zenith House, North Holme Road, Louth Lincolnshire, LN11 0HQ

Lower Gornal, 19/21 Lake Street, Lower Gornal, Nr Dudley, DY3 2AY

Lowestoft, Rishton House, Clapham Road, Lowestoft, NR32 1RL

Ludlow, 54 Broad Street, Ludlow, Shropshire, SY8 1GN

Luton, 6/10 Adelaide Street, Luton, Bedfordshire, LU1 5BT

Macclesfield, 10 Bridge Street, Macclesfield, Cheshire, SK11 6EG

Maidstone, Unit 1 North Court, South Park Business Village Armstrong Road, Maidstone, ME15 6JZ

Mallaig, Mallaig and Morar Community Centre, West Bay, Mallaig, PH41 4PX

Malton, 3 Milton Avenue, Malton, North Yorkshire, YO17 0LB

Melton Mowbray, Crown Building, 50/52 Scalford Road, Melton Mowbray, LE13 1JY

Merthyr Tydfil, Government Buildings, Castle Street, Merthyr Tydfil, CF47 8TX

Middlesbrough, Maxwell Road, Middlesbrough, Cleveland, TS03 8TE

Mill Hill, Unit 9 Grannard Business Centre Bunns Lane, Mill Hill, London, NW7 2DQ

Minehead, 39 Blenheim Road, Minehead, Somerset, TA2 6BH

Mold, Government Buildings, St Davids Lane, Mold, CH7 1LH

Monmouth, Old Dixon Road, Monmouth, Monmouthshire, NP25 3DP

Montrose, Harbour Offices, South Quay, Ferryden, Montrose, DD10 9SL

Morden, 10 Tudor Drive, Morden, Surrey, SM4 4PE

Nelson, Cobden Street, Nelson, Lancashire, BB09 0AH

Newbury, Newtown Road, Newbury, Berkshire, RG14 7EB

Newcastle-Under-Lyme, Parklands Clayton Lane, Trent Vale, Stoke-On-Trent, ST4 6PQ

Newport (Isle of Wight), 23 Medina Avenue, Newport, Isle of Wight, PO30 1EL

Newton Abbot, Vander House, Brunel Road, Newton Abbot, TQ12 4YQ

Newton Stewart, Job Centre, 6/8 Queen Street, Newton Stewart, DG8 6JL

Newtown, Ladywell House, Newtown, Powys, SY16 1JB

Norris Green, Falklands Approach, Parthenon Drive, Norris Green, L1 1BR

North Uist Island, C/O Post Office, Lochmaddy, North Uist, HS6 5AA

Northallerton, Elder House, East Road, Northallerton, DL06 1NU

Northampton, Gladstone Business Park, Gladstone Road, Northampton, NN5 7QG

Northwich (Northern), 4 Felix Road, Winnington, Northwich, CW08 4BU

Norwich, Jupiter Road, Hellesdon, Norwich, NR6 6SS

Nottingham (Chalfont Drive), Block 6 Room F4 Government Buildings, Chalfont Drive, Nottingham, NG8 3RF

Nottingham (Gedling), 21/22 Main Road, Gedling, Nottingham, NG4 3HP

Nottingham (West Bridgford), 24 Musters Road, West Bridgford, Nottingham, NG2 7PL

Nuneaton, 54 Vernons Lane, Stocking Ford, Nuneaton, CV10 8AA

Oban, Cameron House, Albany Street, Oban, PA34 4AE

Orkney Island, Pickaquoy Road, Kirkwall, Orkney, KW15 1RR

Oswestry, Mile Oak Industrial Estate, Maesbury Road, Oswestry, SY10 8GA

Oxford (Cowley), James Wolfe Road, Cowley, Oxford, OX4 2PT

Paisley, Textile House, 3 Duke Street, Paisley, PA2 6RF

Peebles, Tweeddale District Council, Rosetta Road, Peebles, EH45 8DN

Pembroke Dock, Pier House, Hobbs Point, Pembroke Dock, SA72 6HJ

Penzance, 1 Alverton Terrace, Penzance, Cornwall, TR18 4JH

Perth, 111 Rannoch Road, Perth, Tayside, PH1 2DF

Peterborough, Building 5 Westwood Estate, Saville Road, Peterborough, PE3 6PY

Peterhead, Government Buildings, Constitution Street, Peterhead, AB42 1SE

Pinner, 221 Tolcarne Drive, Pinner, Middlesex, HA5 2DZ

Pitlochry, The Hall, West Moulin Road, Pitlochry, PH16 5EA

Plymouth, Endurance House Parkway Court, Longbridge Road Marsh Mills, Plymouth, PL6 8LR

Pontefract, Baghill Station, Station Lane, Pontefract, WF8 1RB

Pontypridd, 18 Pwllgwaun Road, Pontypridd, Mid Glamorgan, CF37 1HH

Portsmouth, Fort Southwick, James Callaghan Drive, Fareham, PO17 6AR

Preston, Chain Caul Road, Preston, PR2 2PD

Pwllheli, 33A Cardiff Road, Pwllheli, Gwynedd, LL53 5HT

Reading, 220 Elgar Road South, Reading, Berkshire, RG2 0DE

Reddish (Northern), 26/28 Broadstone Road, Reddish, Cheshire, SK05 7AE

Redditch (Worcestershire), Elm Road, Redditch, Worcestershire, B97 6HJ

Reigate, 7 Slipshatch Road`, Woodhatch, Reigate, Surrey, RH2 8HA

Rhyl, Victoria Road, Rhyl, Denbighshire, LL18 2EL

Rochdale, Blueberry Business Park, Unit 5 Ground Floor, Kingsway, Rochdale, OL16 5AF

Rotherham, 80 Doncaster Road, Rotherham, South Yorkshire, S65 1NN

Rothesay (Bute Island), C/O Dept. of Employment, 9 King Street, Rothesay, PA20 0DE

Rugby, 5 Newbold Road, Rugby, Warwickshire, CV21 2LQ

Sale, 36/38 Poplar Grove, Sale, Cheshire, M33 7ER

Salisbury, Rougemont Close, Salisbury, Wiltshire, SP1 1LY

Saltcoats, 31 Old Raise Road, Saltcoats, Ayrshire, KA21 5RB

Scarborough, Cayton Low Road, Eastfield, Scarborough, YO11 3BY

Scunthorpe, Off Ferry Road West, Scunthorpe, South Humberside, DN15 8UH

Sevenoaks, 45 Argyle Road, Sevenoaks, Kent, TN13 1HJ

Sheffield (Handsworth), Richmond Park Road, Handsworth, Sheffield, S13 8HF

Sheffield (Middlewood Road), 508 Middlewood Road, Sheffield, South Yorkshire, S06 1TQ

Shrewsbury, 5 Yeomanry Road, Battlefield Enterprise Park, Shrewsbury, Shropshire, SY1 3EH

Sidcup, Craybrook House 15 Sidcup Hill, Sidcup, Kent, DA14 6HR

Skegness, 7 Briar Way, Skegness, Lincolnshire, PE25 3NR
Skipton, Foundry House, Carleton Road, Skipton, BD23 2PA
Slough, Grays Place, Slough, Berkshire, SL2 5AF
South Norwood, 112a Portland Road, South Norwood, London, SE25 4PJ
South Shields, Bedesway, Bede Industrial Estate, South Shields, Tyne & Wear, NE32 3EG
South Uist Island, C/O Tourist office, Lochboisdale, South Uist, HS8 5TH
Southall, 285 Allenby Road, Southall, Middlesex, UB1 2HD
Southampton (Forest Hills), Forest Hills Drive, Southampton, Hampshire, SO18 2NT
Southampton (Maybush), Green Lane, Maybush, Southampton, SO16 9FP
Southend-On-Sea, 11 Prittlewell Chase, Southend on Sea, Essex, S50 0RX
Southport, Eastbank House, Eastbank Street, Southport, PR08 1HE
Spalding, High Street, Spalding, PE11 1UJ
St Albans, Beauver House, 6 Bricket Road, St Albans, AL1 3JX
St Helens, Atherton Street, St Helens, Merseyside, WA10 2JY
Stafford, Unit 7 Greyfriars Business Park, Frank Foley Way, Stafford, ST16 2RF
Stevenage, 3 Drapers Way, Stevenage, Hertfordshire, SG1 3DT
Stirling, Government Buildings, 2 St Ninians Road, Stirling, FK8 2HF
Stoke On Trent (Cobridge), 8 Elder Road, Cobridge Stoke On Trent, Staffordshire, ST6 2HE
Stonehaven, Stonehaven Fire Station, Brickfield Road, Stonehaven, AB39 2JQ
Stornoway (Lewis), Fishermans Mission, 1 Quay Street, Stornoway, Isle of Lewis, HS1 2XX
Stranraer, 3 Ashwood, Stranraer, DG9 7NQ
Strontian, Dalmhor House, Strontian, PH36 4HZ
Sunderland, 1 The Cloisters, Stockton Road, Sunderland, SR02 7BD
Sutton (Surrey), Helena House, 348 High Street, Sutton, Surrey, SM1 1PU
Sutton-In-Ashfield, Outram Street, Sutton in Ashfield, NG17 4FU
Swansea, Valley Way Road, Llansamlet, Swansea, SA6 8QP
Swindon, Marlborough Lane, Swindon, Wiltshire, SN3 1RA
Taunton, 2 Scotts House Cook Way, Bindon Business Park, Taunton, TA2 6BG
Telford, 35 Horton Wood, Telford, Shropshire, TF1 4FR
Thornaby, 1 Brus House, Thornaby, Cleveland, TS17 9ET
Thurso, Naver House, Naver Road, Naver Business Park, Thurso, KW14 7QA
Tilbury, Montana House, Russell Road, Tilbury, RM18 7AE
Tolworth, Douglas House 1b Douglas Road, Tolworth, Surrey, KT6 7RZ
Trowbridge, Wiltshire Drive, Trowbridge, Wiltshire, BA14 0RF
Tunbridge Wells, 8 Upper Grosvenor Road, Tunbridge Wells, Kent, TN1 2ES
Ullapool, Ross & Cromarty Service Point, North Road, Ullapool, IV26 2XL
Upton, Arrowe Park Rd, Upton, Wirral, CH49 0UL
Wakefield, Bradford Road, Wrenthorpe, Wakefield, WF02 0RA
Wallasey, 17c King Street, Wallasey, Merseyside, L44 8AT
Wallington (Mint House), Mint House 6 Stanley Park Road, Wallington, Surrey, SM6 0PY
Wanstead (Hermon Hill), 2 Devon House Hermon Hill, Wanstead, London, E11 2AW
Warrington, Warrington Business Park, Long Lane, Warrington, WA02 8TX
Warwick, Unit 7 Charles Court, Budbrooke Road, Warwick, CV34 5LZ
Watford, CP House, Otterspool Way, Watford, WD25 8HU
Wednesbury, Knowles Street, Wednesbury, WS10 9HW
Wellingborough, Belgrade Business Centre, Denington Industrial Estate Denington Road, Wellingborough, NN8 2QH
West Wickham (kent), 56 Glebe Way, West Wickham, Kent, BR4 0RL
Weston - Super – Mare, Plott 11 Sunnyside Road North, Industrial Estate, Weston Super Mare, BS23 3PZ
Weybridge, Rear of Clive House 12/18 Queens Road, Weybridge, Surrey, KT13 9XE
Whalley Range-Manchester, 14 Milton Grove, Egerton Road North, Whalley Range, MO16 0BP

Whitby, Unit F11, St Hilda's Business Centre, Green Lane, Whitby, YO22 4ET
Whitchurch, The Lodge Paul Moss, Doddington, Whitchurch, SY13 1EP
Wick, Unit 5E4, Wick Industrial Estate, Wick, KW1 4QS
Widnes, Everite Road, Widnes, Cheshire, WA08 8PT
Wigan, 4 Mesnes Park Terrace, Wigan, WN1 1SU
Winchester, Christchurch Road, Winchester, Hampshire, SO23 9SY
Winchmore Hill, Capitol House 794 Green Lanes, Winchmore Hill, London, N21 2SP
Wisbech, Albion House, Albion Place, Wisbech, PE13 1AM
Wishaw, 150-160 Main Street, Wishaw, ML2 7LU
Wolverhampton, Ashland Street, Wolverhampton, West Midlands, WV3 0BX
Wood Green, The Gatehouse Woodhall House Lordship Lane, Wood Green, London, N22 5JW
Worcester, Stanier Road, Warndon, Worcester, Worcestershire, WR4 9FE
Workington, Stanley Street, Workington, Cumbria, CA14 2QG
Worksop, Slack Walk, Worksop, Nottinghamshire, S80 1UR
Worthing, Westmorland House Strand Parade, Goring by Sea, Worthing, BN12 6EA
Wrexham, Brynycabanau Road, Wrexham, LL13 7BF
Yeovil, Maltravers House, Petters Way, Yeovil, BA20 1SH
York, Murton Way, Osbaldwick, York, YO19 5UN